THE SEARCH FOR INTIMACY

Also by Elaine Storkey:

What's Right with Feminism
Mary's Story, Mary's Song
Contributions to Christian Feminism

The Search for Intimacy

Elaine Storkey

Hodder & Stoughton

LONDON SYDNEY AUCKLAND

British Library Cataloguing in Publication Data
A record for this book is available from the British Library

ISBN 0 340 48899 9

Typeset by Hewer Text Composition Services, Edinburgh
Printed and bound in Great Britain by
Cox & Wyman, Reading, Berks

Hodder and Stoughton Ltd
A division of Hodder Headline PLC
338 Euston Road
London NW1 3BH

To Alan Storkey

Contents

Acknowledgements

Although I am the author of this book, much of the material I work on comes from others. It is there in the lives of people I know: in those I have counselled, students who have shared things with me, members of my family, and friends. Their trust has been very important to me. I hope I have treated it with respect.

Former colleagues in the Social Science faculty of the Open University played a very significant part in my earlier thinking, although they may not recognize their ideas now. Friends from the Greenbelt Festival and Örebro Missionsskola, Sweden, have provided annual opportunities for me to develop these thoughts in their programmes. Other colleagues and friends have invited me to test my ideas in university lectures, conferences, and workshops and have given me excellent feedback. I am indebted to Helen Gardyne, and to Chris and Jocelyn Grantham who have twice organized an extended speaking tour round New Zealand. My visits to Australia, the United States, Brazil, Canada and many parts of Europe have similarly refined and developed the work which is presented here. Even the BBC World Service and Radio Four's *Thought for the Day* have invited me to try out and broadcast some of the thoughts I have wrestled with in the book. Beverley McAinsh, Tim Dean and Christine Morgan deserve especial thanks; they along with Amanda Hancox, John Newbury, and David Coombes and Alison Hilliard have all taught me much about communication.

A deep debt of gratitude is due to Margaret Killingray, Sue Beresford and all my colleagues at the Institute for Contemporary Christianity who have each lightened the load I carry as Director, and enabled me to complete this book. Their supportive team work models what the book tries to express about work relationships. Members of the Council have given additional encouragement, not least its chair, Dennis Osborn. Working with John Stott and

John Wyatt on issues of personhood and medicine has been particularly rewarding. Others who have contributed indirectly include Mary Stewart Van Leeuwen, Philip Sampson, Peter Oliver, Roy McCloughry, Ruth Hanson, Fran Beckett, Helen Gardyne and Cathy Kroeger.

I want to thank the editors at Hodder, Carolyn Armitage and James Catford who have been continually supportive and generous in their patience. Trisha Dale did a fine job in copy editing. My parents, Anne and James Lively have always believed in the project and our sons, Amos, Matthew and Caleb each improved my competence to write it. They have gone from childhood to teens or teens to adulthood during its gestation and Amos's marriage to Helen beat its completion by one month. Finally I thank Alan, my intimate partner in marriage, parenting, friendship, work, worship and leisure (what leisure?) for more than a quarter of a century. His love is there in each chapter of the book.

Preface

It came as a surprise to his colleagues when one of the young men in the accounts department of a large firm committed suicide. There had never been any indication that he had problems. He did his job well, earned a decent salary, and lived in a comfortable flat. Not that anyone had ever visited him there, or knew much about him at all really. But that, as they explained, was because he kept himself to himself. As far as anyone knew he had no close relationships, no health or sexual anxieties, and no family worries, for his parents were long dead.

When his papers were searched in the hope of finding something for the coroner, they came across a dozen notebooks of autobiographical poetry. The life story of the man no one knew unfolded itself. His shyness at school, his feelings of social inadequacy, and his awkwardness with women were spelled out painfully in descriptive words and sharp images. His one relationship was with his aunt who had brought him up. She had been quiet and introspective, unmarried and totally committed to nurturing and rearing her sister's orphan. She had loved him fiercely yet always felt inadequate to the task. He wrote of this woman with warmth and poignant tenderness, yet with the longing also to be free from her over-protective love. Her death from cancer had filled him with desolation and grief and a guilt with which he had never come to terms. A month after she died he began to write poems to her. Soon he was writing each day, sometimes gently, sometimes angrily. He confided to her his loneliness, his longings for closeness, his deep need of a friend. The words he had never been able to share with anyone poured eloquently from the pages. The poems had grown more intense and more desperate, showing an ache for any recognition from other people: love, appreciation, hostility – anything but indifference. The final decision to end his life came on a warm, June evening with the smell of honeysuckle wafting through his window. He felt inescapably alone, empty, and without significance.

It is dangerous to generalize from tragic stories of individual experience. Yet if I were to put forward the thesis that in our contemporary culture there is a deep and widespread longing for close relationships, there would be no shortage of evidence. The thousands of friendship clubs, matrimonial agencies and meeting centres all point to the fundamental desire for human warmth. There is a need which lies deep in the human psyche for the security of being loved just as we are. Yet that need is not always fulfilled. Crisis clinics, alcoholism centres, counselling agencies, and divorce courts all indicate how difficult it can be for people to draw close and stay close to others.

In offering this book on intimacy I want therefore to help people to think about themselves and their relationships. I want to do so in the context of the culture which surrounds us, and the changes which press in on us. Whether the spotlight is on friendship, mothers and daughters, colleagues at work, marriage and sexual intimacy, or coping with the past, my hope is that people will find help in its beam. Most of all, I hope that the book will not only be an aid to understanding relationships, but that it will give many people the courage to make them better.

Longings for Closeness

The Idea of having to die without having lived is unbearable.
Erich Fromm

Even though we have seen rapid and unprecedented changes in Western society over the last few decades, the search for intimacy is as profound and as persistent as ever. For the longing to draw close to others seems part of our very humanness. One writer observes, 'We may be well fed, warm and free from physical violence, but we are liable to become insane in solitary confinement.'[1]

Yet the contemporary search is a problematic one. Some writers suggest it is also becoming a desperate one. There are so many ways in which people experience isolation from others in our society; so many barriers to close relationships erected within our culture. One counsellor documents the despair of loneliness in many people's lives. He reports what was told him by a woman laboratory technician:

No one knows what it is like down here. I am so far away from everything and everybody, like in a dungeon . . . Sometimes I get so lonely I could scream. And when I get out of here sometimes I think it's worse. I don't think there is a human being on earth who cares about what happens to me from five on Friday to nine on Monday.[2]

The traditional response to loneliness has been to urge such people to form some relationships: join a congenial social group, develop family ties, perhaps find a partner. It has been to encourage them to break away from their isolation and develop intimacy. Yet in a culture such as ours it would seem that intimacy is not that easy to come by. Marriage cannot guarantee it. Nor of course can cohabitation, lesbian or gay relationships, one-night stands, or wild passionate adultery. Intimacy might be much sought after, but it is also elusive; all the more so because people are not always clear what they are looking for. It is not uncommon to hear the suggestion that we now have a *crisis* in intimacy: '. . . a time of confusion connected with some change that does not have a design, pattern or single "right" path to follow.'[3] The crisis for many people is related to instability: to rapidly changing norms, with apparently fluid rather than fixed relationships. Or, it is related to insecurity where people know what it is to be hurt and are dogged by fear of repeated rejection.

As the tidal waves of irretrievable breakdown claim more and more victims, broken and hurting people are thrown ashore to cope as best they can. Large numbers of youngsters live with the splitting up of their parents, to struggle on with their own loss. Anxiety about being unloved, about sexual identity, and about the future contributes to the rising suicide rate amongst young people. The sad thing is, of course, as Richard Winter points out, that 'suicide is a very permanent solution to what is usually a temporary problem'.[4] The underlying symptoms are often those of deep depression, and they need to be understood and taken seriously as one of the most painful aspects of life in our society today.[5] On a less dramatic level, both the very young and the very old suffer in countless, daily, ordinary ways when there is no one around who has time to give them. Those who talk of crisis have much material to draw upon.

An investigation of the alleged crisis is only one of the concerns of this book, however. I want also to ask why we seem to need close relationships so much, and what prevents some of us from being able to develop them as we long to do. I shall also be considering areas of social life which have traditionally been expected to meet people's intimacy needs, and ask how they are changing.

At the heart of these issues there is however an enigma. For intimacy is both desired and threatening. We both want our deepest privacy to be invaded, but we also fear it. We want to be able to open up our very selves to the love and scrutiny of another, yet we dread the rawness of being exposed. There is somehow deep in the human psyche that tension between bonding and detachment, closeness and distance. Very often, just at the very point where intimacy seems realizable there is a fear of being engulfed, a claustrophobia, a panic and a bid for retreat. To accept that this tension is there, and to live creatively with it are probably marks of maturity. But for many the fear of intimacy itself can take over. The unwillingness to be completely open to another lies deep in our personhood. How can we ever really trust another to disclose our hearts and show all the weakness there?

There is sometimes a further reason other than the inability to trust others. It is because we never have been willing to face up to ourselves. We do not love ourselves because we are aware that there are ugly, distorted and destructive aspects of us which we often do not want to know about. For many, a lack of deep, inner peace, an absence of profound personal security lies at the very depth of their being, out of reach and out of mind. To travel into these areas would be too disturbing. To let you in would mean an emotional upheaval too great to contemplate. The risk is indeed enormous. How can I let you see what I dare not even face myself? How can I expect you to know me and still love me?

So it is not only tearful children, angry with their parents, who play the game of 'go away a little closer'. It is the game which resounds through our culture. The search for intimacy is on.

Intimacy and Gender

It is impossible to write a book on intimacy without being drawn into a discussion on gender, for many writers have debated whether or not men and women do have the same needs for intimacy. And whilst some have suggested that male-female needs correspond to each other in some intricate and complementary way others have pointed to differences between men and women which frustrate the very attempt at deep, reciprocal relationships. There is a hint of truth in the wry quip by one of the Marx brothers: 'No wonder I have problems. One of my parents was a woman and the other was a man.' This is not an issue which engages only comedians or psychologists. Preachers, theologians, biologists, and sociolinguists are all currently caught up in the debate; some fiercely defending stereotypes, others inviting us to reread and reassess much of what we take for granted. I hope to steer through the minefield of arguments and cover an exciting terrain without too many casualties.

Issues of gender concern us also in the areas of friendship and marriage and fellowship. But there are other considerations here too, which come up regularly in the context of the breakdown of marriage, or barriers to friendships. The meaning of those very relationships needs to be opened up. For running throughout the book is a rejection of a 'neutralist' approach to human relationships. Instead, there is an acceptance that all relationships have a normative structure, an underlying meaning-framework which gives them depth and brings greater freedom and enrichment for those who live within them. Exploring these frameworks probes the very definition of what it is to be human and relational.

What is Intimacy?

There is one major problem in even beginning the task of this book. It is that the very word 'intimacy' can be confusing. It has already been debased and belittled. One Sunday newspaper frequently reports in its accounts of rape or sexual assault: 'He was intimate with her', thus confusing intimacy with sexual activity, even activity which is anything but intimate. But rape is not sexual closeness; it is personal violation; it is utter contempt and disregard for another human being, and therefore the very opposite of what it means to be intimate. In popular jargon the word 'intimacy' is also attached to countless other situations, producing images which range from family togetherness round the Christmas tree, to romantic and misty-eyed lovers who are oblivious of all but each other. I will need to describe my own uses of the term if I am going to avoid such confusions.

At its most basic *intimacy is knowing that I am not alone in the universe.* But that *knowing* is not simply a cerebral process. It is something I experience, and live within; something which shapes my understanding and acceptance of reality. Sometimes intimacy is there almost unconsciously as we live in a comfortable taken-for-grantedness with those for whom we care deeply; sometimes it hits us in wide awake amazement as we are suddenly overwhelmed by the wonder of love; our whole being expands with joy and light. Intimacy is the sharing of closeness, of bonding, of reciprocation. It is the engulfing of warmth and care. It is the experiencing of *Another*.

When we experience other persons in this way a miracle takes place. We are taken out of our own self-centredness, into the life and orbit of human beings whom we recognize to be at least as significant as we are. We want to know those persons. We want to be known. We want a state of understanding to exist between us. And as we face the demands of that knowing we make decisions that we will be real, we will share ourselves with honesty and not hide behind a presentation or a mask. The relationships themselves become characterized by a new openness and personal commitment, as we find ourselves moved by a desire to accept those other people, and to seek the best for them. The level of relating is beyond the routine or the functional, for we each begin to share our very souls with each other and receive in return that sense of belonging and of being at home.

Of course we can only enter into this level of relationship if there is an acceptance and trust, a willingness to let someone else into those private areas of feelings and fears, believing that we will not be betrayed. And there is no doubt that such relationships need time to develop. It is possible to experience immediate intimacy with someone we have just met: there can be that recognition of another person's depth, a glimpse of their humanness, a reciprocal sense of excitement, enjoyment and closeness. But if this is to flourish and grow, then it still needs to be nurtured over time.

Intimacy is the close bonding we have with other people. It is the experience of sharing life together, that what happens to these others matters deeply to me, and what happens to me is just as important to them in return. And we can know this *friendship intimacy* with any one we care about, with members of our family, with good friends, with those with whom we have been thrown together in times of everyday or profound experience. It is an intimacy which is at its root not about sex, or even about physical closeness. It is the satisfying of a longing for love and personal significance in the heart of Another.

Nevertheless, it is possible to confuse sex and intimacy. For to be intimate is to be naked, and sex takes people into nakedness with each other: into the joining of bodies and knowing the comfort of physical touch at its most available. Yet the magnet of sex for so many is not simply excitement, but the longing for greater closeness. And often where there has been no true intimacy in sex there is the dwindling of self-worth and self-respect when the excitement fades. That is why the loneliness which follows an encounter which is only physical can be devastating. There is much truth in the comment: 'Sex is a wonderful *symbol* of intimacy. But as we know, symbols can be empty of real meaning.'[6]

Giving oneself sexually best grows from an already deep relationship. It is 'not a step that establishes deep intimacy, but one which presupposes it'.[7] *Sexual intimacy* is more than physical sex. For sexual intimacy means giving our mind and emotions as well as our body fully to that other person; it means joining our futures in the present, acknowledging our commitment to each other; it means exposing ourselves with complete transparency and deep vulnerability. The place of *troth* in such relationships is central. For in exposing our bodies as well as our feelings we run very considerable risks. Our bodies are so closely identified with who we are. They contribute to our sense of self, to our own value and esteem. If people do not treat our bodies with love, we find it hard to believe that they could possibly value us.

In our fragile humanity the possibility of betrayal is frighteningly real. Fear of sexual inadequacy, doubts about trusting a partner, or suspicion that one's body is just being used for the consumption of the other are daily experiences in the lives of countless people. For many, sexual betrayal is a hurtful and violating experience. Others try to avoid pain by cultivating uncommitted sexual relationships; where they can come and go without any loss of autonomy, without any need for troth. But pain is not that easily insured against. Unfaithfulness remains traumatic whenever any real giving and receiving has taken place, and sexual intimacy is not possible without self-giving. Adultery is most of all painful for the faithful partner who stays and loves. It can be experienced as a sense of rejection at the deepest level: 'He took all there was of me, and it wasn't good enough.'

The reality is then that sex must not be depended upon to initiate intimacy. It can only grow out of it. When there is also friendship in that relationship, and a bedrock of faithfulness and commitment rooted in vows made to each other, the intimacy has good soil for the growth to take place.

There is another level of intimacy which I have not mentioned. It is *intimacy with the self*. Each of us has our own growth towards self-knowledge, towards a deeper awareness of who we are and what matters to us. To develop our own selves in a way that enables us to be giving to other people this awareness needs to be fostered and nurtured. Yet even here there is a more profound issue still. It is that the deepest form of self-knowledge is never achieved solely in our separateness. It is also in relationship; it is in knowing who I am, not as an autonomous self-referring being, but in my connectedness with others. Ultimately it is in my unique relatedness to God that I most fully encounter myself.

Intimacy with myself involves me in being critically self-aware; ready to assess influences from the past, ready to understand where I need to change. It uncovers for me those areas of weakness or bitterness in my life; it helps me to learn to love myself, and accept myself, whilst rejecting what in me is harmful or destructive. True intimacy with the self means experiencing the reality of repentance, forgiveness, healing and joy. Intimacy comes when I grow in love and learn to give myself to others.

Many people long for this personal knowledge and wholeness, and are willing even to seek it through prolonged and painful therapy, and yet it so frequently eludes them. One of the results of living in our contemporary culture is that the majority of people are assumed to know themselves, but are given little opportunity to make their own acquaintance. We are invited to cut ourselves off from any deep inner life, and stay caught up in routine and habitual patterns which so easily put to sleep any desire for probing and reflection. And so one of the most disturbing, and fearful human questions is still 'Who am I?'. The vital thing is to know where to go for an answer.

Conclusion

Intimacy has many faces but its requirements are similar in each case. It is dependent on the readiness to let go of self-delusion and the longing to be real. It is inextricably linked with an openness of sharing and a willingness to be known. It is the caring commitment that reaches out to another in trust and vulnerability. It is the giving of time, the giving of love. It is the bedrock of deep relationships, the daily nourishment for human closeness.

Yet the search for intimacy has come upon a harsher climate than that which naturally provides it with gentle warmth and clean air. The biting chill which has settled is not one in which relationships easily flourish. The result is a loneliness which infiltrates the lives of many, and cuts people off from each other. But before we can find the way forward to a more sustaining environment we need to know what kind of place we are in now and what kind of changes might be necessary. For there may well be much ground to cover before our longings for closeness are to be met.

2

Intimacy and the Public World

One does not need to be a doctor to realize that the whole world is sick.

Paul Tournier

The relationship between intimacy and the 'public world' provides the key context for our search for close relationships.

Henri Nouwen makes a perceptive observation reflecting on a trip to New York.

Sitting in the subway, I am surrounded by silent people hidden behind their newspapers or staring away in a world of their own fantasies. Nobody speaks with a stranger, and a patrolling policeman keeps reminding me that people are not out to help each other. But when my eyes wander over the walls of the train covered with invitations to buy more or new products, I see young, beautiful people enjoying each other in a gentle embrace, playful men and women smiling at each other in fast sailboats, proud explorers on horseback encouraging each other to take brave risks, fearless children dancing on a sunny beach, and charming girls always ready to serve me in airplanes and ocean liners. While the subway train runs from one dark tunnel into the other and I am nervously aware where I keep my money, the words and images decorating my fearful world speak about love, gentleness, tenderness and about a joyful togetherness of spontaneous people.[1]

The contrast between the images of intimacy, and the reality of alienation is one which many have experienced in our contemporary world. There is a promise of love, sexual completeness, happy marriages, but there are other voices too which warn us of something different. We are nagged daily by the news to be wary of trusting others, especially the stranger, and we construct elaborate alarms and devices to protect ourselves from the evil outside. We are told of the excitement and fulfilment of deep relationships yet life in our cities is marked by personal anonymity, suspicion, theft and violence. In fact, far from enhancing the possibility of intimacy, the very way in which society has been structured seems to put people at a distance from each other.

The World of Work

We might illustrate this in the area of work relationships. For many people work is the main preoccupation of their weekday hours, and the friendships between work colleagues are potentially very close. This is especially true where the focus is on people working together to achieve a common aim. Conversations in many canteens, common-rooms or offices range far beyond talking shop or even swapping frustrating work experiences. Certainly teachers share verbal exasperations over lazy or deviant students, and store assistants murmur together over impossible customers, but these are often only the preliminaries to establishing mutual ground for broader relationships. And yet very frequently the potential for relating closely to others is not realized because of the very structure of work itself. For what the person at the till at the fast food outlet knows very acutely is that her worth to the firm is measured in terms of the number of customers who rap out their order to her, and the number of cardboard cartons she cashes up. So relationships are incidental to the work. And they are often fragile too. The person who takes the tea break a fraction too early and stays away a fraction too late puts pressure on others, who have to cope with lengthening queues of hungry customers wanting to collect their fast food five minutes ago and go home. The underlying economic concern – to beat competitors and widen profit margins – means that management concern for the individual employee is very limited within the world of work. The majority of work organizations are tailored round the efficiency of the firm or the requirements of the economy rather than around the personal needs of the workers.

This has an inevitable effect on the kinds of relationships that do develop between those who share the workplace together. For where time is money, and work is dominant, the space and commitment needed to form close relationships are severely squeezed. People so often encounter each other not as whole persons with a family history and an emotional past, but as segments, often as role functions. They experience each other as colleagues with a common language, or competitors incompatibly after the same goal, or both. And it is hard for two people to experience openness and sharing when the success of one depends partly on the failure of the other. So rather than seeking the other's interest, the tendency is to have minds firmly on their own, looking out constantly for an opportunity for advancing in status or higher pay. The result is that they will be cut off from personal contact with each other at a fundamental level. More than one psychologist has pointed out, 'isolated, competing egos do not easily open their hearts to each other'.[2]

Indeed, personal intimacy can be a threat to a corporation because it suddenly opens up an area of vulnerability. Single-mindedness can be disturbed, professionalism can be at risk, loyalty to the firm can come under question. For an employee with a position of responsibility the potential abuse can be considerable. That is why 'unemotionalism' is prized in many high-ranking jobs. A chink of vulnerability brands someone as unsuitable for public responsibilities, and any suggestion that he (or she) is not fully in control is enough to prevent promotion at any stage. But there is a cost. The process can often produce people who are out of touch with their emotional needs and who ultimately find it difficult to sustain intimate relationships. Inevitably, it also limits their management capacities.

The public world of work, as currently constructed, fears intimacy. Competition, aggressiveness and emotional distance cannot sit comfortably with a concern for the feelings or the deeper needs of others. It is so much easier to stab a competitor (or a colleague) in the back if he is not seen empathetically as another human being, a person with hurts, or vulnerabilities or deep longings. It is less problematic to require an employee to put in unwanted overtime if no consideration is given to her own needs for rest and peace before she begins her routine at home. Once there is an acknowledgement that behind the role there is a person, then the issues become so much more cloudy, and the decisions not nearly so easy to make.

No area of work seems to escape this ethos. Even in the professions which address people's personal needs, there is no guarantee that the same awareness of needs is brought into the workplace itself. More than once I have heard therapists, clergy or social workers bemoan the fact that what they believe about the importance of sharing and openness does not seem to affect the way they relate as colleagues. And many live with the inbuilt frustration of knowing, and indeed even preaching, a better way forward, but remaining trapped in old rituals themselves. This, of course, is not always hidden from those on the 'receiving end'. I have listened to people who have sought help from clergy or counsellors and been disappointed to see the extent to which those people have problems of their own in establishing good relationships. There is an inbuilt dilemma in the very training of some of these professionals. For the police officer, social worker and doctor are all encouraged to draw up professional boundaries to relationships and, sometimes for sheer survival, to avoid becoming personally involved. Consequently, many of the most caring professionals are trained to offer their expertise but not their love. Therefore to let the barriers down with colleagues and to close the distance between public and personal life can often be doubly hard.

The world of work then is not the best arena for discovering human depth, or for fostering intimacy. Yet when real human encounter does take place it can transform almost any work situation. The sudden word of tenderness from a tired shopper to the middle-aged woman on the till who is weary and cramped and longing for eight o'clock produces a moment of intimacy. The awareness that someone empathizes, does not need to be told but simply understands how she feels, closes the distance and brings encounter. The quiet, gentle sympathy and reassurance of a colleague for the young man who has made a mess of an important assignment opens up communication and eases the pain. Moments of real human insight do occur every day, and are wonderful, but they are so often hidden amid the pervading work ethos.

Neighbourhoods

The case for the absence of intimacy in the public world goes beyond work and professional life. It has increasingly been structured into the very developments of towns and communities.

For many decades British towns and housing estates have been moving away from providing the close-knit neighbourhood ethos previously taken for granted in many areas, to a greater emphasis on individual privacy and self-containment. Widespread housing demolition, creation of new towns, and the spread of detached suburbia have all affected the way people live and the meaning given to community. For some, climbing the ladder of success often brings the need to uproot and relocate; for others, living in a depressed area has forced the choice either to move and hunt for work, or stay and face permanent unemployment.

This has all left its mark on the locality. A generation or so ago it would often have been possible to get a glimpse of the lives and interests of people in a specific area by simply visiting the small neighbourhood shops and noting the goods for sale. The shops were run by those who knew their customers well and saw them regularly. They would cater for their individual needs and quirks: a particular brand of tinned tobacco, a specialist magazine, large-sized fleecy vests! People would shop with their neighbours, negotiate with each other at the butcher's over the last pound of sausages and try to maintain some level of privacy over their domestic finances. They would also often live within walking distance of parents, brothers and sisters, and be in daily contact with those whose lives had touched theirs for many years. Now the average family moves every eight years, and the neighbourhood shops have given way to supermarkets and hypermarkets often set out of town and accessible only by car. There, wants, rather than needs, are catered for by a bewildering plethora of prepacked, pre-weighed goods, and an anonymous assistant on each of a dozen checkout tills. People on the move increasingly have little expectation of being known, being understood or being personally involved in the routine events of everyday life. They are consumers. In patterns of shopping at least they have learned to accept anonymity and indifference as a way of life.

This comes home to me in a personal way. When I was a young girl in Yorkshire my mother would sometimes walk with me on a Sunday afternoon to see the house where my grandparents had once lived, and the house in which she was born. By that time the surrounding streets had changed; there were a few more houses encroaching on the open fields, favourite old trees had been felled outside the long walled garden of a country estate, but for her the area remained unmistakably significant. And although I had never lived in that house myself, its location was always full of meaning for me too; an aunt and uncle still lived next door; several of my mother's many other relatives lived or worked within a few minutes' walk, and old neighbours would come out to greet us and pass the time of day. The walk might often be rounded off by visiting my grandmother in her present home and talking about the changes!

When I met my husband I was interested to discover he also had strong childhood attachments to particular neighbourhoods. His big extended family had long local roots in Norfolk and London, and after our engagement we had reciprocal experiences of being taken home to meet seemingly dozens of cousins, aunts and uncles in the same areas, who all needed to affirm our choice of a future partner! Yet this sense of location is all but lost to my children. They have lived in five different homes in two continents, and if they want to visit grandparents or any of our brothers and sisters it now involves at least a three-hour car journey along major motorways. What is more, I have never been able to show them my own first home in Yorkshire: it was blanketed under town development and new housing schemes decades ago. And although a few elderly relatives remain scattered around and enjoy our visits, the complex community life I was brought up with has long since disappeared. There, in the heartland of my mother's county, as in the great metropolis of London, people follow predictable patterns of car dependence, commuting to work and distant supermarket shopping.

All this is important because even though workplaces and neighbourhoods rarely offer *intimate* relationships they are quietly relied on to provide people with daily contacts which are significant to them. There is a good deal of study which shows that people need as well as close relationships those of a less demanding nature. There is great value in being part of a bigger context, of having some place or function in the order of things. It is true that people who live on their own and those who live within family households both seek some larger community.

My own family unit has found this in two main ways, by maintaining relationships with the extended family and through wide Christian networks. Although geographically distant from both sets of grandparents we now live close to one of my own cousins and to many of my husband's. An advantage of living in the capital city for him is that he has been able to renew contact with the brothers and sisters of his parents. The long childhood years he spent putting down roots with his aunts, uncles and cousins means that they will always be a very significant part of his life, and of all of ours. So we regularly get together with any excuse for a full family celebration! In a similar way the wider Christian community provides a vitally important reference point in our lives; some Christian friends have stayed close to us for many years, and remain a consistent source of support and commitment. In a local sense, the fellowship of our home church offers a neighbourhood focus for each of us, and has provided a growth base for our children.

Other people may find their larger community elsewhere: identification with others with the same national origins, a political party, a local football supporters' club, Scout or Guide movements, the Civic Society. Patterns of dependency on these groups can often be very marked, and people can feel very disorientated if the network is even temporarily removed. This is one reason, for example, why people in the armed services frequently find it difficult to revert successfully to 'civvy' life. The fixed social structure and relationships of their previous communal lives all announce that order and familiarity in which they had a meaning and a role. In a similar way when their neighbourhood has been communal and close-knit it is easy to see why some unemployed people find it difficult to move areas to take up work. All their social roots have been put down in the one locality where they feel significant. This is one of the reasons why people who do move to find work also can feel isolated and bereft, even though they may have been given a new set of relationships in their jobs.

This gives weight to the idea that even in our changing neighbourhoods regular human contact seems to remain important. As Anthony Storr points out. 'It is generally accepted that most human beings want to be loved. The wish to be recognized and acknowledged is at least as important.'[3] In the course of an average day most of us encounter people whom we would not regard as intimates but who still contribute to our social context and to our sense of well-being. The newspaper girl, the postman, neighbours, people on the bus, bank clerks, parents at the school gate, and many others may all have familiar faces with whom we exchange a greeting. What is interesting, of course, is that many of these people know us more than we know them. Those who work on the post or on newspaper deliveries often know their customers in many detailed ways: the time they get up in the morning, their reading habits, the number of letters they receive and from where, the breadth of their social contacts, the time of day they leave for work and how quickly they pay their bills! And if these significant people disappear and are replaced by others then we feel a personal sense of loss, as well as a temporary disordering of our affairs. Yet we usually know nothing about the lives of these people and we do not need to in order to value the relationship we have with them. For what is valued is simply the recognition of mutual interdependence, the acknowledgement of the fact that we exist and are significant enough to warrant a greeting.

The Growth of Individualism and Economism

I have been identifying some changes in our culture which have affected the way we relate to other people. And although I have focused on changes in neighbourhoods or work and consumer patterns I could have chosen many others. The interesting thing is that such changes do not come out of thin air. Obviously they relate to advances in technology, to population trends, and needs within the economy. But they also connect with underlying philosophies of society. For these can influence even how other needs are perceived. And amongst the whole web of ideas and attitudes which lie beneath these changes two are particularly significant for this book.

The first is the influence of individualism. An individualist philosophy has long been a part of British and American cultures, although in Britain it battled hard with a concern for social welfare and collective responsibility, particularly in the postwar years. By the 1980s and early nineties it was evident, however, that in Britain, as in America, individualism had won. In fact the whole emphasis on social concern became discredited, and even the concept of 'society' was challenged. One of the frequently quoted statements of Mrs Thatcher, that there was no such thing as society (only individuals and their families), became thoroughly enshrined in a political and economic creed for over a decade.

Individualism holds as sacrosanct (at least in theory) the sovereignty of the individual. Individual choice, rights, freedom, ownership and morality have become central concepts of British culture, and to challenge them is the worst form of modern blasphemy. Individualism has therefore made it possible to give unqualified public approval to the drive for individual success, individual affluence and individual profit. It has also offered a public invitation to millions of people to love themselves more than their neighbours. The argument advanced by Michael Novak that individual freedom to accumulate leads to generosity and benevolence sadly is not borne out except in a few cases in British society. Instead it seems more the case that a concentration on private success and gain does not easily translate into concern for other people.

And in that lies a fundamental dilemma. For what becomes increasingly evident is that an individualist perspective is essentially centred upon strong individuals. For they are the ones who have the resources and the drive to pursue these acclaimed goals. Weak individuals, however, become penalized. They indeed are likely to be robbed of their 'individual' status and be lumped together. It is a common complaint of the unemployed, the poor and the disadvantaged that they are seen simply as numbered entities: card carriers who must fit the system for the system is too big and unwieldy to yield to them. This ethos seems to be present even in those who operate the caring services. Daily contact with the 'failures' of a success-oriented society can harden those who work with them, for example in administering welfare benefits. Suspicion of potential thieves or scroungers, and disdain for the inadequate so often becomes embedded into the way relationships are conducted or the messages that are unconsciously communicated. It is easy to become callous and indifferent to the needs of people when they can all be grouped under one impersonal classification.

Even though it works at best only partially, and at worst produces great injustice, the influence of an individualist philosophy has extended way beyond the 'public' world. As well as being the philosophy behind patterns of taxation, transport, education, the deregulation of Sunday trading and the decline of social welfare, it has become the framework within which people think about every area of life. So, inevitably, it has affected personal relationships. Sexual ethics, family living and even leisure patterns have all come under its influence. I would want to argue that it has indeed proved one of the biggest barriers to intimacy, and shall be looking at some of its effects in later chapters.

The ultimate irony of individualism is that although it starts with a declared concern for the fulfilment of the individual (through individual choice, individual rights, individual sovereignty), the outcome is almost always a society in which the individual is devalued and isolated. Ronald Rolheiser makes this final point graphically:

> As we become more of a *Gesellschaft* society we seek our privacy and freedom with a passion, not wanting any inter-dependence forced upon us. We want to be free to choose the persons with whom we will relate. So, at marriage, we break away from our own family to try to create our own private, nuclear family. We seek our own private life, with a private house, a private car, a private office, and not content with that, we want within our home a private room, a pri-vate telephone, a private television and so on. And once we have attained that, and systematically undercut many of our interdependencies with other people, then we wonder why we are lonely.[4]

Economism

In Western culture, individualism has been accompanied by the growth of economism, the widely assumed notion that the fun-damental value of anything has to be given in economic terms. This idea has been so powerful that it now dominates the mind-set with which people approach any event or transaction. Every-thing must have a price tag. The question is 'Does it pay?' And the question is asked not simply in the world of busi-ness, town planning and corporations. It is raised as a way of calculating the value of virtually any activity. And so hav-ing a baby, enjoying music, going to church or caring for the environment are seen in economic terms, even when the eco-nomic might be the least important aspect. Two decades ago,

Schumacher made this point very eloquently in his book *Small is Beautiful*:

> In the current vocabulary of condemnation there are few words as final and conclusive as 'uneconomic'. If an activity has been branded as uneconomic, its right to existence is not merely questioned but energetically denied . . . Call a thing immoral, soul-destroying or a degradation of man, a peril to the peace of the world or to the well being of future generations, as long as you have not shown it to be 'uneconomic', you have not really questioned its right to exist, grow and prosper.[5]

It is amazing really how we have let this view penetrate so many areas of society. Somehow we have been lulled into thinking of this as normal. 'Surely there must be a "bottom line"? Of course everything must pay!' And month by month this perspective has been taken into education, into health care, into social work, into ethics, into the church. In any of these areas it can be demonstrated in many ways.

Take the growth of managerialism, for example. When the economic is the most crucial aspect of any enterprise, then the most important people in that enterprise are the managers. This has, of course, long been held true in business and industry, and reflected very much in salary levels. But this industrial model has been imported into areas where management skills were once thought of as far less significant than professional expertise (if indeed they were thought of at all!) Now we hear the protest from many headteachers that their role is no longer that of a professional teacher leading a committed staff of other trained professionals. But they are asked to be managers who are there to think about 'productivity', to attend to budgets, to make the school 'competitive', to attract more good calibre pupils, to work out how to cut economic corners, to manage tight resources. And the same is increasingly true throughout the professions, whether in medicine, social work or probation care.

This has gone along with another shift. There used to be a great concern about causes, for coming to grips with reasons for things that happened. In trying to understand issues it would be normal for certain kinds of questions to be raised:

'Are we understanding things aright?' 'How can we discover what causes the patterns we see (of crime, or poor educational achievement or breakdown of marriage)?' 'What is behind the way in which people learn?' 'What further research should be developed in these areas?' But now there is almost a weariness in trying to find causes or in raising the question 'why?' Instead, there is an assumption that we all know why. Marriages break up because partners are tired of each other. People do not learn because they are stupid or because they are not taught properly. People commit crimes because they are bad.[6] Reasons are simple and obvious, so we do not need more knowledge, more resources, further research, extensive and futile probing of the 'whys'. Instead, we need to concentrate on putting things right by managing the way people behave. And so questions about causes have been replaced by questions about procedures. The preoccupation is not with understanding people but with ensuring better management. We need efficiency. We need more rigorous competition. We need to avoid being uneconomic. So we must regulate and manage human behaviour.

Some of these arguments are sound. It is important to exercise good stewardship of resources, and to ensure social and work structures do not collapse through inadequate organization. It is also important not to allow specific ideas about causes of human action to become great, unchallenged orthodoxies that we all bow before. Yet I believe we must remain very cautious about the underlying shift. For when important questions about human relationships are reduced to questions about managing behaviour, much of the human dimension has already been dismissed. People are no longer being taken seriously. The aim instead is to regulate them within a predetermined (economic) system.

We must notice that this is entirely in keeping with the whole thrust of economism. For economism reduces all value to the economic. It believes that there are no mysteries, that anything which is real can be sold or exchanged. Even public ethical questions ('Is it right?') are in danger of being replaced by economic ones ('Can we afford it?'). Economism says, sometimes in a shout, sometimes in a whisper, that material values are the fundamental basis of reality. So it has profound implications for the way we approach daily life. For it gives us a false measurement by which to assess the real value of things.

We can see its hollowness quickly when we apply it to the area of intimate relationships. The private lives of many business tycoons give assent to what the Beatles sang decades ago, that money can't buy us love. (Ironically, the biographies of John Lennon published in the 90s have come up with a similar sad conclusion.) Yet this remains a counter-cultural message. For economism drives us to believe the reverse; that an expensive holiday produces a peace with self, that the newest kitchen delivers a blissful marriage, that an abundance of television sets (all tuned to individual channels) brings a contented family. It confuses affluence with emotional satisfaction, material well-being with intimacy. The sad thing is that those who believe this lie pay the price.

The deepest problem with the philosophies of individualism and economism over the last two decades is that they are out of step with the most fundamental needs of human beings, and have therefore proved inadequate in relating to who we are and what matters to us. A point made by Olthius offers a succinct summary: 'We live in a "things-first, people-second" society which makes genuine love difficult. Instead of being taught to love people and use things, we are more often taught to love things and use people. Such a climate provides precious little room for sharing, caring and being oneself.'[7] Consequently, a culture which has slowly grown based on the centrality of the individual and the economic has left us dissatisfied and deeply lonely. For our value is always more than economic. Economism fails to acknowledge the amazing non-economic richness of the world God has made. The reality of most things that surround us cannot be understood, let alone exhausted, in economic terms. The beauty of a sunset, the gentleness of a baby's face, the mellowness of an old friendship, the power of prayer and worship cannot be reduced to economic categories without destroying their very meaning and integrity. And ultimately we are not and were never intended to be individuals. In our very created personhood we are people-in-relationship. The reality of this touches down into every social situation, for our lives inextricably involve and are affected by other human beings. We live with others in households, we cluster in neighbourhoods, we drink the same water, drive on the same roads, breathe the same atmosphere, suffer the same pollution, face the same recession and die of the same diseases. In this world, where others do exist and matter, to experience our own significance in the context of those others is crucial.

These two ideologies ultimately lead us into emotional bankruptcy. It is often with painful hindsight that many come to recognize the sobering fact that a commitment to individualist materialism and a commitment to intimate relationships are almost incompatible.

Growth of Violence

Many people who would not necessarily reflect on social change theoretically still have their own observations about society. One is that it is marked by growing violence. The experts might well contest this, of course. Violence is nothing new. Brutality towards other people has occurred in almost all societies throughout history, and the brutality evidenced in former epochs was of a chilling and bloodthirsty kind which we in modern civilized regimes shudder to think about. The very instruments of torture preserved for us in museums of antiquity are light-years away from life in our pleasant leafy suburban areas. What is arguably more true is that in the decades since the end of the First World War British society has been the least violent in its history.

Yet there is a sense in which the knee-jerk reaction of the person in front of the television set is well founded. The sense of stability has been undermined by many events during the more recent years. Spectacular acts of sadism, many of which have involved children, have brought ripples of horror into people's everyday lives. And there is evidence that a new culture of violence has begun to grow in the West closely attuned to the prevailing ethos. Even though the precise reasons behind this growth are not clear, they do seem to be part of a mentality which devalues people and seeks sensation and self-gratification.

The statistics themselves are striking. Over the last twenty years there has been an enormous rise in crimes of violence against the person. In 1971 in England and Wales 47,000 such crimes were recorded. By 1993 the figure stood at an alarming 201,800.[8] One of the most frightening trends is the use of dangerous weapons, especially firearms, in other kinds of crime. For example, in 1972 there were 182 cases of firearms being used in offences of 'criminal damage'. By 1991 this had gone up to 12,000,[9] a rise of almost six and a half thousand per cent! Any particular offence represented in these statistics might not be directed against the person, but the implication of the figures is very clear. If people get in the way, they can quickly be obliterated.

Many elderly people feel understandably isolated and vulnerable in the face of this violence. They wall themselves up inside their homes and are afraid to answer the door after dark. They know they are of no account to anyone who is prepared to attack them in order to take whatever goods they might have. Similarly, members of ethnic minorities often have to live with the recurrent possibility of racial antagonism because of hatred targeted against them. Then there are parents who are anxious for the safety of their children, and children are taught not to trust strangers. One effect is that well-meaning strangers are often reluctant to approach a child in distress for fear that they too will be brought under suspicion. In the tragic and much publicized murder of James Bulger in 1993 a number of adults had to live with the memory of having seen the child being led away by his young murderers, and feeling unable to intervene. The number of missing children grows weekly, and every new publicized incidence of child abuse produces alarm and shock; not least when it occurs at the hands of those within the family or household, rather than from strangers.

Unprovoked violence of all kinds has a destructive message. It is that people have no deep intrinsic value. It is a message which is shouted loudly in the sadism and ugliness evident in many contemporary films. What is more, the long-term impact on those who survive violence can be very profound. Physical wounds might heal, but emotional scars linger for years, and in some people present almost insuperable barriers to trusting others fully. Even more than that, the sense of self-worth and of personal value may not be regained until much later in life, and sometimes even never at all. To be treated as someone who does not matter, who can be used and disposed of is a fundamental affront to our humanness, particularly if the experience is a prolonged one. Yet it is part of living in our contemporary culture and, whether we are personal victims of violence or not, ultimately it affects us all.

Sexual Violence

One area of violence has other undertones. It is sexually driven. Women are the specific target for many violent encounters, and many of them fear attack or rape whenever they walk alone in certain areas in British cities. A study done in the London Borough of Wandsworth pointed to the fact that more than sixty per cent of women interviewed, from different ethnic backgrounds, said they were afraid to leave their homes at night.[10] And even though the many 'self-defence' schemes might help women in some situations, in acts of real violence there is little that can be done for protection. A rape victim who was a karate expert told of her experience of utter fear:

> I thought I was really strong and that I could fight and was tough. But the violence that was coming from this man really frightened me. He really paralysed me. Now I actually view men with suspicion. All men I see as potential rapists and violent. I have since talked about it to friends who have had similar experiences.[11]

Sexual violence often belongs to a cult of the erotic which uses women's sexuality to enact punishment. This destructive woman-hatred is evident in most forms of hard pornographic literature, and videos. Therapists often describe how those who have become addicted to it find it very hard to enter into any kind of intimate relationship without deep psychic complications.

The 'success' of the pornographic industry is a good example of the success of the prevailing ideologies of individualism and economism. This is evident even in the soft porn available at almost any newsagent. For pornography is the ultimate in individualist sexuality. No relationship is involved, no other human being to care about with real needs and longings. Nor can any disease be caught. It simply exists as an erotic visual aid for individual gratification. What is more, sex is reduced to an economic category. Pornography does not present sexual activity as having integrity in an intimate bonding, full of love and warmth. But it is displayed as a cheap commodity which can be bought and sold in ever more debasing and dehumanizing forms. The saddest thing is that pornography can never be a substitute for relating to another human being. It can only widen the loneliness.

Conclusion: A Postscript on Postmodernity

What I have been documenting might be described as a loss of confidence in the public world with regard to many of the key features of modernity. It is not only that the public world has become isolated from warmth and closeness between people. It is also that belief in those humanist ideals which have flourished since the eighteenth-century Enlightenment has declined. Social progress, progressive secularization, and the ability of human beings to direct their affairs in a rational way are no longer held as axiomatic. Instead there is cynicism towards these very utopias of modern society. We see this not least in the shift away from the deference given to scientific or political movements, and the reluctance to allow theories of experts to interpret and direct and shape public thinking. For *postmodernity* now exhibits scepticism about such 'grand narratives', towards the very idea that there are big systems of truth and explanation which will give us the key to understanding the world aright. Instead, the culture of consumption turns everything, including truth and knowledge themselves, into marketable consumer items. Citizens become consumers and goods themselves are valued not for their use, but for the *meaning* they bestow. People find significance in the very act of consumption to the extent that 'I shop, therefore I am' has become one of the slogans of postmodernity. Inevitably, this reinforces advertising as a key feature of postmodern society which curiously blurs the content with the medium. Along with the goods that they present to us, the images which are used to present them become products consumed for their own sake. There is seemingly no limit to what can be commodified. Inevitably, not just sex but many other forms of intimacy have been put on the list.

The need for intimacy is a crucial part of our human longings. Yet the conditions in which real intimacy can develop and grow seem to be increasingly absent in the world we inhabit. The confusion between image and reality, between person and consumer feeds into the brittleness of the public world, further accentuating the loss of coherence and integration. Even language seems barren, a 'sounding brass' or a 'tinkling cymbal'. James Olthius comments: 'Troth, openness, authenticity, warmth, integrity, sensitivity, understanding, commitment seem to be only words. Manipulation, double-dealing, efficiency, coldness, suffocation, loneliness, alienation appear to be the realities.'[12]

It comes as no surprise, therefore, to read that loneliness is a sad and constant companion for many people. And yet the irony is that even this becomes exploited by the economism of our postmodern consumer culture, with no longer any attempt at subtlety. Lonely? You can buy or rent your own 'date' on video, especially selected just for you (and anyone else who pays) for viewing in a darkened room, with or without explicit sex. Wanting relationships? You can share intimate talk for hours on (highly profitable) telephone chat lines with people of similar sexual orientation, all available for just 49 pence a unit by ringing one of these numbers . . . The total price for such mass-produced, disembodied 'intimacy' is simply a video shop subscription, a large phone bill, and a greater emptiness than ever when you switch off the set or put the receiver down.

I believe that the perceptions of Henri Nouwen with which I began the chapter are very much on target. Intimacy is so regularly promised, but so rarely delivered. And the conditions required to bring about change in this area are very wide-reaching. A culture which is fragmenting and increasingly focusing on surfaces rather than depth is not likely to have the inner coherence from which critically to address its own pathology. For more is needed than glossy magazines telling us how to increase our libido, or how to be more assertive in our relationships. Even seminars which help us towards greater individual openness, or conferences which increase the level of awareness in the caring professions and the churches only scratch the topsoil without disturbing the sprawling roots of the problem. For changes to be introduced that will be effective for good, some of the fundamental assumptions of our culture must be understood and challenged in a way that works healing into the political, social and economic areas and encompasses all levels of public life. But the 'private' – issues which lie deep within the human psyche – must be reached. At the most fundamental level what intimacy itself means in human life, and what it means to be a human person will need to be addressed. In that respect we have not even begun.

3

Intimacy and the Private World

Today we find many people in a state of confusion and disillusionment about relationships. Feelings of discomfort, disenchantment and alienation have reached epidemic proportions.

Jacquelyn Carr

For most people in our society life comes in two compartments: their work life and private life. And usually, although work is something that may be talked about, their private life is their own affair. The label 'private', of course, does not necessarily just involve areas of sex or relationships. It can include opinions on a whole range of ideas or topics which people do not want to be opened up to the scrutiny of others. 'We never talk about religion and politics,' muttered a smooth host to me at a dinner party. A pity, I thought afterwards, it would have done much to improve the evening!

But this division between public and private is more than just a social convention at dinner parties. For more than a century it has dominated the way our society has been organized. It separates our lives into two, and lies at the centre of how we understand relationships. In most people's minds, the last word you would use to describe the public world is 'intimate'. For the public arena is by its very nature hard-nosed and tough. It is the world of economics and negotiations, efficient management, and impersonal bureaucracies. In this scheme of things, close relationships, sexuality, marriage, love and home life belong somewhere else. They belong in the 'private world'.

The gap between these two worlds is wide, and some people have difficulty in bridging it. They find either that they are consumed by the public world: they become workaholics, organization people, single-minded careerists where all of life is work. Or they feel trapped in the private: the bereaved and elderly who feel isolated, a parent alone with children, a woman who describes herself as 'only a housewife'. But for most others there are well-worn highways which carry their daily lives between the two, from the hard competitive public arena to the personal, private one. And these highways are important for it is in this second, shadowy realm that all the hidden emotional and deep needs of people have traditionally been deposited. In the private world the whole language is different. It is now possible to talk about love and feelings, about yearnings and hopes. It is permissible here to acknowledge our fears and our vulnerability.

Although the division between public and private is deeply entrenched in our society it presents us with three problems. The first is that the division is an impoverishing one. People whose commitment is predominantly to the private world find their official contribution to society devalued, and indeed made invisible in all official statistics. In turn the public realm can be vacated of deep human values and warmth, and left harsh and often ruthless. In one sector, human relationships are crucial but often exploited; in the other, people can be simply secondary to the efficient functioning of the firm.

A second problem is that the division is an artificial one. It is not true that the public world is the world of work and the private simply the world of relationships. Relating to others in a caring way often requires a great deal of work. The fact that in the UK there are around six million carers reminds us that as much work goes on in the so-called private sphere as in the public one, but it is largely the work of the unpaid, done mostly by women. This work, though 'voluntary', is often demanding and even sacrificial, yet remains part of the hidden gift economy which underlies so much of what goes on officially in Britain.[1]

The third problem is probably the most pertinent one for this chapter. It is that the private world is becoming overburdened. It is increasingly asked to mop up the tragedies and heartbreaks which have their roots in the so-called 'public' area. Yet at the very time when it is becoming severely overstretched, it too is lacking resources. For where does the private sphere get its strength and power to counteract the loneliness which lies deep in the roots of society? Where does it get its stamina to combat the effects of the rat race, powerlessness and redundancy? We cannot create and sustain a cocoon in society which will insulate us from the damaging effects of the way we conduct our public affairs. In reality, the opposite is true. The underlying values which dominate the public realm pervade the private also. For example, individualism and its focus on self has not been contained within the world of economics and consumerism. It has invaded personal relationships at their very heart, reducing other people to being 'the punctuation marks in the dry and windy monologue of our own self-centred existence'.[2]

The search for intimacy is more than a 'negative reaction to a wider, more impersonal universe'.[3] But it is intensified by the parallels between the values of the public world and those of the private. For domestic violence mirrors violence in society. Child abuse is another way of commodifying people. Even something as everyday as job frustration can be carried into private life in the form of anger or irritability. Just as the pressures increase, so does the demand for better and deeper relationships. The result is that for many people even close relationships can no longer meet the depth of their search for human intimacy, and resolve the sense of isolation in their lives.

Marriage and Family Life

Marriage and family life have usually been thought of as the traditional way the private realm most effectively caters for the intimacy needs of society. Yet, at the end of the twentieth century these time-honoured institutions may possibly be under greater threat in Britain than at any time before. Marriage particularly has come under fire; both because it seems to have failed to provide the intimacy it promises, and because it has not been strong enough to withstand the pressures of stress, boredom and financial difficulties. The argument has been that, far from meeting the deepest needs of people, marriage has been very often responsible for some of their deepest problems. For some it has been destructive and has brought brokenness and misery. For others it has merely become empty and tedious, full of repetitive tasks but without the framework of love and commitment to give them meaning.

Examining the Statistics

Current statistics on sexual behaviour, marriage and divorce rates all indicate massive changes in the way people live in the part fifty years.

1. Sexual Behaviour

The idea that sex belongs only to marriage finds little favour with the majority of today's population. Studies on sexual behaviour from the Kinsey Report in the USA in the 1940s through to the *National Survey* in Britain in 1994 chart this very significant move. For example, in the 1960s, Michael Schofield's survey of British adolescents reported that 17 per cent of girls and 34 per cent of boys had experienced intercourse by the time they were 18, irrespective of whether they were married.[4] Twelve years later in Christine Farrell's report, these figures had risen to 55 per cent of girls and 69 per cent of boys.[5] These trends were confirmed and updated in 1994, in the authoritative *Sexual Behaviour in Britain: The National Survey of Sexual Attitudes and Lifestyles* which studied the shifts over forty years.[6]

In the 1950s almost half of all women waited until they were married before they had sex. In the 1990s this had dropped to four per cent. A fifth of men were virgins on their engagement in the 1950s (14 per cent on marriage) and the figure today is under one per cent. Because men clearly showed a lower commitment to abstinence than women even four decades ago, women were previously left to reinforce the relationship between chastity and marriage. They have largely abandoned that task. Now women as well as men are likely to have had sexual partners from at least their late teens and the small percentage who stay celibate until they marry usually do so because they have strong religious or moral convictions, no longer because it is the 'done thing'.

2. Marriage Patterns

The changes in sexual behaviour feed into the marriage figures themselves. During the last twenty years there has been a marked fall-off in the 'popularity' of marriage. From 1971 to 1990 the pace of this change became dramatic. The rate for first marriages was more than halved, and the numbers of those cohabiting more than doubled. By 1992, 18 per cent of unmarried women and men were cohabiting. Remarriages rose from 20 per cent to 35 per cent as a proportion of all marriages, although fewer of those who had divorced were remarrying.

3. Divorce Figures

Marital breakup has similarly increased. United Kingdom figures over a long period show a growing rate of divorce throughout the century, but one which accelerated very quickly after 1971, when the Divorce Reform Act became law. In the mid-eighties there were almost half as many divorces as there were marriages (175,000 against 393,000 marriages), and between 1971 and 1990 the divorce rate more than doubled (rising from 74,000 to 153,000). By 1990 a quarter of all divorces in England and Wales involved at least one partner who had been divorced before. The rate in Britain is now higher than any other country in the EEC, more than one and a half times that of France, Germany and Belgium, although it still lags behind the average figure for the USA.

Some details are also significant. One of them concerns the length of marriage. Fewer marriages are surviving those first few months. A tenth of all divorces in the UK are now between couples married for less than two years. At the other extreme, those who have stayed together for years also separate. A fifth of all divorces are between those who have gone through more than twenty years of apparently successful marriage.

The other statistic concerns the male-female ratio. More than three-quarters of all divorce petitions are filed by women. Again this figure has been growing, in fact since the 1950s. In 1961 women applied for rather more than half of the divorces. By 1971 it was around two-thirds. Since the mid-eighties it has topped three-quarters. It is interesting too that most divorces to wives have been granted on the grounds of the 'unreasonable behaviour' of their husbands.[7]

Statistics are important for showing overall trends, but each individual example is significant in its own way. Every incidence of divorce makes some statement about the failure of the marriage to provide an intimacy which holds people together and sustains them. Each couple who decides to live together without a 'marriage' is making some statement about the irrelevance for them of the traditional institution. Every act of adultery says something about lack of commitment, contemporary pressures and the restlessness around us.

Expectations of Marriage

It is very difficult to argue that marriages which end in breakdown do so because of common factors, just as it would be difficult to identify certain things about marriage which would please everyone. Yet when we do look for explanations some conclusions keep recurring.

The first is that many people are unsure from the outset what they want from marriage. They are unclear what makes marriage different from cohabitation or indeed from living on their own. Some have felt comfortable with the pattern provided by their parents and echo that model in their own relationship. Others do not, but are unsure what to put in its place. Women in particular seem less content with 'traditional' role-dominated marriages than was formerly the case, and this is true not just of young women, but also of those who divorce their husbands after many years of being together. What might have been assumed in marriage relationships two generations ago is no longer acceptable for some today.

Another explanation is that more conflict is likely to arise in marriages today, and people find it more difficult to handle. This is probably connected to the fact that roles and processes of decision-making are no longer so clear-cut as they once were, but are fluid. Conflict over money, sex, use of time, housework, work patterns and eventually children can all start within the first few weeks of marriage, and either build up to breakup or end in an unsatisfying stalemate. Then, some argue, that there is less emphasis on long-term *commitment* in marriage than there used to be. Wedding vows are now seen more as a declaration of hopeful intent rather than as a permanently binding, 'for better, for worse'. With the increasing legal ease of divorce few people feel that they *must* stay together because they have promised to do so.

One other conclusion is the most difficult to quantify. It is that many more people today are uncertain about their personal identity and are struggling to know who they are. So those who entered marriage in a mood of optimism – born out of romance, love and a sense of shared values – can find that time corrupts these. Instead, a mood of frustration and unease can weaken their commitment to their partner; even more so if it goes along with a shifting sense of their own identity. 'I don't know who he is anymore,' disclaimed a wife of her irritable and much absent husband. 'I just know he's not the person I married.'

Each of these conclusions makes a valid assessment of the pressures on marriage today, and together they assemble a formidable picture. There is no lack of evidence to support them. Take the suggestion that people are unsure what they want from marriage. Even this observation itself is couched in contemporary language. It belongs to a period where there are options, styles, different possibilities within marriage, and where individual choice is regarded as paramount. A couple may indeed be looking for lifelong companionship, troth and a willingness to give all that they are to one another. But that certainly cannot be taken for granted. Marriage can just as easily be seen as an end to loneliness, a increase in status, an acceptable base for child rearing or a quest for self-knowledge. For many people the search for intimacy in marriage is bound up with the search for themselves. And as the search for self becomes profounder and more intense it can mean that marriage has a greater burden to bear than it was ever intended for.

There is plenty of evidence too about the repudiation of traditional gender roles. The fact that three-quarters of all the divorces granted are petitioned for by women is itself significant (although it also partly reflects the reality that women are often left with the task of ending the marriage). I was interested in the account of a recent divorce petition brought by a young wife against her husband. She argued that he treated her predominantly as a servant, requiring her to do all the household chores, showing no interest in her educational and social needs or in spending time with her outside the home. The divorce was granted on his 'unreasonable behaviour'. I wondered if the much older women in her family ever made quiet comparisons with their own early expectations of marriage. Today even though in family households women still do most of the housework, cleaning, cooking and ironing, it can bring resentment when such chores are never shared, or when such work is simply taken for granted. The old quote 'It starts out when you sink into his arms; it ends up with your arms in his sink' even now has a contemporary ring.

The stability and security of fixed domestic and marital work roles, important to previous generations, seems now prized less than a commitment to mutuality and sharing. Women whose mothers or grandmothers might have accepted a marriage defined by home and domestic duties are now making more strenuous demands of reciprocal understanding from their own relationships. Very often having no marriage is seen as preferable to marriage which is predominantly functional.

The issue of conflict handling is also a substantial one. Many young people enter marriage with little or no notion as to how to resolve disagreements and conflict between them. Often the only role model has been their own parents whose own 'resolution' was to separate. Consequently, rows can bring fear and high levels of anxiety, with the partner who is more desperate for appeasement 'giving in' to save the situation. Although this might be a good way to end conflict initially, it can also perpetuate a pattern of dominance and bullying which is harmful in the long run.

Yet although most of the conclusions offered can be backed up with these sorts of arguments I am not yet convinced that they inevitably spell a drop in the level of commitment within marriage overall. It is often alleged that people give up too easily in marriage today; that the high divorce rate indicates an unwillingness among couples to make their union work. That is certainly true of many, but by no means of all. Those involved in counselling often have a different story. We see people who are struggling hard, even desperately, with their relationship, but who often feel they have conflicting or even incompatible needs within it. In fact, when marriage does not produce a close emotional partnership, especially early in the relationship, it can bring an enormous sense of being let down.

The increase in demand for marriage counselling itself emphasizes the high expectations many have of their lives together, and the high level of satisfaction they initially seek in that relationship. And the disappointment can deepen if there is little sustained progress even after counselling towards a more satisfying relationship. The trouble is that emotional depth, companionship and intimacy cannot be produced on demand. Sometimes, even when much struggle and effort to communicate has taken place, the problems remain; especially where partners are unevenly matched in their temperamental needs. It is often only after years together that these kinds of difference resolve themselves, and the couple discover that they have grown together, and loved together, and that their relationship has found its own depth of sharing. But some cannot stay around that long. The sad fact is that in spite of the greater demands of emotional fulfilment there is for many an inability to begin to relate or to sustain a relationship at the depth demanded.

Two final issues are important. We have to remember that most adults spend so much of their time in the 'public world' which does not equip us for caring, deep, intimate relationships. How can a person who has been taught that what matters is the ability to get there first, no matter what it costs, suddenly switch to making sacrifices for someone else? And how can a competitive man at work learn to adapt to a 'strong' woman at home? Even for those who are committed to a relational way of living, the transition is often a difficult one, and the success rate is not always high.

The other is that, because marriage is required to produce such high quality interpersonal relationships, there seems to be a strong reluctance to endure a dissatisfying relationship, even if it means living without a permanent 'bonding'. And although many who do break up go on to make later, successful marriages, for others there remains a considerable question mark over the belief that marriage is indeed the best way of meeting our deepest requirements for intimacy. There are in particular two strong lobbies in society today who challenge this idea most strongly.

Feminism and Marriage

Many of the changes in marriage which have come about in the last half century owe something to the influence of feminism. The suggestion that women should have at least as much equality in relationships as men has been one which has found its way into the everyday framework of most people's thinking. The outworking of reciprocal marriages, of equal partnerships, of the needs of intimacy have all been stressed by feminist sympathizers for decades.

Yet there are other feminists for whom this is all too little and too late. Radical feminists' *repudiation* of marriage has gone on for at least twenty years. They have argued that marriage has traditionally been arranged around the demands of a male-dominated society, rather than with an equal concern for women's needs. Consequently, women have been penalized by marriage. Women have had their independence withdrawn, their self-confidence damaged, and their love exploited. This is true, they would insist, both within legal marriage and within patterns of cohabitation. For patriarchal relationships do not depend on a wedding ring to be effective. In fact there is no evidence at all to suggest that the majority of women who live with men outside marriage are more confident, more secure as persons, or more free than those who marry. In some cases there is evidence that they can be even more exploited, especially when children have been born into the relationship.

There has therefore been a prolonged and powerful challenge to the assumption that women find their deepest fulfilment in *dependency*: being housewives, building up a partner's career, rearing children, providing a warm, private retreat from the public world. There is scepticism towards the many appeals made to justify these roles: women's biology, hormones, natural abilities, psychology, need for protection, the sacrifices of motherhood, doing one's duty, or 'the will of God'. Feminist writers feel they have seen through these smoke screens to the resulting oppressive nature of marriage relationships.

Although some feminists urgently press for us to learn the lessons from the past, and reorder our understanding of marriage upon more egalitarian lines, these others are far less optimistic. For them any attempt at 'modern marriage' shares intrinsically the same problems as all marriage. It locks women into oppression. Writing in 1984, Carol Smart voiced widespread doubts that even in a new form marriage is capable of meeting its ideals of intimacy, understanding and flexibility, arguing 'there is little sign of it in the magistrates' domestic courts, the divorce courts and in battered wives refuges'. For her the only viable option was 'not to extend the legal and social definition of marriage to cover cohabitees or even homosexual couples, it is to abandon the status of marriage altogether'.[8]

The Challenge from the Gay Community

Most of the feminist arguments about marriage are echoed by those from the gay community, for the allegation that marriage has always served male interests provides a platform for lesbian writers. In their book on lesbian mothers, Gillian Hanscombe and Jackie Forster use the same argument as Smart to challenge the whole ethos of conventional marriage and the nuclear family. For them the arrangement is wrong because it is wrong for women. Nothing will finally be right for women so long as the legal marriage contract continues: 'One radical change in the law would strike at the heart of patriarchy: the abolition of the marriage certificate.'[9] They argue that such an abolition would lead us to reject many other assumptions about love and relationships:

> Women [must] 'fall in love' with a man and then 'get married' to him. It is becoming more obvious as our century wears on that many women are refusing to comply with this teaching. The demand is too high. The demand is, quite simply, that women should be able to bring together their romantic feelings, their sexual needs, their maternal drives and their capacities for work. All in one place.[10]

These authors are convinced, therefore, that women's intimacy needs can very often be better met by other women rather than by men. There are those who describe their own journey into lesbianism as a growing consciousness that traditional heterosexual marriage means 'men first'. It reinforces male centrality and so makes intimacy and equality impossible. For them the very institution of marriage, contracted by law and legalized by the State, is there to promote patriarchy. Consequently, the way ahead in the search for intimacy is to dispense with old institutional structures, and indeed with men too. Even in parenting, they would argue, lesbian couples can provide as good, if not better upbringing for children than a traditional 'nuclear' family. Their arguments are now part of the battle for no discrimination against lesbians in fostering and child custody.

The challenge from the gay community is not only limited to a lesbian-feminist attack. The normality of heterosexual marriage is undermined by the very growth of alternatives, and by the reiterated suggestion that there are other viable and widely travelled routes to intimacy and emotional happiness.

Two rather different approaches have been articulated. The first is the live-and-let-live argument. Here those who identify themselves as homosexual or lesbian are asking simply that they be seen as normal human beings with equal dignity, intimacy needs and capacity for loving to those of any other people in society. A homosexual identity was not their choice, but 'something finally acknowledged after years of turmoil and bewilderment'.[11] The labelling and belittling of our culture of those whose emotional leanings are towards their own sex has meant that many have found it impossible to feel good about themselves, and have lived lives of deceit and denial. Those who have now come to terms with their sexual orientation see it as something close to their sense of identity, rooted in their very nature and personhood. So, many of them would argue, to be denied the rights to expression of intimacy, love and physical affirmation because of some quirk of biology or psychology is painful and unfair. It is to be branded morally deficient or a criminal.

The other approach is more assertive. The argument here does not depend on an individual's homosexuality being somehow physically or biologically rooted. For a gay lifestyle is no less valid even if it is simply a matter of choice and sexual preference. What is under attack instead is the norm of heterosexuality. There are claims that numerically the gay community is a significant proportion of the total population (some suggest ten per cent) and that bisexuality is almost as common as 'straight' heterosexuality at certain periods of life. (One author talks of 'one third of the nation's population'.[12]) Homosexuality is therefore both morally and statistically on a par with heterosexuality, and consequently those structures based on a 'heterosexual power elite' must be challenged.

One of those structures is the whole 'institution' of monogamy which is now targeted as both oppressive and unrealistic. It is seen as particularly oppressive to homosexuals whose lifestyle includes having more than one sexual partner. In the book *We Speak for Ourselves*, Jack Babuscio makes the point that 'in a society where passing for straight is for many of crucial importance, casual affairs and anonymous encounters will be easier to sustain than stable relationships'. He therefore claims the right for gays to choose either multiple or monogamous relationships and wants to divide off 'mutual commitment to an emotional sense of responsibility' from 'simple pledges of erotic fidelity'.[13] The issue of multiple relationships versus monogamy goes beyond the debate in the gay community. For it is not possible to have a homosexual group in society where regular sex with different people outside a marriage bond is accepted as a norm, whilst arguing that for heterosexual people the 'rules' should be different. So when a psychologist is called in to substantiate Babuscio's claim it has to be the whole structure of monogamy which is put under attack:

> Of the thousand or more different societies that have been carefully studied, less than five per cent claim to expect monogamy. Ours is one of them. There are no societies on record, including ours, that can demonstrate working monogamy. Where both parties, for moral or any other reasons practice real monogamy it kills the spontaneity. The quantity goes down, the quality goes down, and sex becomes routine. The non-sexual parts of the relationship suffer as well.[14]

Although the 'live-and-let-live' approach has many friends and allies outside the gay community, the more aggressive approach has far fewer. It has been criticized both for its misrepresentations and its refusal to recognize the consequences of its demands. Claims about the size of the gay population have particularly been challenged, as has the methodology used to determine that size. In *Sexual Behaviour in Britain* the estimated percentage of the UK population involved in homosexual relationships was found to be not ten per cent but nearer one per cent.[15] Almost 94 per cent of the sample claimed to be 'exclusively' attracted to the opposite sex (4 per cent 'mostly'), and only 0.5 per cent said they were exclusively attracted to members of the same sex. Then, the claim of the 'healthiness' of multiple partnering has also been criticized as special pleading. The counter arguments have called for the recognition that the spread of HIV, serious anal damage, and other sexually transmitted diseases has occurred as a result of the undermining of monogamy. Even though there is often a reluctance to make this connection for fear of accusations of bigotry or lack of sympathy, the psychologist Jack Dominian feels the consequences have to be faced. He points to the repercussions of the weakening of sexual faithfulness in society, and the endorsement of promiscuity as a viable way of life. As well as physical effects there are moral, social and psychological ones:

> The consequences of promiscuity are anything but harmless . . . the presence of promiscuity gives rise to a sinister devaluation of

human meaning. The characteristics which emerge are mistrust, lower expectations, destabilisation of relationships, and above all, the impoverishment of the potential of one of the most meaningful human acts.[16]

Dominian and other writers have pointed out also that too ready a celebration of change in this area puts more strain on celibates of either sexual inclination. For in spite of all we read to the contrary, there are still large numbers of people who are committed for personal, moral or religious reasons to developing intimate relationships that do not involve sexual coupling. There are also those who believe in the age-old relationship of friendship!

Gay campaigners see nothing remarkable in the alleged growth in homosexuality and lesbianism. They argue that a large gay minority lies hidden in most societies, but in less repressive, more enlightened cultures it is able to 'come out'. The evidence for this, however, is shaky. There have certainly been several times in history when an overt homosexual culture was evident; for example in ancient Greece, where it went along with a despising of women as less significant than men. Yet in other periods it seems absent altogether. During these times even though there was much romantic literature where sex was discussed explicitly (and often with a vulgarity which is unfashionable even today) it was inevitably seen as sex between a man and a woman. We have to bear in mind, therefore, that cultures themselves produce different forms of sexual behaviour, and different forms of sexual identification. People *learn* to experience themselves as homosexual, or lesbian, and to express themselves as gay. And much of that learning experience and expression depends largely on the overall cultural values which lie on a deeper plain.

The present level of homosexual experience, even though it is below that often claimed, seems to be a particularly contemporary phenomenon. For even though the gay movement stands for community and collectivity, especially when it comes to establishing networks or lobbying parliament, the underlying arguments are very individualist. In one sense it is very critical of the dominant cultural ethos, but in another it relies very heavily on the prevailing ethos of individualism in the culture to grant it support. The claim is for the fulfilment of individual emotional and sexual needs as defined individually, irrespective of what other ethical considerations might be offered. This, more than any deep psychological need, lies behind the insistence on the 'right' to multiple partnering. It is there too in the demand for acceptance of paedophilic behaviour. The language of individualist rights sounds entrenched in Ken Popert's assertion:

> Gay liberation, before anything else, stands for the integrity and inviolability of sexual desire, the right of men and women to choose their sexual partners according to their needs. No matter how well-intended or how good the end, we can never allow anyone to prescribe our sexuality.[17]

The gay community has indeed been counter-cultural in many aspects. And for this it has had to suffer animosity, personal rejection and ostracism. But it is also very much a product of the prevailing culture. The fact that it is in precisely these societies at this point in history where homosexuality has experienced the greatest growth and in some areas, acceptance, is no accident. At a fundamental level it is not out of step with secular cultural values. It is just a beat ahead.

One further observation needs to be made before we leave this section. Even those who have rejected both celibacy and heterosexual marriage for what to them is a more meaningful expression of their own sexuality have not necessarily found deep intimacy in a gay lifestyle. Some of course have not sought it, yet for others this has been a deep longing. Even for a convinced homosexual there is nothing about sex with other men that automatically brings emotional fulfilment. In fact gay and lesbian relationships are as prone to anguish and heartbreak as heterosexual ones. Insecurity, unrequited love, jealousy and desperation are not only to be found in male-female couplings. They can be even more evident elsewhere. Henry's story is a common one:

> I suppose my problem was that I never believed anyone could really love me. I was always selling myself short, measuring against erstwhile or imaginary competitors . . . What I wanted was a relationship that would last a lifetime. I was so concerned that Peter and I should remain together for always that I guess in time I had become his jailer. The more I tried to hold on to Peter the less he seemed to like me.[18]

Henry was not an adolescent experiencing early infatuation, but a 39-year-old man who longed for intimacy and security. These deep human needs are not exclusive to heterosexuals, nor is the vulnerability they bring. Many other stories would illustrate how the rivalry, boredom, manipulation and abuse in other kinds of relationship are part of the homosexual scene also. An old colleague of mine, a woman who had gone from an unhappy marriage into a series of lesbian relationships, ruefully advised a more 'idealistic' younger woman that possessiveness and unfaithfulness are not unknown within lesbianism. They can damage and hurt people as destructively there as anywhere else. In fact it can be worse for some of those who have turned their backs on the majority view, and vested their faith in the gay or lesbian community. Without the traditional family support systems and with a higher level of anonymity and anxiety there can be a much greater degree of instability and distressing exploitation for those who see themselves as gay. And when they experience betrayal or deep hurt there, they can be left feeling that there is nowhere else to go.

This is one reason why the issue of homosexual acceptance has become so large in religious organizations. The desire of gay people to find a home especially within the church has thrown up dilemmas and heart-searching for more than two decades. The response has not always been made with wisdom. On the one hand, the notion of a 'gay church' where the worship of God and the celebration of an unrestrained homosexual lifestyle are virtually synonymous is deeply problematic. For frequently the theology within these churches is such that it prevents people from hearing what the Holy Spirit might be saying in conviction and challenge. It stifles the possibility of biblically reassessing the lifestyles which are being celebrated and shuts out anything which might call for repentance and change. On the other hand those churches which loudly denounce homosexuality as 'filthy, lewd and an offence to God' do so at the cost of serious damage and pain to some who are struggling to make sense of their sexuality and their faith. Without the affirmation of God's love for human beings as the context within which all other issues are tackled, the church becomes a place of judgement rather than of wrestling in love. The most understanding work is often done through patience and long-term care, helped by those within the church who have most direct experience of struggling with sexuality, yet who also know the power of God's love in their lives.[19]

Disillusionment with the Family

Along with a sustained challenge to the sanctity of marriage and importance of monogamy has come a questioning of the ideology of the family. In fact the timing of this has been interesting. Just as many branches of the church have 'rediscovered' the family and developed family-centred celebrations, worship and liturgies, outside the church the family has increasingly come under fire.

The influence of individualism has helped to erode the idea of the family as a collective unit, and to replace it with the idea of the home as a household of related individuals. Many aspects of communal life have all but vanished. One cynic has said that being in family with one another has about the same relationship as a Big Mac has to french fries and a medium coke. Eating meals together, visiting relatives together, spending leisure time together are now less prominent on the agenda of many families, especially when the children move into teenage years. Even watching television together – a typical pastime of the television boom of the fifties to seventies – was less common by the mid-eighties. The boom in computer games, Walkman audio sets and video hire has made individual home-based leisure more of a normality, and today's children live in a world which is mediated electronically. Sociologist Norman Denzin points out crudely that the postmodern child 'is cared for by the television set in conjunction with the day-care centre'.[20]

Sociologists of the 1980s raised the question whether the communal family model was ever more than an ideology. For the segregation of parents and children, husbands and wives was very evident in family life even a few decades ago. For men, the focus was far less on the home than the local club or pub, and families were much more class-based in the time they spent together, and the leisure they shared. Very interesting accounts of this can be found in many studies on the family in the fifties and sixties.[21]

Feminist theorists have argued, therefore, that far from being a unit which met people's shared needs the family has been a 'location where people with different activities and interests in these processes often come into conflict with one another'.[22] There are differences between liberal, socialist and radical feminists as to how these different interests are to be identified, and the debates between them are often as significant as the debate between feminist and non-feminist.[23] But whether the key concern is sexual division of labour, or the issue of sexuality and violence, the patriarchal nature of 'family' is seen as given.[24] For many feminists unease with this model does not stem from any endorsement of individualism, but from a longing for something deeper: 'The feminist critique of the family is not a critique of love and affection, it is not celebration of individualism and isolation, it is a critique of the oppressive context in which these needs are met (if indeed they are met there at all for the majority of people).'[25]

Part of that 'oppressive context' is the very division of public and private and the way in which domestic life is dependent upon and even dominated by work in the 'public' world. So where a family lives, who works to earn money, how frequently they move, where children go to school are all decided not by the family themselves but by the job of the breadwinner(s), and the demands of the firm. And even within the family it is usually the man's job, the man's career, and the man's needs which come first, with the wife and children subsumed under the man's work requirements. The result is a situation which is far from the popular ideology.

The spotlight over recent years has also been on more sinister problems within the family. The increasing evidence of widespread abuse, violence and sexual violation within the family has presented the biggest challenge to its integrity as a haven and retreat from the harshness of the outside world. Official statistics offer us only the tip of the iceberg, and we really have no foolproof way of determining how widespread is such abuse, for in this 'private area' of society it is possible for vulnerable people to be abused in secret. Abuse has a marked effect on the search for intimacy, whether it is suffered by an adult – a wife, a parent – or by a child. Low self-esteem, little sense of personal value, and a fear of trusting others can become part of a person's outlook, and when this goes back to childhood it can be very hard to discard. The power of the past is in itself a key factor in people's relational lives, and will be the subject of a later chapter. Many people in our society are coming to the search for intimacy with a history of deep hurt and misery. And many go away sorrowful.

The Growth of Therapy

In view of all that I have said, it is easy to understand why counselling and therapy has mushroomed over the last few decades. People need help with their 'private lives'. Marital intimacy, and the ease and warmth of close relationships cannot be taken for granted. For some people their counsellor is very likely to have the biggest present impact on their emotional development and sense of personal well-being. This is especially the case in some areas of the USA. In fact there is a joke in California that whenever a friend offers to introduce you to a date for the evening, the first question you must ask is 'Who's his therapist?'

Counselling people towards intimacy can sound very strange. Secure people often believe that intimacy should be spontaneous and personal. It should simply happen in the context of the right relationships. But so often before any such 'right' relationship there have been many wrong relationships, not necessarily of that person's choosing. Much therapy proceeds, therefore, on the assumption that we need to learn how to be intimate. We need to learn how to be released from the past, and to live in our present. For many counsellors, intimacy is something which can be organized and developed in that people can be helped to reflect on themselves and on the way they relate to others.

Professional therapists provide an interesting bridge between the public and the private worlds. Their work is public. Therapy is their job and they are trained and paid to perform this skill. But the things they are dealing with are essentially very private and personal. Counsellors are often given confidences, or show insights about a person that no one else has ever glimpsed. They become skilled in helping a person to relate to her own emotions, to face up to his own needs. For some people the counsellor can quickly become the mainstay of their lives, a shelter from anxiety and the stepping-stone to a new maturity. Essentially, counsellors only succeed insofar as they work themselves out of a job.

For some, individual counselling is not the best form of help. Group therapy or support groups provide for them the means of responding to some specific problem in their lives, like alcoholism or incest. Others come together on the issues of sexuality or gender. For more than two decades women's groups have been important in focusing issues for those who want to identify with other women and explore common experiences in a predominantly male society. Where women have moved into organizations which have until relatively recently been male precincts it is often very important to establish some network where they can get together and raise or share issues, whether these are of professional frustration or sexual harassment. In areas where there are still marked divisions between women and men these groups are even more important. Within the church such gatherings have been a lifeline for women who often feel at odds with the stereotypes they encounter each week, yet powerless alone to come to terms with them.

A more recent phenomenon has been the growth of men's groups which are different in nature and ethos from traditional male groupings, such as work, drinking or social gatherings, or from sexually orientated gatherings such as gay clubs. The aim of these groups is to provide an arena for men to explore issues of emotions, identity or relationships. Whether they develop the 'wild man' ethos of finding 'primitive roots', or explore patriarchy and their place within it, these groups are deliberately self-conscious, identifying manipulation, competitiveness, dishonesty or lack of trust. The fact that many men have reported difficulties in taking on this agenda, even when they have been committed to the task, may indicate something about the way in which they experience emotional restraint. The idea that feelings are embarrassing and it is an asset to be emotionally invulnerable lies as a conventional barrier to openness with other men.[26]

In a context where people are less likely to group in neighbourhoods almost any regular group can take on a life of its own. I meet with a very unlikely gathering of people for an hour and a half each Friday lunch time. We comprise a monk, two Jewish rabbis, two psychiatrists, a Baptist minister, a hospital chaplain, a college lecturer, a medical visitor and her vicar-husband! Over a period of ten years we have got to know each other well. Even though we are different in religious, ethnic, gender and professional backgrounds the group has a warmth, stability and openness which makes it a safe vehicle for reflection and sharing together in trust. It has also enabled each of us at one time or another to make more sense of our own reactions and relationships to others outside the group. It has demonstrated to us in a personal way one aspect of the reality of intimacy.

Conclusion

The last few decades have brought so many changes in the area of personal relationships. In particular the apparent stability and rigidity of former patterns has given way to much greater fluidity, and nothing has been left without scrutiny. Questions about the meaning of sexuality as well as about the morals of sex have all become part of the discourse of our age. Ours is not the first generation to ask these questions, but it may have been the first to find the assumptions of its predecessors so unacceptable.

One other fixture of the past which is being vehemently shaken at the end of the century is the whole distinction between public and private. This demarcation has always been an artificial one, for the public is personal and the personal is political. There is ultimately nothing which can remain hidden behind closed doors, unaffected by what goes on in the public arena. Those who work in the public world are also people with emotional needs and longings for intimacy. Those who were abused at home are also the decision-makers in civic life: men who train soldiers, women who operate on patients.

Yet, ironically, it is not a desire to give credit to the private or to restructure the public but the slide into postmodernity which has produced the greatest challenge to the distinction. For when the big themes of the past are no longer interesting, it is the everyday stories which take centre stage. And when this is put alongside the insatiable urge of consumerism, it is not surprising that an absorption in personalities not policies becomes the flavour of the month. Long gone are the days when the media wrapped a respectful silence around the private lives of 'the royals', bishops or ministers, and focused only on that which was deemed to be in the public domain. Now the private is the most public aspect of what they do. We can find out what they had for breakfast. We can read all about their extramarital affairs. We can debate whether they might have bulimia, or cancer, or AIDS. We can listen to their taped phone calls for a charge of 49p a unit. Some newspaper reporters kindly spend days and nights outside their homes, documenting who comes in and who goes out, photographing what goes on in the garden, the dining-room and even the bedroom if the curtains are left open.[27] Playwrights and novelists make up whatever they want and we watch it. So this breaking down of the public/private split is not in order to rediscover or reshape community or to work for justice. It is purely for consumption, in a society where anything can become a commodity.

I ended the last chapter by highlighting the need for changes in the public world to reach far beyond an obsession with economic growth, or more consumer products. The need was for a greater understanding of what it is to be human. In the light of the fragility of our intimate relationships that need has become even more evident, for it is now recognized that they are too important to be relegated to being the half-time refreshments for the rat race. Research done by social psychologists has thrown much light on the issues considered in this book, and I would acknowledge my own debt to many of their writings. Yet no psychologist is neutral, but each one has a framework of interpretation, a way of making sense of human experience and the reality we live in. As we turn now to look at the origins of intimacy I hope to uncover some of these and make evident what directs my own understanding.

4

The Origins of Intimacy

One of the greatest human longings is to be close to someone.
Fisher and Hart

In all the debate on the changing climate of intimacy in society one point seems to remain clear. It is that the needs for human intimacy continue. In his book *Men and Friendship* Stuart Miller claims that 'needs for intimacy are as perennial as human cultures'. By this he is not referring to sexual needs, although that was often the misconception of people even in his own research. He has in mind rather the needs for closeness and reciprocation from other human beings.

We do not have to look for evidence of these needs. It lies everywhere around us and can be seen in dozens of little cameos plucked out of everyday experience. We encounter it when we watch the joyful reunion of old friends, the affectionate cuddle between grandparent and child, the anxious waiting at the bedside of a sick relative, the fondling and snuggling close of a young couple in love. Within every society, enshrined within rituals and protocols, customs and folklore our need for intimacy persists. It is indeed the 'normal condition of the human race'.[1]

Anthropologists studying societies far different from the British attest to the great variety of cultures in which these needs are expressed. Robert Brain's book, *Friends and Lovers*, describes the experience of closeness among men, in his study of the African Bangwa. He describes how the young men would frequently be found for many hours 'in each other's company, holding hands when they walk in the market'.[2] Studies of polygamous societies will often show the unexpected intimacy which might develop between an old wife and a much younger wife in a very patriarchal household, where because of the structure of male dominance husband-wife intimacy is less likely to be the norm. There is intimacy which develops between those who face an enemy together or work on survival expeditions. The sheer variety of patterns of intimate relationship show that whatever the social context such needs have to be met in some capacity or another.

More evidence can be provided when we look at literature and the arts. Our needs for intimacy shout at us through the pages of diaries, letters, biographies, novels. They are the subject of profound poetry, they are the inspiration behind much music, film, drama and art.

The books which have become classics in the West often tap into this wealth of personal relationships. Novels like Charlotte Brontë's *Jane Eyre*, or Jane Austen's *Pride and Prejudice* identify the various layers of intimacy and illustrate the differences between relationships which are intimate and those which are not. Many novels show intimacies of friendship, such as C. P. Snow's novel *Strangers and Brothers* which portrays the deep relationship which grows among companions at an Oxbridge college, each one of them tapping into profound experiences of identity and love. Or Tolstoy's *War and Peace* where the real meaning of human closeness and bonding becomes focused at the end of the novel in the death of Alexis. Many more show the pain and struggles for intimacy as in *East of Eden* by John Steinbeck, where the poignant and sometimes tragic relationship of two brothers and their father dominates the last third of the novel. In Alice Walker's colloquial womanist novel *The Color Purple*, the journey to intimacy is a long one through violation and negation before new love and acceptance bring healing. The failures and complexities of intimate relationships are a key theme. Penelope Lively's Booker-prizewinning *Moon Tiger* describes a dying woman reflecting on the key relationships of her life: those with her mother, her brother, her lover, her husband and her daughter. The result is a skilful mosaic of memories in which recollections of a search for intimacy are replayed by the different people in the narrative. Favourite children's stories also evolve around the theme of intimacy. Sometime it is family- or neighbourhood-based, as in Louisa M. Alcott's *Little Women*, or in *Anne of Green Gables*, or *Heidi*. Sometimes it is found in the struggle for self-knowledge and growth as in the popular, humorous *Adrian Mole* stories. It is there in biography, as in

Shadowlands, the unexpected love story of the Oxford don, C. S. Lewis and American divorcee Joy Davidson, or in Corrie Ten Boom's book, *The Hiding Place*, where the warmth and love within her close Dutch family allowed people to share their hearts with each other and enveloped others who came into its orbit. The list is inexhaustible for the theme of human intimacy is taken up in almost every kind of literature. Whether we read the plays of William Shakespeare, the love sonnets of John Donne, the perceptive novels of George Eliot, or the social commentaries of Charles Dickens we are confronted again and again by the centrality of its power and importance.

But all this evidence points to a bigger question. If it is true that almost all human beings do share some deep-seated needs for closeness and warmth, why this is so needs some explanation. For example, are these needs produced when people get together in groups, or are they innate within the individual? Are they derived from the process of forming stable societies or part of some biological evolutionary development? If we can come close to probing the *origins* of intimacy, then it will surely help us to grasp more of what is involved in the search for intimacy today. It will contribute to a better understanding also of the conditions under which close relationships flourish. Although the question 'where does the need for intimacy come from?' is rarely raised in such a direct way, many thinkers have addressed it obliquely. And some interesting and widely differing arguments have been put forward. I want to focus on four.

Intimacy as Biological

One of the most widespread notions is that intimacy is fundamentally biological. It is related most of all to procreation, and to the transmission of genes. Its purpose is to continue the human race. Although it may be overlaid by cultural and social overtones most of us experience it as a natural, essential part of the human condition.

This view has been developed in a more sophisticated way by numerous theories. Most of them rely heavily on evolutionary assumptions, and see biology as the underlying basic 'given'. What they have in common is their focus on the survival of the species. This is the background against which we must examine any characteristic which plays a central role in human life. So when we look at human individuals and human societies today we see characteristics which are the results of countless eras of successful evolution. They have been successful precisely because they have been useful in maximizing reproduction and ensuring growth to maturity.

1. Harlow's Monkeys

Just two examples of this approach will illustrate it. The first is Harlow's famous work in the 1970s on the *socialization of monkeys*. Harlow wanted to investigate the part played by 'closeness' in the way monkeys developed their social life. From a wide number of studies he identified different relationships and bondings that were important in the experience of the monkey. These included bonding with mothers, with adult males, and age-mates. He then documented what happened to infant monkeys when normal bonding with these was absent. When the infant monkey was deprived of the caressing, stroking, clinging and holding which would be usually provided by its mother, relational problems occurred later. In particular, these monkeys began to have considerable problems in relating to peers in adolescence. Other deprivations were also significant. When 'normal' affection – from adult to young males, and between those of the same age – was absent this seemed to affect the development of adult heterosexual relations. Not surprisingly, Harlow's conclusion was that an infant monkey's experience of love or intimacy is very important for its maturation. The need for ongoing warmth and closeness – what humans would call 'intimacy' – is more than simply a sexual urge, for affectional ties exist not simply in relation to sexual coupling during the mating season. 'Closeness' involves a whole range of relationships. This same need is evident amongst many species and is built into our own human biological structure. What we call 'love', therefore, is seen to have an evolutionary, biological origin, and is manifest among humans and non-humans alike.

Most animal theorists only draw parallels or inferences to human behaviour, or to human social life. My second example makes much wider claims.

2. Sociobiology

The theory known as sociobiology conjectures that ultimately all human behaviour, human societies and human relationships can ultimately be explained in relation to biological development.[3] The sociobiologist appeals to evolutionary adaptation and speculates on how we generated strategies which have ensured our genetic survival. One of the answers involves 'love'. What we understand to be love or intimacy is really an evolutionary phenomenon, tied in with natural selection and sexual selection. From the beginning 'love' increased offspring survival which gave it a distinct advantage among early humans; it clearly provides the best conditions for the transmission of one's genes to future generations. So, the argument goes, 'love' is simply a sophisticated range of intimate relationships which the evolutionary mechanism has developed over time to help perpetuate the species.

The argument develops in an interesting way for some sociobiologists. At the centre of the argument is the notion of the 'selfish gene'. In Richard Dawkins' phrase, human beings are 'survival machines', who are prepared to invest in the next generation, often at apparent cost to themselves to ensure the survival of their genes.[4] It is not simply that humans as a species have a generalized drive for survival. But each human individual is driven to pass on his or her specific genes to generations yet to come. The implications are fascinating.

Females become pregnant and males do not. What is more, a man can technically father hundreds of offspring, whereas it is quite difficult for a woman to manage more than twenty. The 'parental investment hypothesis' suggests they might therefore need different strategies to maximize the passing on of their genes. Males need to widen their access to sexual partners, and develop aggression to ward off competitors. For them intimacy is geared to achieving and maximizing sexual access to females. But females, who can produce a much smaller number of offspring, must maximize their reproductive strategies to ensure that all their children reach adulthood, and in turn reproduce. So for females, intimacy is to safeguard that access, and to produce a stable environment.

Many of the differences believed to exist in courtship and relational patterns are argued to come from this distinction. Patterns of aggression in men or domesticity in women are all part of the way in which our biology has directed our social relationships. For intimacy here is not about self-conscious choice or open personal disclosure. It is to do with maximal reproductive strategies, and optimal conditions for the continuance of our genes.[5]

Although these examples are taken from quasi-academic arguments, the ideas behind sociobiology have a much longer history in gender stereotypes and folklore. We encounter the notion of the 'naturally promiscuous male', for example, in judges' sentences in rape trials, in soap operas and in the popular press. It even used to be part of older sex education programmes. It is so widespread in fact that many people see this as a 'given' in society, and something which can be changed only with effort. This idea is reinforced humorously in Garrison Keillor's *Book for Guys*: 'A monogamous man is like a bear riding a bicycle. He can be trained to ride it, but he would rather be in the woods doing what all the other bears are doing.'[6] The same idea is behind the quip that 'women grow old gracefully, men grow old disgracefully!'

These ideas might be popular but they do have problems. The methodology of the approach is problematic. Gleaning evidence from animal studies and then projecting these on to human relationships contains in itself some very questionable assumptions. It accepts without examination the notion that we can explain human behaviour in exactly the same way as animal behaviour, because humans are only a sophisticated form of mammal. This has then to ignore all the evidence which suggests there are very significant differences between the ways in which human beings relate and animals interact. It also has to ignore vast cultural and historical variations within human societies themselves. The method of explanation is also disputable. It is largely a posteriori, that is, as a series of untestable hindsights. Observing, for example, that men rape women more than vice versa, an explanation is then produced that suggests there is within males a genetic 'predisposition' towards promiscuity and sexual aggression. But this is not capable of being conclusively examined one way or the other. Yet even with such a spurious epistemological foundation the sociobiologist is not deterred from erecting a very ambitious building.

Finally, however, the theory is *reductionist*. It reduces complex sets of characteristics and phenomena, namely human societies, human intimacy and the varieties of human relationships, into a simple, unidimensional explanation. In so doing it erodes both the intricate diversity of human action and behaviour, and the moral basis for our behaviour. For there can be no condemnation of acts which exploit other human beings rather than enrich them; no preference for intimacy rather than hostility; no concern about male aggression or brutality. On this model our behaviour is ultimately explained with reference to what is perceived to be our biological and genetic make-up, evolved over time. Morality is nothing more than a series of social taboos which various societies have developed. In the end our biological structure, as interpreted above, is what determines the way we live.

Intimacy as Social Construct

Amongst those who reject the reductionism of the biological position are those with a powerful counter theory of their own. It is that society 'creates' intimacy. It may *appear* as some kind of 'natural', innate force within us, but in reality intimacy is a social construction. It is created so that society can operate successfully. It is constructed in the context of the contractual obligations which people make to each other, because it is a vital part of the process of forming and maintaining stable communities.

This might seem a strange argument when we think of the very un-intimate ways in which many societies function today. The idea that human intimacy has its origin in the vast bureaucratic structure of contemporary urban life seems far-fetched indeed. Yet although much of life in the West is now characterized by fragmentation and individualism it was not always so. In fact our past is tightly bound up with patterns of corporate living and intimate relating. According to Barbara Tuchman people in medieval Europe lived collectively in 'infinite numbers of groups, orders, associations, brotherhoods'. She claims: 'Never was man less alone. Even in bedrooms married couples often slept in company with their servants and children. Except for hermits and recluses privacy was unknown.'[7] Stuart Miller makes the same point: 'Until not very many years ago, two hundred at the very outside, one was born into intimacy, lived and worked in it, and died in it. In this sense no one has ever been alone before now.'[8]

The 'social construct' argument has more weight, therefore, than at first glance. For there is an intrinsic relationship between intimacy and society. Without close and familial relationships there is no social cohesion, there is no effective organization of societies. And those who defend this position argue that we have developed attitudes, emotions and patterns of living which ensure that society will not be a war of all against all. So, we 'fall in love'; we form close bonds with others; we make implicit pacts which ensure our mutual protection; we each perform specific roles, often developed along gender lines. Families themselves are sophisticated social organizations which exist not primarily to maintain genetic survival, but to give an identity and a place to their members. Even bureaucracies, which very obviously outlaw intimacy, can only operate if there is also a vast area of society which is arranged differently.

In traditional societies we see the power of this theory manifested most clearly. It is demonstrated by the power of the clan. Sometimes this takes on sinister overtones. The 'family business' of the Mafiosi spells out most effectively that relations of intimacy are in effect a way of organizing and regulating the strength of the family. It is interesting why Mario Puzo's novel *The Godfather* is such compelling reading. In this riveting story the key to the whole network of relationships is not the biological ties nor even emotional bonding. It is the implicit family and social agreement which itself defines intimacy, justice and the meaning of relationships. Commitment to this overrides all other considerations, whether ethical, emotional, political or legal. The Family constructs morality. Consequently, 'The greatest crime any member of the Mafia could commit was to tell the police the name of the man who had just shot him . . . *Omertà* (silence) became the religion of the people. A woman whose husband has been murdered would not tell the police the name of her husband's murderer, not even of her child's murderer, her daughter's raper.'[9]

The Corleone family is a powerful social force. *Loyalty* to the family counts more even than blood relationship. So a 'biological outsider', such as Tom Hagen the lawyer, has greater admittance into the warmth and closeness of the old Godfather's circle of intimates than many members of the same family. And when Michael Corleone succeeds his father and becomes the new head of the Family he withdraws his protection from any who have in his eyes betrayed the implicit agreement or understanding which binds them together. As a result both his sister's husband and his own brother pay for disloyalty with their lives. Even marriage and sexual bonding and marital commitment are second to the Family contract. For ultimately Michael's wife, Kay, is herself rejected and closed out, deprived of her children and the intimacy she once enjoyed.

Of course, *The Godfather* provides a particularly brutal example of social construction, within a complex net of political intrigue, and organized crime. To quote it as the main way in which society constructs intimacy would be to invite the dismissal of the view as a serious explanation. In non-Mafia societies the social organizing of intimate relationships is just as evident. In most cultures there are often quite explicit proscriptions about those with whom we may be intimate, and the purpose of intimacy is socially designated. Engels argued that in capitalism marriage itself is one of the main means whereby the system is kept intact. The wife and family become part of a man's private property. Futhermore, family connections, aristocracies, old boy networks and brotherhoods all contribute to the various power structures of the Establishment, and keep the political and economic power in the hands of a few. In other societies arranged marriages maintain the power of the family, in both social and economic terms. The caste system, ethnic groupings or religious hierarchies often have a strong say in who relates to whom. The argument, therefore, that *intimacy is defined largely within the social system* has some articulate exponents. They would claim that although intimacy might have elements of emotional bonding, it would be wrong to think of it as something biological. Essentially, it has a social origin, and serves a social function, existing both to build up and reinforce various power systems within society, and also to protect individuals from those power systems. From this perspective even sexual intimacy is not innate or natural: 'Sexuality must not be thought of as a kind of natural given which power tries to hold in check, or as an obscure domain which knowledge gradually tries to uncover. It is the name that can be given to a historical construct.'[10]

The arguments are coherent. Without the bonding and closeness of personal relationships it is difficult to see how societies would hold together or survive. What is more, it is possible to see great social variations in how intimacy is constructed. Different historical epochs or societies produce very different patterns. Intimacy between a father and a baby is, for example, a very contemporary construct, related to changes in our concepts of masculinity and manliness; the current images we often see in advertisements of close involvement and manly tenderness towards a baby would have been rare indeed a few decades ago. But even the intimacy between a mother and a baby may not have been there throughout history. Certainly it was not so evident in the pre-industrial period when babies were handed down to wet nurses, and where infant mortality was very high. Some very fascinating studies show how parent-child relationships as well as adult relationships were affected by the prevailing economic conditions.[11]

Yet it still seems too reductionist to claim that the very *meaning* of intimacy is given by its social conditions and context. Particular societies might shape and contextualize intimacy in certain ways, but this does not make it simply a social construction. Rather, the fact that something recognizable as closeness exists in all human groups suggests that it exists *prior* to human society, coming before social arrangements and influencing them, as much as it is influenced by them. Even if we only observe it in people's social and personal relationships, intimacy can no more be defined as a creation of society than as a product of evolution. It is rather something to do with our very humanness itself.

Intimacy as Autonomous Choice

Many people who delve into the subject of intimacy resist both the social and biological reductionism of the two perspectives I have just outlined. A third and widespread notion is that intimacy originates in ourselves and our choices. This comes out strongly in modern relationship manuals where the usual underlying view is that 'intimacy is a choice rather than an instinct'[12] and that this choice is an *autonomous* one for each of us. Far from being prescribed for us, intimacy then is something *we* manufacture; it is what we create for ourselves when we 'opt for closeness'.

It is important to note how far this idea parts company with those of either the sociobiologist or social contract theorist. We can be successful or failures in intimate relationships, but this does not depend on either our biological 'performance' or on the society we live in. It is rather related to our own self-awareness and our capability to undergo 'regular personal and social redefinition'.[13]

When intimacy is defined within either biological determinism or mutual social protection it is now seen as shallow. People whose 'intimacy' is little more than an instinctual animal drive, for example, might experience sensuality but not true emotional and intimate depth. Or those whose 'intimacy' is confined to traditional extended family and neighbourhood living are likely to be trapped within ideas of duty or gender roles which might be far from intimate. Indeed it is highly debatable from this perspective whether what passed for intimacy in older societies or in tribal rituals was intimacy at all. It was much more concerned with economic survival, with maintaining stability and fighting hardship. But if intimacy is linked with freedom and autonomy it can only really exist in a context where there is space and energy for both self-knowledge and depth-knowledge of other people.

Under this view of intimacy choice is therefore ultimate. For some this means that there must be no fixed ethical system which is absolutely binding on us, or which can be allowed to limit our autonomy. This is expressed strikingly in a comment from a gay writer who is objecting to those who say we must look to 'nature' or to traditional morality for directions on how we should live: 'Man is a creative being, constantly correcting his ethical insights and altering his universe into something better that will give added meaning to his life. Nature cannot be the guide for man's actions; it is man who must impose upon nature his own dreams and values.'[14] The focus is therefore on our own wills and decisions which are paramount. Self-creation, self-direction and self-definition provide the bedrock for the development of intimacy, and choosing our own goals is the process. Even the concept of commitment has a different nuance. It is now a commitment to autonomy and authenticity, a pledge to the goals we have chosen to pursue. 'Making the commitment to our goals means, in part, agreeing to accept responsibility for our own lives and acknowledging we must find our own answers and make our own decisions for there is no one best way to live. Each of us is the author of his or her own life.'[15] It is a development of what Erich Fromm insisted: 'No power transcending man can make a moral claim upon him. Man is only responsible to himself for gaining or losing his life.'

In his book *Habits of the Heart* Robert Bellah, an American sociologist, tells the story of Brian. Brian moved from an adolescence of 'hell-raising and sex' to marry, have three children and hold down a responsible job. But the job became his life's focus to the extent that overwork and total career involvement crowded out his close relationships. In the trauma of marriage breakdown, Brian experiences a 'conversion' to a new set of values which sees intimacy as much more central and important. So second time round, his new wife and family come first, and the job is demoted. But there is something odd about the 'change'. It stops short of being a real conversion story. We see how far short when Brian tries to explain why his present life is better than the former one. His basic values have not changed at all. Ronald Rolheiser comments: 'In the end, his reasons for doing what he is now doing, and believing in its worth, are little different from his reasons for pursuing pleasure as an adolescent or business success as a younger adult – it makes him feel good. Crassly put, he did his thing then, and he is doing his thing now.'[16] Autonomous, self-directed choice is the meaning of his new intimacy. But this has been the meaning of all that he valued in life before. At the deepest level it is not Brian who has changed, nor his beliefs, only the goals which will bring him what he wants.

The central ingredient of such choice is *freedom*. There are not, and there must not be, constraints on my right and liberty to choose. Freedom and choice are what it means to be human. And this commitment to personal freedom is embraced as a fundamental principle, despite the scepticism of the cynics. 'Freedom', says one joker, 'is being able to do what you please without considering anyone except your wife, the police, your boss, your insurance company, your doctor, your airline, the internal revenue, the government authorities and your neighbours.'

The problem with the notion of autonomous freedom is, of course, that it is unreal. We are never ultimately free simply 'to do our thing'. We live within the constraints of our structured humanness, in connection and relationship with other human beings. So there are always limitations on our freedom, and on our capability of choosing. We have to listen to the needs and longings of others. We have to negotiate ways of living with differences. We have to recognize the need to make sacrifices for those we love. If we can do none of these we are trapped within the mind-set where, as Sartre suggested, 'Hell is other people.' That is why Santayana warns us that 'Absolute liberty is a foolish challenge thrown up by a newborn insect buzzing against the universe. It is incompatible with more than one pulse of life.'

Intimacy may involve freedom and choice, but it is not defined by it. God invites us to choose, but always within the created and normative structures in which God has placed us. Otherwise we find that we have no freedom, only bondage to the penalties of ignoring our creatureliness. As Rolheiser observes: 'Freedom is always experienced in relation to some lord.'[17]

Intimacy as New Age Connectedness

Over the last two decades there has been another growing movement which has shown interest in the meaning and origins of intimacy. The New Age movement has captured the interests of many in considering this area. Yet its own course is on direct collision with the one I have just mapped out. It utterly rejects the concept of autonomy as being the key and instead asserts the centrality of intrinsic *connectedness*. Nor would it accept either the biological or the social arguments as valid. For it would see each of these as part of the same rationalistic perspective on the world. In opposition to any view I have already examined, New Age writers would argue that our needs of closeness and intimacy have fundamental mystical origins. They lie in our relatedness to the entire cosmos.

What fuels much of the popularity of the New Age approach is its ecological awareness. For in an overcrowded planet we do not have the space or the right to be isolationists and self-centred. There is an urgency about the need for intimacy for unless we have a new sense of cosmic community then the future of the world is in doubt. One author comment. 'It used to be "love one another if you want to be perfect", but now it is "Love one another if you want to survive."'[18]

Many writers argue that the current crises result from the failure of modernity. The fragmentation of contemporary life has been roundly rejected by the New Age. It is suspicious of the separation of emotional, physical and social nature. It is tired of a society which cuts every operation into small 'rational' segments, and measures performance as a mechanism for attaining efficiency. Such forces as 'rationalism, professionalism, economic and physical mobility and individualism' are seen as 'all tending to destroy intimacy'.[19] The time is ripe for a new look at relationships and at their origins in the universal life of the planet and beyond.

Pat Collins outlines the issue well:

> As the scientific materialism of the last two or three centuries gives way to this holistic perspective, attention will shift to the importance of interconnections which are governed by a universal blueprint and purpose. In other words, intimacy of ever-increasing degrees of intensity is a characteristic of the relationships that should pervade the whole of creation, from the realm of sub-atomic particles to the experience of genuine human love.[20]

Human intimacy, then, is not to be explained by some biological or genetic drive, by types of social expediency, or by individual autonomous choice. It is to be understood by its place in the interconnectedness of everything that exists.

Within a New Age framework our intimacy has no boundaries. We are just as intimately connected to the earth, the stars, the trees and animals as we are to each other. What is more, everything is imbued with *spirit* so that it makes sense to talk of communing with the planets or with the seas or winds, because we share one cosmos and are all part of one deep spiritual force, *Gaia*. The planet itself is seen as having psychic as well as physical and kinematic energy. The earth's psyche in particular is in pain and suffering as a result of the coldness of human beings: 'The dark energy forms that our aggression, anger, fear and resentment have created are the most destructive contribution we have made to the planet's decline . . . the earth is a living being with feelings and emotions.'[21] For those within a New Age framework there is more at stake, therefore, than the basic human needs of warmth and closeness. There is our responsibility for the spiritual damage of the cosmos. The ecological crisis is itself a psychic problem caused by bad vibrations from human activity.[22] What we put down, for example, merely to atmospheric or weather conditions is really *Gaia* telling us of her pain. Human love is therefore only one small aspect of the intimacy available to human beings. And it can be a dangerous aspect. For within New Age thinking it can lead to selfishness, to exploitation or to rejection of the fundamental claims of the rest of the universe.

For the New Age adherent, true intimacy helps us to understand our relationships beyond human ones, and it does this most powerfully by the experience of *fusion* or *integration with the divine*. In leading us to realize the true nature of the cosmos, intimacy draws us into relation with the nature spirits and shows us we are one with them. This is in many ways the same sense of *merging* which is present in some Eastern religions and is also much sought-after in drug-induced experience. Many who have experimented with heightened states of consciousness through hypnosis or drugs know the power that this 'merging' can have over the psyche. There is one now classic account of a psychological experiment where subjects were asked to gaze for long periods at a blue vase. The sense of merging with the vase, of the vase being in them, and feeling so deeply attached to the vase that they experienced disappointment when it was taken from the room was a common response. Even without drug use, prolonged meditation had produced some kind of union and identification with the vase, which they experienced as love and intimacy.[23] This is very similar to what is described in much New Age writing, although there it is also connected with the sense of 'spirit' and 'spiritual union'. Robert Ogilvie Crombie describes how he became aware of his identification, his 'merging' with Pan, the god of woods, flocks and pastures:

> He stepped behind me and then walked into me so that we became one and I saw the surroundings through his eyes . . . The moment he stepped into me the woods became alive with myriads of beings – elementals, nymphs, dryads, fauns, elves, gnomes, fairies – far too numerous to catalogue.[24]

This quest for a loss of individual autonomy, or even loss of individual consciousness, is not new. There are elements of it in most religions. Even writings of the Christian mystics have been interpreted along these lines. Yet there are some very significant differences. Fundamental to Christianity is the notion of *willingness*, of personal choice which we offer up to God. In a deeper relationship with God we find ourselves. By contrast, the intimacy within New Age framework is a deprivation of identity. A merging with the spirit of Gaia does not involve deeper awareness of our own being. It is a take-over, a loss of humanness, a surrender of personal involvement, an abandonment of choice. And in this sense it is also dangerous. From a Christian point of view it opens us up to the elemental spirits of the universe without discernment. We do not know whether these spirits who take us into themselves are good or evil. We do not know whether these mystical beings help or hinder our own growth as *human beings*. We do not know whether they reveal to us the truth about reality, or offer us a delusion. Tapping into the spirit world of the universe can only be done with prayer and deep wisdom. To offer ourselves into merging and union with something of which we know so little, on the basis of heightened experience of connectedness, can be costly. And it can take us further away from, rather than more deeply into, real intimacy.

Intimacy from a Christian Perspective

Christianity relates in a critical way not just to the New Age understanding of the origins of intimacy, but to each of the very different views I have outlined. For each of them presupposes certain things about the nature of human life, and indeed about personal identity. Yet there are also elements within each which a Christian position would endorse. For every one of them goes a long way to explaining the ubiquitous nature of our needs for intimacy, and points to aspects of our lives which are important. The danger is that they each see themselves as total explanations, ruling out the possibility of any other and making absolute a certain starting-point, whether it is biology, society, autonomy or connectedness.

In the experience of most people, and I suspect in most cultures, intimacy involves all of these aspects and more besides. Certainly it is *biological*. As any adolescent knows something significant happens to our bodies when we draw close to other people. The variety of our sensations is wide. We can experience anything from a sense of peace to palpitations, depending on the particular kind of intimacy we are encountering. Our close relationships bring us so many bodily feelings – states of high physical anxiety, expansive mellow enjoyment, or intense sexual relief – and the degree of 'biological' interaction can be high.

Then again intimacy is *social*; it takes shapes and derives its institutional forms from its specific cultural settings. In one society, extended family relationships might provide the main focus for intimacy, in another it might be marriage, in yet another it might be same sex companionship or informal clubs. Most societies will have each of these expressions of intimate relationships in some degree or other.

It is true too that intimacy involves *choice*. We, and no doubt people throughout the ages, have chosen those to whom we would draw close. Sometimes indeed this has not coincided with the choices made for people by others, and the conflict has sometimes produced relationships which have suffered lack of deep encounter. In most societies people choose their friends, their companions and their confidants. In some they also choose their spouses.

And finally we also experience *connectedness* in intimacy. Indeed, one of the ways we can discern the real from the sham is the level of involvement we feel with the life and worth of the other person. We are taken out of ourselves into the needs and feelings of another. The sense of knowing and being known can be very important to those whose intimacy needs are deep. We are often taken away from fragmentation into wholeness. And this wholeness can extend to our relationship with other aspects of the world we live in, so that, even if not in a New Age sense, we do begin to recognize the integrity of all creation.

Trying to grapple with the origins of our need for intimacy must lead us beyond an entrenchment within apparently incompatible viewpoints, to an acceptance of the importance of elements in each. But to do that we need to find a different starting-point. We cannot absolutize the biological, the social, the autonomy of choice or the 'mystical' without shrinking our area of discourse to something which is narrow and poverty-stricken. Intriguingly, within a Christian perspective not one of these explanations is seen as ultimate, and yet each is seen as having essential features which are true. All the points I have just outlined would form part of a Christian understanding of the origins of our need to form intimate relationships. It is their own bid for totality which makes them biased or lop-sided.

What holds these different areas together within a Christian framework of reference is that they are all seen within the norms of *createdness*. For the one idea which has not yet surfaced in the discussion is the idea that our search for intimacy might be a response to *created* needs; that we have deep-seated requirements which are intrinsic to our created human personhood. This is not surprising since most theories about our intimacy needs assume that human beings are not created, that is brought into being by a creator. Instead the options presented are that we are the products of chance evolution, of cultural construction, or are autonomous human agents. Even in New Age thinking there is little reference to human createdness. For them god is not creator but a pantheistic god-in-everything, and human particularity is not recognized as fundamentally distinct from the rest of the universe.

The notion of createdness reorientates the discussion and introduces very different key concepts. First it puts the idea of biology in perspective. For human biology is itself structured according to norms laid down by the creator, and does not simply generate its own drives, instincts or strategies for procreation. Put another way, there is a biblical unfolding of our biology which sees it not as self-referential, but as related to feeling, rationality and morality. Similarly, human societies do not 'construct' their members simply according to expediency, but they do so in response to (or denial of) basic human values which are imprinted into our humanness by a creator God. We may not choose autonomously, as though we were responsible only to our own wills. But our choices themselves are structured. They are good or bad choices, they are wise or foolish, compassionate or harsh, careful or reckless. Whatever we do and however we live is therefore entered into as those who live in a universe structured by norms, where we ourselves are created by God.

Createdness has two further implications which go even more strongly against the autonomy of the age. One is dependency. Far from being independent and on our own we are utterly dependent on the God who made us, and in whom, in the words of St Paul, 'we live and move and have our being'. The second is our relationality. We are not isolated individuals, but we are locked into an intrinsic and inescapable relation both with God and with others whom God has made.

Intimacy as Imaging God

The origins of our intimacy are therefore in our creatureliness and in our *ontological* relatedness to God; they are there in our very being. The Bible has its own graphic way of describing this relationship. It talks of human beings as the *image of God*. The metaphor here is a powerful one. It suggests that human beings have no independent existence outside God. Just as a reflection in a mirror has only a derived existence, and cannot exist in and of itself, so we too have only derived existence from God. Whether we acknowledge it or not, our very identity as human people is bound up with the existence of God and with the norms with which God has structured the universe.

One of the ways in which we do image God is in our relationality. For here too the Bible uses imaginative language to convey the notion that God's very self is relational. God is interpersonal. God is one being, God is three persons. And the irreducibility of the Godhead suggests powerfully that at the very centre of the universe there is not isolation and aloneness, but deep, divine personal encounter. The three persons of the Trinity are described as being there from before the foundation of the world. United in an eternal relationship, the creator, the redeemer, the empowerer are presented to us as God. We listen in to their dialogue, we overhear the Son's prayers to the Father. We encounter the Spirit's wisdom and encouragement and we know, but cannot comprehend, that this mystery of fusion and separateness holds the key to understanding our own humanness.

The reality of God is therefore a reality of intimacy; the intimacy of deep relationship where each person of God knows the others in a depth of understanding which is inaccessible to us. What we can know, however, is what God has disclosed to us: that the name of this infinite intimacy is love. And it is a love which calls us into relationship. For we can also know union and deep connectedness with God, not as a *merging*, but as *indwelling*. In the fourth gospel Jesus himself talks about this deep intimacy: 'In that day you will know that I am in the Father, and you in me, and I in you.' (John 14:20) It is an image of *abiding*, of knowing union. It is where the Spirit of Christ comes to us, and lives with us and fills us with God's love. But we each retain our own personality. God does not invade us; God does not negate us. Instead we receive God's Spirit in our spirit and cooperate with our creator in the way we live.

Because we are each an image of God, we too are inescapably relational, and in need of deep intimacy. In our own humanness we carry this same interweaving of separateness and bonding, of individuality and relatedness. In the story of the creation the book of Genesis tells us that only one thing was pronounced to be 'not good'. And that was that the human man should be alone. So where there was one human being, there became two, not made now by a separate act of creation from the dust of the earth, but by the re-creating of the man to form man and woman. And so God made community, fellowship, family, sexuality and friendship. God put intimacy, the image of Godself, into the very heart of creation, and Jesus prays that his people might be one. The very notion of the *body of Christ* communicates that deep sense of closeness which we are to share with one another. We are to be in union with one another. But we are to retain our distinctiveness.

And so we seek intimacy with other people, we search for those with whom we can bond, and draw close. We look for those who will understand us and affirm our value and personhood. We ask of our friends, our family, our lovers that they love our individuality and uniqueness, and that they also give themselves to us in close and deep personal encounter. We seek others because it is not good that we should be alone, but we should live in interdependency and acknowledge our need for intimacy and love.

Conclusion

The origins of intimacy from a Christian perspective are in the nature of the universe itself, not in a pantheistic way, but as derived from the nature and love of the creator. Intimacy is central to our lives because it is part of our createdness and identity as image of God. Yet this means that there are also dangers to intimacy. Because it is so close to the reality of who we are, to the core of our human personhood, we can begin to identify it as *the* meaning of our human life.

Gerald Priestland, in *My Pilgrim Way*, spells out with succinct clarity the truth about the origins of intimacy:

God is Love. But the lover needs a beloved. So God made us for himself to love. This is not selfishness on his part, since love is not worth having unless it is freely given, and that freedom gives us the power to reject God's love. Giving us that power is a huge and unselfish sacrifice on God's part. Once we recognize God's love and return it, then only is love circulated and complete. Unrecognized and un-responded to it is love crippled and frustrated.[25]

Ultimately, the search for intimacy is the search for God. Yet so many people are unaware of that truth. Instead they stop short at the search for intimacy itself. There is an insatiable thirst for deeper relationship, for greater encounter, for more complete marriages. Yet the search is a restless one and an uprooted one. The results are what we see around us in our broken society; damaged people, with painful memories, moving from relationship to relationship to try to find one which will give them the depth of affirmation which their needy souls long for. And the result is that instead of drawing people closer to the source of their identity and humanness, intimacy becomes an idol, something to be worshipped and sought after because we need so much to experience the love which is our human birthright from our creator.

What we need to know, however, is that we cannot experience the fullness of intimacy until we understand that it goes deeper than anything we might find in the greatest human encounter; until we realize that its origins lie far beyond ourselves, or our universe, to the very creator. And when we come face to face with the reality of this truth, we can accept the gift for what it is; the reminder to our hearts of who we are, and whose image we bear.

5

Barriers to Intimacy

We have forgotten how close human beings once were to one another.

Stuart Miller

In the light of my conclusions in the last chapter it is perhaps not surprising that the intimacy people search for so often eludes them. God may seem far away, or even non-existent. For some, relationships hardly get off the ground. For others who do have friends or partners, there can still be that deep loneliness of heart and a longing which seems to have no name. The perennially rising divorce statistics testify to the failure of many relationships to have delivered the intimacy they once promised. And more evidence is provided by the decline of friendship and the breakup of family relations.

The reasons why intimacy eludes us are complex. They can be linked to the prevailing social ethos of individualism and economism, where people have been turned into commodities, their sexuality for sale in pornographic images; or into consumers, their value measured only in what they can be persuaded to buy. A society which robs people of their personhood in these ways is not one in which intimacy flourishes. Or they can be linked to personal attitudes which get in the way of drawing close to others. This chapter will consider both these kinds of barrier. But individualism and economics are not the only forces in contemporary society which undermine intimacy. We need also to look at the effects of the patriarchal structure.

Dominance and Patriarchy

In the West we often think of patriarchy as belonging to Islamic or other male-dominant cultures where women have few freedoms.

This affects not only marriage and family relationships but also worship and work. Amongst Islamic communities, even in Western countries where they are in the minority, the male rule in the home, the mosque, and the economy is well established. In one study of women's work in such a community in Britain, Swasti Mitter comments that the same 'servility, subservience and passivity' which wives and daughters-in-law were expected to show their menfolk at home were reproduced in its factories.[1] Other studies on low paid women in Britain in the 1970s and 1980s found that the lowest pay occurred amongst women of Asian background who worked in textile and other firms run by men from their own communities. Surveys in Wolverhampton and Leicester noted too the long hours, the lack of any union regulation and the poor conditions which were accepted as normal in these jobs.

Yet pointing the finger at other groups can often be a way of ignoring the record of Western cultures in this area. For patriarchy is just as alive here although it might take a different form. How many women in Britain and America can be found in the top echelons of the professions, or business, or manufacturing or government? In almost any area the answer is pathetically few. Medicine is an interesting example where now almost half the entrants to medical schools are women, yet fewer than two per cent of top consultancies in areas of thoracic, heart, lung and brain surgery are occupied by women. In some areas of surgery there are no women consultants at all. In all other areas of work too women have had to struggle for equal pay, in spite of the legislation which technically ensures it. In Britain some women have gone to the European Court for a ruling in their favour.

But work is only one aspect of male-female inbalance. It is also there in politics, education, the professions, wealth and poverty, the home or the church. In fact we are so used to living within a patriarchal society that we accept many of its values as normal. Only recently has the idea that men are much more equipped for positions of authority and leadership been challenged. And those who challenged them were often labelled 'feminist' or 'strident'! It is suggested that those who want equal opportunities for women have a chip on their shoulder or that they have a grudge against society, because they have not got where they wanted to be. Often it is only when male dominance gets 'out of hand', in violence or sexual abuse of women, that some people recognize a deep problem here. And even then there are those who insist it is always the woman who is to blame.

A patriarchal power structure inevitably affects intimate relationships. One of the ways it does so is to give established power to men but emotional responsibility to women. Whereas men have predominantly controlled the *public* arena women have been given the tasks of managing the *private* sector of life which has often meant that men have been relieved of the responsibility of emotional engagement and development. Harriet Lerner observes astutely:

> Males are not rewarded for investing in the emotional component of human relationships. In our production-oriented society, no accolades are given to men who value personal ties at the expense of making one more sale, seeing one more client, publishing one more paper.[2]

But within close relationships there have been other problems, by now well established. In the past (and in the present too, as far as some are concerned), men have been invited to see themselves as the ones 'in control' in marriage and family relationships. They are the ones who call the tune. The pleasant old custom of 'giving the bride away' reinforces the idea that the woman moves from the authority of the father to the authority of the husband, although many who still accept the custom now reject the implication. Some Christian writers have not helped at all in this respect, with volumes of books on the permanent leadership of the man in marriage, in the church, in the family, and so on. But there are two main practical problems with this teaching (and more theological ones). The first is that authority and intimacy do not easily fit together. If the relationship is one where the wife is always having effectively to 'ask permission' of her husband, and where his views are what ultimately count, then mutuality, listening and shared responsibility are far less important. Yet these are precisely the qualities which are crucial in an intimate relationship.

The second is that alongside this teaching of male headship there is rarely the balancing teaching of male humility and emotional vulnerability. I have listened to many women married to men who have absorbed all the ideas of headship and authority, but who have never been given any help or advice on how to express and develop their feelings, or to allow other people to get close. Consequently, some women find that though these men may make authoritative pronouncements, and perform well publicly, at home they are effectively emotional cripples. This often has to be masked by assertion, or distance. In some cases the closer the woman becomes and the more aware of his weaknesses the greater the retreat from the husband. So the relationship deteriorates and the man is unable to seek help. For he is a man, and called not to be weak but to be authoritative, and for him it is a sign of weakness to admit there are deep emotional problems in his life.

A later chapter in the book will explore some of the gender issues connected with people's understanding and experience of intimacy. The only point I want to make here is that the way in which men have been required by our culture to be 'strong', 'powerful' and 'single-minded' has not made it easy for some of them to defy the cultural stereotypes and learn also to be intimate.

Personal Barriers to Intimacy

Although the effects of patriarchy are very widespread I do not believe, however, that it can be offered as an explanation for all the barriers to intimacy which exist between people. The reasons for the lack of intimacy can lie profoundly in our own selves and our emotions. They can lie in our judgementalism, our resentment of others, our unforgiving attitudes, our reluctance to trust, our lack of humour and play. They often lie quite deep in our personal struggles with our own humanness. Sometimes they may be rooted in that tension between detachment and bonding, separateness and connectedness deep in our human psyche. All too often they result from the fact that we do not know intimacy with ourselves. Many people struggle with problems with their own ineffectiveness in relationships, until the pain of persisting becomes too great to continue. In the rest of this chapter I want to try to identify some of the most recurrent barriers.

Over-Detachment

I have pointed a number of times to the twin needs we have within us of separateness and connectedness. We navigate these needs throughout our lives and are affected by them differently at various stages. They can occur in a polarized way in the same person within a few hours. A mother with three small children can feel a deep sense of bonding as she nurses the baby and dresses the toddler. Four hours later, if she is still on her own with the children who are fractious and constantly crying and clutching at her, the need for separateness can become overwhelming! Closeness with others, and space for our own personal needs are important to all of us. Some people feel called to a whole life of separateness: taking even vows of silence to follow a contemplative or meditative way of life. And yet usually these vows are maintained not alone or in isolation but within communities. So the separateness is purposeful and chosen, and occurs within a context of communal support and encouragement.

There are, however, many people who simply find it difficult to sustain close relationships with others. Detachment and bonding cannot be held together in any creative tension for them, because they do not really understand what is necessary to any bonding. The result can be over-detachment. Such people can be seen by those who relate to them as remote, incommunicative and reserved, and it can be very difficult to develop an enriching association with them which reaches any kind of depth. In some of these people there is a persistent need for autonomy. All kinds of activities might be pursued as a way out of having to spend emotional time with others. And the result can be that often unrealistic and unreasonable demands are made of those who would be close to them. Such people can, often unconsciously, see themselves as the norm. Their needs and interests are the ones which are always assumed as the most important, and a self-centred lifestyle is slowly built into any relationship of which they are a part. Indeed, they can resent the intrusion of others on their own autonomy, and they make for themselves a great requirement of independence, and demand for personal time and space. The effect of all this can be that they are not happy to be with other people who require anything from them. Even the brief conversation of others can irritate, providing an unwelcome distraction from their own thought patterns.

A typical scenario grows up in some families. At the end of the day's work the man arrives home tired and uncongenial, at the same time as his wife. She too feels frustrated by the day but the children each require attention. The woman takes off her coat and, because she is a mother, listens to the children's complaints, stories and requirements, as she makes her way to the kitchen to prepare supper. The man goes to the lounge and switches on the television set or picks up a newspaper. Untroubled by what might be going on in the rest of the house he relaxes. It is not that he is averse to housework. He readily washes up and clears away after the meal, happy to have no help from the others. Later, he might write some cheques to pay the bills or clean out the shed. He is not lazy or over-demanding. He simply does not want other people crowding in on him.

If this is an isolated occurrence there is no overriding problem. We all need time to get our bearings before we can relate meaningfully to others, even others in the same family. But if, as is sometimes the case, this person requires detachment as a way of life, then there is going to be little bonding or intimacy in his relationships. Without some interest from her husband the wife may feel frustrated and resentful, her self-confidence diminishing further with every impatient or dismissive word from him. If she is strong she may begin to form her own autonomous lifestyle where she no longer relies on his companionship and affirmation. The children will soon get the message that they are of little interest to their father and withdraw, quite likely rejecting also the compensatory attentions of their mother. Consequently, family times spent together will at worse become strained, at best formalities, where every person goes through the ritual of relating, but where the hearts of each of them are elsewhere. The pattern continues unbroken until the children grow into adulthood. The end result is a constant repetition of the situation described by Rolheiser in *The Restless Heart*:

> We all dutifully put in time and put up a façade of pretence, while our hearts and our fingers fidget, anxiously awaiting the moment when our duty is done and we can finally get to bed, or to the phone or the car, and to the place where we really want to be.[3]

Over-detachment both leads to loneliness, and is a product of loneliness. It builds up iron walls of privacy between people, where time to oneself becomes sacrosanct and even thoughts are private. Communication consists of discussion about the time of meals, or which channel to watch on television. The sad thing is that the effort needed to break this pattern is more difficult with each passing month until, some years hence, it becomes impossible. The sorrow of such empty relationships can become a dull ache at the very centre of one's being. Moving away from such patterns of over-detachment is not easy. Even to admit there is a problem can be difficult, for often the person who lives a life of withdrawal and self-containment sees this as perfectly normal. What is wrong with keeping thoughts and feelings to yourself? So for such a person if a problem exists at all it must be with the other. Locating the problem 'out there' as 'your problem not mine' is one of the most common protective mechanisms.

Yet even with the acknowledgement that there is a problem, there are difficulties in resolving it. For the very closeness which makes some people seek their own company and keep their own counsel still inhibits them from communicating about private issues. For them it can all seem so irrational and untidy. Conversation about feelings or emotions is accompanied by embarrassment and is impatiently dismissed as self-indulgent navel gazing. I know one man who breaks out in a visible sweat whenever canteen-table talk becomes focused on emotional or personal things! He generally falls silent, his face looks anxious and he leaves the room at the first opportunity.

All these issues need to be faced, however, if there is to be progress in ability to relate to others. Sometimes it might mean that habits of a lifetime have to be put under scrutiny, and strong drawbridges, rusty for years, have to be gently lowered to allow people to walk across. 'I know now that all my life I feared invasion' one man confessed to me. 'But I'm beginning to discover that letting the wall down can be liberating.'

Bonding and Possessiveness

If a constant desire for detachment can present a powerful barrier to intimacy, so can a consuming need for bonding. The longing for another person to end the loneliness within can mean that we grab at relationships, and then when a special one has come our way, we stifle it, choking it of air and space to breathe. Many things can lead to this desperate possessiveness. For one man it might be the realization that here at last is someone he can love, and from whom he can receive love. And he needs this love quite urgently, for he finds it very hard to love himself. Past hurts and deep insecurity have eaten away at his self-esteem, and he has never come to understand who he is within the love of God. Consequently his own poor sense of self makes this new possibility full of fragility. And his inbuilt distrust, passionate jealousy, and fear of loss can suffocate the very relationship he wants to flourish.

For another woman it might be the sense of the biological clock ticking away. She has always assumed that one day in the future she will settle down in a permanent relationship. But waking one morning, still tired and full of cramp, she realizes with a pang that she is growing old on her own. She will run out of time. She might never have the children she longs for. And her desire for an intimate relationship becomes doubly intense as the fulfilment of another desire becomes dependent on it. So she looks out for the person most likely to remedy this situation, perhaps pressurizing him into the kind of relationship he is not fully committed to. And as her own anxiety grows, and the depth of her need becomes apparent, the man begins to feel owned and controlled and overwhelmed by her emotional demands. When he can cope no more, he shakes free, leaving her devastated and terribly alone.

Possessiveness can occur in any intimate context. Even quite small infants learn it. They can be seen regularly making a bid for the sole attention of their mother. Recently I almost had to abandon a visit to a friend because her three-year-old quite simply did not want to share her with me. With a child's transparency he banged, shouted and screeched until we finally gave up our conversation and focused on him! Adults are usually more sophisticated but the same possessiveness is evident enough. It can be there in relationships between single people who might have been close friends. But the needy one draws an exclusive line around the friendship, shutting out other contenders in an effort to make the friend solely his. It can be there in empty marriages where partners live in bitterness and resentment towards each other but draw their emotional solace from the child who holds them together. It can be there after divorce when the mother desperately needs the assurance of her daughter, and experiences loss, fear or even betrayal when the girl begins to relate to her father's new partner. It can be there with an elderly parent, who finds it difficult to face the independence of the daughter or son who lives with them and cares for them, and tries every means of containing the relationship. For the ones who have to satisfy this need, it can be draining and exhausting. They can feel owned and manipulated, strained or even torn in two. So overwhelming can be the possessiveness that it can ultimately stifle even the freedom to act. Henri Nouwen tells a moving story which illustrates this poignantly:

> I vividly remember the story of a student who was invited to stay with a family while studying at university. After a few weeks he realized how unfree he felt and slowly he became aware that he was becoming the victim of the crying loneliness of his hosts. Husband and wife had become strangers to each other and used their guest to satisfy their great need for affection. The hosts clung to the stranger who had entered their house in the hope that he could offer them the love and intimacy they were unable to give each other. So the student became entangled in a complex net of unfulfilled needs and desires, and felt caught between the walls of loneliness. He felt the painful tension of having to choose between two lonely partners and was being pulled apart by the cruel question: Are you for him or for me? Are you on her side or mine? He no longer felt free to go and come as he wanted; he found himself gradually unable to concentrate on his studies while at the same time powerless to offer the help his hosts were begging for. He had even lost the inner freedom to leave.[4]

There are nearly always reasons for people's possessive behaviour towards others: a deep need of love, affection and warmth; fear of being left alone or unloved. And yet it drives away intimacy as surely as a forest fire will drive away the birds who would otherwise find their peace and rest there. For ultimately the person with whom they would be intimate becomes subordinate to their own all-engulfing need. And they are left with little of themselves to share, except pain and fear.

Intimacy grows best between people who have found space in their lives to get to know themselves. It flourishes most effectively when people are able to enjoy connectedness with others, and also given space to develop their own sense of separateness. But this fine balance is not always there at the beginning of any relationship. It is something which often needs to be talked over, prayed about, and worked at. And when there is mutual acceptance of the other's needs, and mutual concern for the other's anxieties and vulnerabilities then both self-containment and over-possessiveness can be dealt with. But the commitment has to be mutual: one person cannot make it work alone. And the concern has to be for the other: for where the focus stays on myself, even for understandable reasons, it makes the search for true intimacy just that much more difficult.

Fear of Risk and Exposure

An intimate relationship can act as a searchlight to other areas of our lives. When someone cares for us, we experience a new sense of enjoyment about ourselves. Very often we find we have a great desire to be the sort of person we see reflected in the concern of the other. Things about which we have never felt particularly proud now become a greater source of shame. We would hide them even from ourselves in the bid to recreate ourselves anew.

We are often afraid to show our love because it is such a risky endeavour. We feel raw, tender, exposed. We fear rejection, humiliation. We are not sure at the end of the day whether we really are that lovable to anybody. And this distancing ourselves from the sheer possibility of intimacy can produce some very odd behaviour.

Take the 'playing-hard-to-get' syndrome. Some people seem trapped in this ritual. How extraordinary it is that the moment those people find they are interested in another and long to spend time with that person, from that moment so much energy is committed to pretending the opposite is true. I know of a woman who felt deeply attracted to a man who started coming to her church. She thought about him each day, got his phone number, learnt his birthday, found out where he was from. She was always conscious of where he was in the room, or whoever he was speaking to. But whenever he approached her at church or at the end of a meeting she would pretend to be in animated conversation with someone else, just including him out of friendly politeness. She was terrified that he might guess how she truly felt and pity her. She wanted to convey the image of being popular, strong, self-sufficient. She wanted him to know that she was not dependent emotionally, and that she was not longing for him just to come along and ask her out. When he accepted what he assumed to be the hint, and took no further initiative, she then very obviously ignored him, hoping that he would notice he was being avoided and that in some miraculous way this would lead to a declaration of his love.

But of course it did not! Because even though he was a caring person who had found himself attracted by the vivacity and warmth of this other, he too was not without his own insecurity. He had been hurt twice in the past and was cautious a third time about taking risks. And as the time went on and the games persisted, he found it harder rather than easier to let go of his reluctance and take the first initiative. For the longer it continued the bigger the initiative became. Eventually, it seemed tantamount to an abandonment of his own independence. It was like laying everything he had on the line, and risking rejection when all he really wanted was time to get to know this person and test the possibility of a deeper relationship. Consequently, he never made any further move, and she was never able to overcome her pride and take that step herself. Fear of not being accepted and fear of looking ridiculous ultimately prevented both of them from moving openly and generously toward a relationship they would dearly love to have had.

This kind of insecurity has sometimes been linked with sexual repression, with the suggestion that sexually 'liberated' people do not suffer such hang-ups. I do not believe it.

The fear of rejection in relationships which have begun as casual, sexual ones is no less intense than that same fear elsewhere. In fact it can have an added dimension. For people are often afraid of their inadequacy at physical intercourse. Outside the context of a committed and faithful relationship some people feel insecure and vulnerable in this area and always on trial run, needing to perform well. The scorn or rejection of those who find their performance lacking does not lead either to a greater sense of self-esteem or to a fertile ground for the growth of intimacy. It is not comforting either to suspect that opportunist sex, rather than personal value motivated the relationship. There is also the spectre of sexual jealousy, which once roused can have terrifying consequences.

Although in my illustration I have identified the fear of exposure as a barrier to an intimate relationship ever getting off the ground, in fact it can be a problem for people who have been together for years. Within friendship, marriage, or family relations there can still be a problem with letting someone in to those profound, personal areas which we have never disclosed to anyone. Adult children have said that their parents never knew them, and they have never felt free to disclose to them who they really are. Some married partners also can stay together for years and yet not know some fundamental things about each other. The relationship can be one of fear of opening up or exploring these areas, because what is lacking is the trust that there will be empathy and understanding. And when one person in the relationship takes the risk and begins to open up something which for them is very personal, the slightest hint of insensitivity or impatience can mean that this issue is packed away again. And it will be harder to introduce a second time, and indeed it may never surface, but be instead one more lost opportunity for sharing and growth.

Inability to Make a Commitment

Some people have great difficulty in committing themselves to another. I have known people who have been going together for years and where one person has been unable to make a commitment. Some people go through elaborate processes of living together, or moving in and out of living together, with 'no strings attached', with the expectation that either in the end there will be some permanence to the relationship, or they will split and find new partners. Sometimes, of course, this 'temporary arrangement' can go on so long and the couple become so bonded that commitment has already crept in through the back door when nobody was noticing!

A Christian view of relationships does not see commitment as an optional extra, but as central to their very meaning. A committed relationship is one which offers a place of safety, not so that the partners can move into a rut and take each other for granted, but so that they can experiment and explore, and grow together. That is why Christianity places commitment and troth prior to sexual intercourse. It provides the context for a relationship which can celebrate bodily what the couple know with their hearts.

Yet some people find commitment very hard. They want their autonomy too much to be able to give themselves wholly to another person. In particular one of them might find the idea of marriage terrifying, even though that is what the other might be hoping for. And that other person might then hang on and on, hoping that one day it will change and the way forward will be made more easy. The longer the relationship has been there the harder it is to let it go.

Paula had gone out with Tim for five years. In the early years they had talked about marriage, but had felt neither of them was ready. They were both studying and then job-hunting, and then trying to settle into a new work environment. They found jobs close to each other and continued the relationship. As time went on Paula's commitment to Tim grew and she found she wanted more than anything to know that he was also committed to her. But although he never went out with any other woman, Tim could not bring himself to that point. Especially, he continued to feel unready for marriage, and always required more time. Paula's need for having some long-term aim, and his fear of it, became a tension within the relationship. Whenever she raised the question of the future he would become defensive and anxious. She would be impatient and sometimes tearful, and they both would feel unhappy.

Eventually Paula explained openly that she needed to know where she stood with Tim with regard to the future. She wanted mutual commitment in their relationship, and ultimately to marry and have children. Tim said he could imagine that he might feel that way in the long run, but not just yet. With remarkable calmness Paula suggested they might leave the subject completely alone for nine months, after which she would ask him for a final decision. Tim agreed. Those months, free from tension and acrimony deepened their relationship, and they relaxed and enjoyed communication and companionship. But when the nine months were up Tim said he needed more time and asked if she could wait the three months before the summer holiday. Reluctantly, but feeling this was not too much, she agreed. When the summer came Tim still felt unready to make such a big decision, and asked for more time. Then Paula felt the waiting had to end. She knew she could not continue with this constant uncertainty, and although it was the hardest thing she had ever done she broke off the relationship. Tim was deeply upset and became quite depressed. For weeks he was listless and strained, but he made no attempt to change her mind.

What was it Tim feared? It is difficult to say. It was not that he did not love Paula. He thought about her a good deal, and she was an important part of his life. But he was afraid of completely giving himself. For him, commitment meant coping with someone else's emotional life. He was at his most vulnerable in the relationship whenever Paula began to make emotional demands on him. Very soon he was out of his depth. Being committed would leave him in a permanent state of vulnerability when he did not have the emotional resources within himself. But he was also afraid of the finality of commitment. He panicked about the possibility of making a mistake. If marriage could have been in two-month stints, even to the same person, it might have been easier for him. But for better for worse, for richer for poorer, in sickness and in health had a frighteningly final ring about it. Paula's painful decision was the only way forward.

Lack of Play and Humour

One of the words that children and adolescents use most to describe the lives of adults, especially those in middle age, is 'boring'. Their work is 'boring', their home life is 'boring', their relationships are 'boring', their conversation is 'boring', their sermons are 'boring'. Sometimes, reflecting on the preoccupations of an average adult day, I have to concede that these critics have a point. Contemporary life for most grown-ups is marked by its solemn weightiness. Inflation rates, recessions and unemployment, crime figures, divorce and premature deaths are the serious stuff we are surrounded with most days of our lives. And they have their way of affecting even the most light-hearted of us. The routines of our lives can easily squeeze out much of the fun which is evident still in more youthful relationships. For many evenings on end, people may do nothing more interactive or interesting than going to the shops, catching up on housework or watching television. People's contemporary lives are often careworn, and although they technically have more leisure time than ever before, they probably have less play.

This should strike us as odd because play and humour are so much part of our humanness. Play is not simply the passive relaxation from work, but the active involvement in other areas of human creativity. It can be both self-absorbing and corporately enriching. When we play the piano or sketch a face, tell a story or write a letter we are getting in touch with another dimension of life. It deepens our awareness of sounds, shapes, patterns, emotions. As well it opens up for us the feelings of other people. Humour is part of play. Good laughter cements social relationships and lightens the heaviness of any situation. People who know how to laugh at themselves as well as how to see humour in dreary situations are like a break in the clouds on a grey, gloomy day. We want to be with them, to enjoy the relief of being 'taken out of ourselves' and to escape from the mundane and ordinary to the larger-than-life.

Most healthy families have their stock of archive humour which comes out regularly on certain cues: Grandad whose budgerigar dislodged his wig and sent it into the lap of the visiting vicar; Aunt Doris who rushed out to buy a lounge suite on hearing they would be moving from London to Nottingham, because she feared there would be no furniture shops north of Harrow; brother Paul who at the age of five so perplexed a burglar when he poured him a cup of cold tea with sugar that the thief left bemused and empty-handed. Family narratives are part of the folklore of our lives and we enjoy the idiosyncrasies and the intergenerational memories. We delight too in the humour of other family groups. A rabbi friend of mine can enliven any situation with his seemingly endless store of Jewish stories. There was the mother who bought her son two fine ties for his birthday, and when to please her he wore one next day for a special appointment she gave him one glance and asked accusingly, 'So what's wrong with the other tie?'

Play and fun are essential in all our close relationships. Young people banter and flirt with each other, communicating that they are great to be with and that life is not for the too-serious. The sad thing is that all too soon when such relationships become intense the fun can disappear. Humdrum routine, boredom, lack of interest in one another's sense of humour can easily replace playfulness. Pranks or jokes can be discouraged as a waste of time, or rewarded with arrogance or irritability. I well remember after three years of marriage receiving a large present for my birthday from Alan. I love surprises and there in front of me was a special one, wrapped in intriguing paper, covered in poems and kisses and promising all the excitement love could bring. To my shame I was neither delighted nor amused when the unwrapping disclosed an old rubber boot and one of his smelly athletics socks! But I was sorry afterwards that my intensity over receiving presents had crowded out my appreciation of his idiocy.

Intimacy thrives on playfulness. Friends or partners who stop sharing jokes or enjoying humour with each other lose a whole dimension of their relationship. As a summer school counsellor with the open university I used to watch people relating to fellow students in the bar or seminar rooms. They would flirt, joke, tease one another, and sometimes act like adolescents, even though many of them had long-term relationships at home. Often I would be aware that those home relationships had become uninteresting and dry, and that playfulness was now only available for these others who were little more than strangers. Yet it is so much more important among those who are close to each other.

Laughter needs time. Humour grows out of sharing. Playfulness demands a sense of fun. But little draws us more completely out of irritation or alienation than the ability to enjoy pranks and jokes and daft stories and see the ridiculousness of life together.

Resentment and Guilt

Long-term relationships often have more chronic barriers to growth than those that are relatively new. People who have been in a relationship for many years may have given up hope of ever achieving the kind of intimacy which they once believed was possible. Very frequently at the bottom of that impasse lies resentment.

Resentment is one of the most persistent problems in long-standing relationships. It can have many sources, some of which might go back decades. Sometimes an unconscious anger at having given way on something which was important later surfaces as resentment of the other and of decisions for which the other was responsible. Concessions coming out of people, or expected from them in a taken-for-granted kind of way generally prove costly in the long run. The sense of having been injured or ignored, having been treated as less than valuable can be buried for a while, but then smoulders destructively for years. That is why in a relationship of two people who stay together resentment is often accompanied by guilt. One person resents, the other feels guilty.

The sad thing is that there is often little that the guilty person can do to take away the resentment. When something has happened so long ago, an apology does not seem to be sufficient. When something has affected the rest of their lives, an apology might be dismissed as ridiculous by the one who is now angry and bitter.

The curious thing is that the closer the relationship the more damage the resentment can cause. In settings where those who have caused the injury are less intimately connected the response is often to ignore them, or to keep them at arm's length. But for those who daily face each other over the breakfast table, or who share the same bed, such resentment and guilt might eat away at their energies and their lives together. I find it interesting how many of these relationships actually do stay intact. Where it is between married people resentment and guilt does not always, or even usually, lead to breakdown and divorce unless it is accompanied by other problems. But the relationship is none the less a permanently damaged one, with one partner always trying to punish the other to show how much they have been hurt, whilst the other moves into a greater and greater sense of hopelessness.

Dorothy and Peter had been married thirty years. Peter had gone into business, but had never been very successful. Dorothy, who had a much better business sense, had given up her own career as a bookkeeper to stay home with her children. She had wanted to fulfil her own ambitions through her husband and pushed him into a bigger business venture than he was capable of. Waiting in the wings, always ready to help, and indeed to rescue him if necessary, she had believed they could make a go of it together.

Peter felt threatened by his wife's competence. It was his business. His partner did not have a wife who wanted to discuss everything and who made him feel small. He disliked Dorothy's manner. He felt she could be very supercilious. She did not understand most of the issues he was working through anyway. Being at home for six years with children had hardly kept her in touch with the business world.

Consequently, he spent more time at work with his business colleagues and less at home with his family. He did not want to spend much money on the house until work capital was secure, and was not interested in his wife's strategies for 'sorting things out'. When, three years later, his business collapsed leaving all the partners with debts his wife took a well-paid part-time job to help clear the backlog. With help from the bank, and a more stable job for Peter they slowly recovered. Six years later they were once more financially stable although not well off.

The anger which Dorothy had contained for nearly twelve years was now deeply seated. Peter had long since apologized for not trusting her judgement, although he had done it in a rather begrudging way. He still felt it was largely bad luck rather than his own inefficiency which had led to the collapse. Meanwhile Dorothy had been counting the cost. Her children were now grown. Her eldest had left home. They had never enjoyed a warm family life. Work and money had dominated their time together. Peter had always put work before the family, and before their marriage. The decisions to cut her out of business discussions, the way her own advice and insights had been ignored, the way she had been both mother and father to the children all simmered inside her as if it had all happened last week. Consequently their relationship grew worse, full of recrimination from Dorothy and guilt from Peter as he increasingly entered her world and her emotions. Finally, any conversation became impossible for it would always be punctuated by references to the past and his inability to do anything in the present which could ever compensate.

Resentment is a way of holding on to the past and tenaciously refusing to relinquish the anger which is rooted there. It is fed by sorrow, a grief fuelled by dissatisfaction and frustration. It is there as a reminder that things could have been so much better, life could have been so much richer. With some people it is also accompanied by anger directed to oneself. Why didn't I put my foot down? Why did I tolerate it?

Yet whatever its source, and however deep the hurt, where resentment is allowed to continue it will kill off intimacy. For at the very root of resentment is unforgiveness. The one who resents can never release the one who feels guilty because they must always pay for the pain of the past. But where there is unforgiveness there is hardness of heart which shuts out the pain of the other and closes off the possibility of both hearts sharing together.

Letting go of resentment is the hardest thing some people will ever have to do, for it demands so much. It leaves us vulnerable, for what happens if we are hurt again? It leaves us exposed, for it requires us to face our own need for vengeance and lack of love. It leaves us empty because sometimes all that is left of our inner life is the anger and bitterness which has consumed us for years.

It is when we face issues like this that we can understand more clearly the meaning of the love which St Paul writes about in his letter to the Corinthian church. That love does not resent, it keeps no score of wrongs. Fundamentally it is demonstrated most powerfully by Jesus Christ himself. For he forgave his own most intimate friends, his disciples, for the way they failed to support and nourish him at his time of greatest need. When all he required was that they should stay awake, and pray whilst he wrestled with the fear of death and separation, they simply slept and left him desolate.

Our own relinquishing of resentment is costly but brings us closer to our own humanness and deepens our relationship with God. And when that letting go is a mutual act it also opens up the future for a new intimacy in our relationships. Years of hurt can give way to the healing process, and a new nourishing and valuing of another can replace an endless roll-call of guilt and recrimination. Lewis Smedes makes a wise observation: 'Forgiving heals your memory as you change your memory's vision. When you release the wrongdoer from the wrong, you cut a malignant tumour out of your inner life. You set a prisoner free, but you discover the real prisoner was yourself.'[5]

In the end, the sense that the past is behind us and today is a new day with infinite possibilities is one of the most liberating experiences of all. But as we shall see in the next chapter we sometimes need to travel through pain first to reach that place.

Conclusion

Barriers to intimacy lie deep in our society and deep in our personality. In fact for many the very complexity of the human psyche and its apparently incompatible needs make the possibility of intimacy with others appear remote. It can seem even more unlikely because of all that has happened in the past and because of the unloving structures which surround us every day.

The Christian gospel has another view on this. It helps us to understand our human complexity, showing how the twin needs of bonding and separateness are important to all of us in our created humanness. It also helps us see how easy it is for those needs to distort our relationships with others. As Rolheiser sensitively observes:

We know that when we interrelate with others we must be careful never to violate their freedom. We must stand before them patiently respecting their inner freedom and dictates. When we deal with others, we may encourage, challenge, and perhaps even prod slightly at times, but we may never push too hard. We must respect the mystery that is the human heart.[6]

More than this, the gospel gives us the assurance that even long-created barriers do not need to dominate our lives. Although the process may be painful and we may require help these barriers can be dismantled, and our entrenched patterns of destructive hurt can be broken down. But it is in its vision for the restructuring of our relationships that the Christian gospel gives us greatest hope. For whether those relationships are structured by society, or family or our personal lives they can be reconstructed, and can become more open and trusting. But at the heart of this change lies the centrality of forgiveness. Without that no bonding can grow and no relationship can know time, depth and intimacy.

6

The Power of the Past

The average punter makes enough mistakes in each day to suffice. There is no point in being crushed by the shortcomings of a whole life.

Michael Riddell

My last chapter ended with a story of how long-term resentment rooted in the past crippled a relationship. In this chapter I want to focus exclusively on the past, because so many relationship problems begin there. What we are now is closely linked with what has gone before in our lives and how we reacted to it. It is almost a cliché to note that when people seek counselling, the central issue is not always the immediate, but is more deeply related to attitudes or anxieties in their personal history which have a much longer history. Understanding the origin of these attitudes is often the first step to being able to relinquish their hold on us.

For good reason psychologists from many different theoretical stables identify the past as important. Although they are likely to disagree profoundly over what it is about the past which is crucial, they might well find themselves in close agreement that many of our individual characteristics emanate from it. The briefest glance at some of the theorists in question would find evidence for this. B. F. Skinner and the behaviourist school, for example, see the past as the *conditioning or learning context* of our present attitudes and beliefs as well as of our behavioural patterns. For, Skinner has argued, we are essentially the product of patterns of stimulus and response which were inculcated in us from birth onwards. We are our *reinforcement history*, where approved attitudes and behaviour have been reinforced by rewards and pleasure, and other patterns discouraged by punishment or pain. So who we are now is almost entirely a product of how we were moulded then. For Skinner it has little to do with notions of human freedom of choice or personal commitment, indeed these are largely spurious. Nor is the focus on analysing the workings of the mind, or the place of the unconscious in the human psyche. Instead human beings are presented more as sophisticated and trained circus animals than freely reflecting mental agents. The past is important because of the way earlier reinforcement patterns have produced in us behavioural characteristics which we now associate with our 'personality'.

Of course behaviourism has its many critics, and has been attacked, not least, for its mechanistic approach to human life, and its denial of freedom. There is no doubt that the assumptions of the behaviourists severely hamper their conclusions. But in that they find a focus in the past they have other bedfellows. From a completely different basis the past is also important to Jung. His particular emphasis on the unconscious highlights the significance not only of our personal history but also our corporate past. We carry about with us the collective memory of those we never knew in the way that young Jewish people carry around with them the memory of the holocaust. The search is now for integration rather than fragmentation, and is born out of the disparate yearnings which have developed over time.

A similar looking back to the past and to personal history occupies Freud who develops his own account of the unconscious. Along with Erikson and other developmental psychologists who have taken their cue from him, Freud writes about the importance of earlier stages of life in the formation of our experiences and identity. His account is also a long way from behaviourism. The emphasis is not now on stimulus and response, or behavioural characteristics but on *inner* experiences. Feelings, especially of anxiety, fear or sexual arousal, can become sublimated and then unconsciously redirected into new situations. Freud emphasizes how our repression of traumatic events in the past can affect our present in apparently quite unconnected ways. And ever since Freud, many others have described the ways in which present fears, neuroses, phobias, or patterns of destructiveness all have their roots in situations long past. Anything, from an irrational fear of sharp objects or avoidance of being left alone to recurrent terror nightmares, has been traced back to specific or prolonged events in people's childhood.

Despite their considerable disagreement at a theoretical level, what these and many other psychologists point to is that our past experiences, our memories, and often those events which lie now beyond the recall of memory can deeply affect both the kinds of persons we are and the ways in which we relate to other people. And in this consensus there is yet another link. It is with what the Christian Scriptures have long ago disclosed to us. These psychologists are developing an insight which is fundamentally *biblical*, although they are doing so from quite different underlying assumptions and taking it in different directions. Put at its most obvious, it is that *our history matters*. Our personal and social past helps to create our value system, our belief patterns, our interests, our sense of self, our areas of frustration, our choice of partner. We see there the reasons for many of the idiosyncratic tastes and preferences many of us exhibit. Inevitably our past experiences can present us with both benefits and problems, with both ease of relationship and complexes. For example, habits and attitudes which might seem irrational to other people can have us in their grip and prevent us from knowing the freedom we would love to know in a relationship. We can see this even on a superficial level. More than once I have been told by someone asking my advice, 'I can hear myself speaking and saying things I vowed I would never say. I even use that whining voice of my mother's I used to despise, but I just don't know how to stop myself.'

It is not surprising that old biblical themes recur even in the work of non-christian psychologists. One is the impact of family relationships, and relationships with other central adults in our infancy. In the Bible, parents are told to be careful how they rear and nurture their children precisely because what goes on in those early years is crucial. The way in which we were parented, treated by our 'caretakers', inevitably deposits with us the presence or absence of feelings of security as well as some sense of our own meaning and value. The encouragements or discouragements we were given to live certain kinds of lives are likely to have repercussions for decades to come. That is why those early Hebrews were advised to communicate wisely with their children, to deal justly and teach respect for others and a healthy fear of God. In short, parents are told to bring up children 'in the way they should go, so that when they are old they will not depart from it'. And when in the Mosaic law (Exodus 20:5) the people are told that 'the sins of the fathers will be visited upon the children even to the third and fourth generation', we understand more of why we need to bring up our children well. For the way any one of us lives has inevitable consequences which affect other people. The evil we do to even one other person can cause ripples which pass right through the generations. So, of course, can the good we do. For biblical teaching is that those who reject wrong patterns of living, or who ask forgiveness from those they have hurt can effect blessings and peace to those who follow them in years to come. Although those predictions were uttered thousands of years ago we can see their contemporary relevance in our own society. Statistics quantify the way in which those who have suffered violence are found so regularly amongst those who now perpetuate it. And it is also true that those whose parents (and grandparents) have taught them to stand against injustice and exploitation are often found amongst the carers and visionaries of the next generation.

The Development of Intimacy

The Bible does not go into detail concerning all the forces that are at work in our personality and growth which make early experiences so important. God usually points us to the fundamental truths and leaves us to work out the specifics. But we do know enough about the process now to make some quite definite statements. Especially we can see how both our sense of self and our understanding of intimacy have been affected by our upbringing. Even those people who have never read any psychology would be able to detect strong pointers in their own lives. For none of us has emerged from nowhere with just this particular package of intimacy needs.

Our childhood itself was inevitably a place of learning. It was in the past that we first learnt who we were and how to relate to other people. It was somewhere back in our personal history where we received our first sense of what was right and wrong, where we picked up our first notions of love and sex. It was in our parents' marriage where we learnt our earliest lessons about marital intimacy, faithfulness and trust or where we encountered unfaithfulness and recrimination. It was when we were very small that we heard our first joke, endured our first teasing, enjoyed our first celebration. At some point in our childhood many of us first discovered what it was like to be betrayed, or to be an outsider.

Whether we are conscious of it or not, therefore, many of the things we feel about ourselves now have their origins in our early years. We may have learnt the power of stereotypes as they were applied to us: whether racial, sexual or physical ones. We may have been given labels which we enjoyed, or detested. We may have been fed information about ourselves which we suspected was untrue, but which we went along with anyway. For all of us spent many influential years listening to the voices of our parents, our peers or our teachers, instructing us, reproving us and telling us what we are like. Each of us has thousands of hours of memory tape recorded from years back which often lie dormant in our memories. Some lie even deeper than that, in fact beyond the recall of memory, yet they still influence us with attitudes, fears or anxieties which we carry around with us.

Those who are strongly aware of the influence of those years might still be able to repeat some of the things which they were told about themselves and some of the words which predominated: they were 'lazy', 'untidy', 'clever', 'pretty', 'a tomboy', 'selfish', 'useless', and so on. Very often these words were a part of underlying attitudes which interpreted children to themselves, and gave them a strong sense of the kind of people they were and the value which others gave them. As they grew older their peers might have found other more hard-hitting epithets: 'Chink', 'titch', 'smelly', 'Paki', 'nigger', 'four-eyes', 'poof', 'vegetable'. The more widely they were used the more the child would have to struggle from being dismissed and isolated. Whether we can clearly recall the past or not our self-image might still be affected by the labels we selected from the many offered us as children.

The effects of parental attitudes last far longer than labels from peers. For even if we can shrug off the unfavourable responses from people our own age, the judgements of those who are older and closer bed down in our consciousness. Not for nothing does St Paul remind fathers not to be harsh or discouraging to their children. For our parents leave us many legacies. If we were fortunate enough to be born to stable, nurturant people who surrounded us with warmth and a sense of well-being we will have been spared much of the later trauma of those who endured a childhood of coldness. If those who were close to us in our early years gave us respect, affirmation and affection, we will almost certainly find it easier to develop stable intimate relationships ourselves than if we suffered hostility and abuse. For, ironically, constant affirmation and realistic encouragement do not usually result in egotism or swollen headedness. They are more likely to contribute to a sense of generosity and openness to others. People who have known *unconditional love* for most of their lives have little to prove to other people. On the other hand, constant blame, recrimination, criticism and any form of abuse leaves those who endure these things far less comfortable with themselves. Such attitudes can even inculcate in people a permanent sense of guilt or inadequacy. They can leave their recipients struggling with bitterness or mean-spiritedness for years.

Analysing the Past

It is sometimes difficult, however, to pin down precisely the contribution of the past in any one person's present experience. Even though some psychological theories, such as behaviourism, present us with an analysis which correlates past and present very closely, most others writers would see their relationship as more complex. There is little obviously clear *causal* connection between past and present in areas of our life, especially with regard to human intimacy. For there is something about human personality which cannot simply be reduced to history, parenting, genes or environment. We often hear stories of identical twins brought up close together, who yet develop quite separate emotional, sexual and personal lives. Similarly, even though two children who have endured cruelty may both suffer emotionally and be deeply affected for years to come, the suffering of each may exhibit very different characteristics. They may show contrasting levels of resilience, different abilities to put the past behind them, and even varying attitudes towards those who have badly treated them. In one way or another, then, even at an early age, we bring our *own responses* to a situation.

I am not wanting here to tap into the old nature-nurture debate, but to make a different point. It is that our capacity for intimacy and for close relationships with other people has many layers. Some were placed there firmly during our infancy, others have been dug up and relaid, some have been put down continuously throughout long periods of time, others have been deposited in a single heightened incident. But in all of the layering we have been both passive and active: sometimes being overwhelmed by the process, and at other times taking charge of it. What is more, it is not at all easy to say for sure which has been which.

To change the simile, trying to unravel the influence of the past is like becoming interested in a very complex movie which is already well into the plot. We can see that the various relationships and the hints of early bits of the story are all significant, but cannot be sure exactly how without a much more comprehensive understanding of the whole. The problem is that because the movie is our own life it is not easy to stop the sequence, rewind, and replay some earlier action to grasp the bigger picture. And even if we did have perfect recall the place where we decide to stop may be arbitrary and we could still not be sure which of our reactions now to those events or experiences are the significant ones.

Most of this will be familiar to those who are in counselling situations. Confronting the power of our personal past is no exact science. The legacy of the past differs for each person, and much of it we can only re-experience with hindsight. Yet even with all the above cautions there has been enough work in social psychology for us to be able to broadly identify situations in our lives which are *more likely* than others to leave a lasting effect on us. The majority of those situations will involve our parents or relatives whose lives closely connected with ours in childhood, and we might be aware of the effects long after we have left the parental home. For many people find themselves trapped in past reactions to parents which have set up long-term habits – defensive behaviour, deceitfulness, fear of judgement, trying to win affection – and it can be difficult to move into real adulthood until these patterns are recognized and rejected. Jacquelyn Carr observes: 'Until we have completed our relationships with our parents, our whole lives are actually *about* our parents. If we are trying to prove or acknowledge something to them, our lives simply become reaction patterns.'[1] These findings are reinforced over again in work with many different people who are struggling to understand their emotional lives.

There are many reasons why people do not complete their child-hood relationships with parents or others and move their relating on to a new level of maturity. Sometimes it is because the love offered has always been conditional, and as a person grows there is still the child within trying to meet the conditions laid down by the parent. It may be because the mother or father is so dominant, aggressive or powerful that a relationship of intimacy and equality never becomes a possibility. It may be because traumas endured in childhood were brutal. Or sometimes it may be because a vital early relationship was cut short by death, desertion or separation. Whatever the reason, however, an emotional blockage can result which make take a long time to clear.

Intimacy and Early Loss

A childhood experience of loss must be among the most traumatic and enduring situations we have to deal with. The death of someone close to us comes not only as a sharp blow, but also turns the world we inhabit inside out. Normality changes. Definitions blur. The first bereavement may present a child with so many unanswered questions and fearful associations, and can be all the more difficult to handle later because the actual death will be largely unremembered. Yet the early feelings stay registered in the awareness of most children and can be reactivated at any point in life. Often without warning, an association or a signal similar to the one received in the early experience will set off sensations of fear or unhappiness, or bring profound depression.

This is true for a large number of children who have been in close contact with another's death. In her perceptive book, *Loss*, Jean Grigor talks of experiencing 'a funny, frightened feeling' whenever she thinks of her father's mother, even though she has no conscious memories of her. This grandmother died when the author was only two, in the child's house, and in her bed, nursed by her own mother. She remembers uneasily that her mother did not like the old lady and that they had a less than warm relationship. So many of the nuances, the attitudes and the complexities of adult feelings are picked up quickly by a child, who usually of course does not understand them, or know how to deal with them. Jean Grigor summarizes: 'No matter how skilfully adults imagine they are shielding a young child from painful exposure to grief or grieving people, that child will have his or her highly perceptive radar switched on, alert for all kinds of signals of distress.'[2]

The distress radar will be on full alert where the death is that of a parent. The loneliness of a child's grief can be very profound, all the more so because it is experienced against the backcloth of a previously predictable security. Now the one who could always provide comfort in time of fear or anxiety is the one who is gone. The other parent who is left is grieving too, and has usually no remedy for the pain. And so the proliferation and confusion of emotions which children of all ages experience in the face of the death of a father or mother make the process a complex one.

Compounding the sense of deep loss is often anger, sometimes anger directed at the parent who has left them. There can also be a niggling sense of guilt, particularly if there has been a long terminal illness and the child has repeatedly been told to 'hush, be quiet, don't disturb mummy'. Or 'don't quarrel or it might make daddy worse'. When the parent dies, how are they to be sure that it wasn't brought on by their quarrelling or noisiness? There can even be a residual fear of going away from home, when the memory that haunts is of being taken suddenly away to a neighbour's house for some hours, to return and find the sickbed empty and people weeping.

For many bereaved children there is the freezing of the relationship, where scraps of memories serve as an ongoing reminder that such a person was once there and was kind, or loving, brave or fun. Protection of the child against any 'unnecessary' details about that parent often means that the picture is a very incomplete one, built of folklore, mental snapshots and fragments of experience. Where the details remain scant with the passing years the emerging adolescent can easily sense a conspiracy of silence against them. Sometimes it is not until much later in life, even following the death of the remaining parent that some children, now as adults, hear stories which give them a very different picture from the one they have cherished for so long. This can bring in a new crisis of identity for some, as the person they thought was real turns out to be only a fantasy.

The experience of losing one who provided a touchstone in a child's emotional life may well therefore have many repercussions. At the immediate level a number of responses are typical: clinging behaviour, being over-possessive towards the remaining parent or grandparent, nightmares of searching for the lost one, or wish-fulfilment dreams where the dead parent is alive and well again. Long-term responses can vary much more. For coming to terms with loss is so often a very private matter in our culture and few children are given any real help with it. Sometimes a child might appear to become more self-contained, showing a measure of autonomy not evident in his peers. Often adults note this with approval. 'He's getting over it really well.' 'I'm very glad about the way she has learnt to cope.' And indeed it can mean that the child can be coming to terms with the grief in a way that develops growth and maturity.

Yet it might mean something else. For some children after the initial period of shock and early bereavement a new detachment sets in. Reluctant to give all that love so fully to another human being who might also die the child can 'close up' and withdraw. It may not be until adulthood, when they make new relationships and become deeply attached to a partner, that they go through the final stages of bereavement. But for others this transition never takes place at all. The effect of loss stays as an intrinsic part of their personality, and the 'closing up' becomes fixed. These people firmly take charge of when and how they will be drawn into any experience emotionally, and may always choose not to allow feelings to develop beyond the stage at which they remain in control. Consequently, they can be left with difficulties in giving up their autonomy. Even if they marry, an inert fear of loss can remain a permanent barrier to a deep relationship. For there is a deep, hidden terror of ever trusting someone again with the weight of their emotional life.

One very sad story which illustrates the paralysing power of this fear was David's. A 'strong, silent type', he had attracted Jackie by his stability and even-temperedness. In the two years before they got married nothing seemed to throw him off course and he exhibited omnicompetence in all the areas where she was weak. A few months after the wedding they moved away to a new area, with some excitement and anticipation. They left behind, however, Jackie's family and women friends who had provided her with a long-term, taken-for-granted warm support network. As the weeks went by, with only David's companionship to rely upon, Jackie began to experience his silence as loneliness rather than as strength. Their conversations never got beyond the place where they had always started years since. He regularly failed to share bits of information or conversation which, had he reflected on it, he would have known to be interesting to Jackie. As Jackie began more and more to miss the effusive affection of her family, David began to show other unexpected characteristics. He was very fearful of 'scenes', and a 'scene' would be anything which involved a raised voice. He was impatient with any 'unnecessary' show of emotion. He would have to leave the room if Jackie became distressed by an image on the television or an item on the news. He became angry with Jackie's tears, and would quietly smoulder whenever she was upset by something he had said or done. Her efforts to get him to be more communicative and sharing were met by irritation. Over a short period he retreated into almost non-communication where only the necessities of everyday functional conversation, or social chat with friends broke the silence.

After a tearful and emotionally heightened 'scene' Jackie threatened to leave him unless he agreed to go with her to counselling. Unhappily he agreed. On his first visit he hesitantly disclosed in answer to gentle questioning that he had been an only child who had lost his mother at the age of four. His father had sent him to boarding school, visiting him rarely, and remaining at home on his own. When he was twelve David realized that his father had become an alcoholic. The two of them were unable to talk about it, and his father died four years later of cirrhosis of the liver. All of this information was delivered in a very matter of fact way, yet David was visibly under great strain. When asked how he had felt about his father's alcoholism he became impatient with the counsellor and asked for the interview to be terminated. Jackie felt enormous progress had been made, and was very grateful for what she perceived as a breakthrough. Yet she returned alone on the next visit to say that David was not willing to come to any further sessions. A few months later he said he wanted the marriage to end. Despite all efforts of family and friends they separated a year later and, like his father, he retreated into solitude and isolation.

It was clear that even after all those years David still could not face the strength of his own pain. Having had to bear two central bereavements utterly on his own with no help from adults, he was not able to let go and become childlike and vulnerable again. It was a tragic defeat. For even the breakup of his marriage seemed to him to be preferable to going through the intensity of emotions he could not understand, for an outcome he could not envisage.

Although the death of a parent is undoubtedly the most significant loss which can be experienced by a child there are many others which are also crucial. The death of a brother or sister brings a particular turmoil, as well as a new anxiety surrounding the child's own mortality. The death of a grandparent can be full of grief and distress, particularly where that relative has given quality time to the grandchild, and even provided an occasional ally against the rest of the world. Similarly, the death of an aunt or uncle, of a close neighbour or friend can each bring powerful feelings of sorrow and loss. In each of the areas even though the pain is shared with parents and others in the family, the child's experience is very specific.

Sometimes, however, the depth of a child's experience does not take place in a community of mutual grief. Because children have their own categories of significance and closeness, the strength of the pain they feel might be out of all proportion to the actuality of loss from an adult perspective. So when a cat or even a guinea-pig dies the sense of bereavement can be as great as anything the child has yet experienced. A child can cry with pain for days following the shock of a pet's accidental death, and can remember the event for years afterwards, even more so if they were directly involved in the accident. Other losses not involving death at all can be very significant. The loss of familiar surroundings when the family moves, the absence of a particular friend who might be taken away from the area, the loss of treasured possessions which are stolen or destroyed all leave a legacy of sorrow for a young child. How the grief is handled, as well as the depth of grief itself both play a significant part in our emotional development. We can move into a maturer adulthood where we are in touch with our feelings, and are not afraid of pain. Or we can be left stranded, marooned on an isolated island of anxiety and fear, where we will practise any kind of avoidance rather than be exposed to such hurt again.

The Effects of Family Breakup

I have written mainly of the effects of loss through death and bereavement. The other loss which has its own specific effect on children is that of family breakup through divorce and separation, and there is a great need for understanding some of the hurts and damage which this can bring.

Many therapists have pointed to the need for broken partners themselves to go through a period of mourning. This is true even when the couple may have been desperately unhappy together. For breakup is still a kind of bereavement, not now grieving the death of a person but a death of all the possibilities of that relationship. Divorce usually marks the final abandonment of the hopes invested in the marital bonding. It is the recognition that this marriage is over, this partner has gone, this love is not returned, these years shared together are not enough to keep the relationship intact.

For children of divorced parents there might also need to be a period of mourning, and a time of consciously working through the changes which the dissolution of the family household brings. For theirs can be a particularly difficult experience. Sometimes the first they know that their parents' marriage is to end is the day that one parent leaves. Even where there were prolonged rows, threats and desperation the experience of divorce is not usually one which children themselves consider. Then there can be that sense of personal guilt, or at least ambiguity. These two people had once been married. Now they are not. Was it my fault? All too often this question has already been answered in the affirmative, unwittingly perhaps by blame thrown in a child's direction.

When one partner goes to a new lover it is not only the remaining partner who has been left behind. The experience of desertion is experienced by each offspring in the family. The sense of being rejected by a parent who is dearly loved can deeply cripple a child's sense of value and worth, and that loss of confidence can remain even when both parents stay in touch with the child. Some children are also quick to 'see through' attempts at compensation especially by a deserting father who brings gifts or expensive outings, but not love for their mother. It can add to the confusion and rejection.

But there are other significant issues too. Children often hang on to the hope of a happy ending. For the deep bitterness, anger or just plain boredom of the parental relationship is not part of their own experience, and for them the issue is inevitably less complicated. Small children have been known to try physically to drag their parents to each other, believing that this is all that it takes to make up. Wallerstein and Blakeslee in their study, *Second Chances*, makes some important points in this respect. These two authors investigating divorce and remarriage compare the effects of divorce with those of parental death, and conclude that 'the children of divorce face a more difficult task than the children of bereavement'. Coming to terms with the fact that the marriage is over is one aspect of this difficult task. The analysis in the report is poignant and shows how children may cling on to the hope that the family will be brought back together again: 'Death cannot be undone, but divorce happens between living people who can change their minds. A reconciliation fantasy taps deep into children's psyches . . . they may not overcome this fantasy of reconciliation until they themselves finally separate from their parents and leave home.'[3]

Although all loss is significant, and the breakup of parental marriage is a deep experience of loss for a child, it is not possible to generalize about the long-term effects of the divorce. How the parents handle the split, and how much the child is affirmed and loved during the process is also very important. Parents who refuse to drag their children into the bitterness, and do not use children as pawns against each other are infinitely more considerate to them than those who do. Parents who are able to explain a little, to ask forgiveness from the child for the hurt they have caused, to ensure that the child is able to have a good relationship with the estranged partner will be already helping their children through some of the worse parts of the breakup. But such responses are not easy. If they were the marriage would probably not have broken up in the first place. The same reasons which drive people to split with their partners also often lead them to want to punish that partner for the damage, waste and betrayal which has left them broken.

There are better and worse ways of having to face the situation of parents' separation and divorce, and thankfully many children are guided through the process with love and care. But sadly, even at its most benign it cannot fail to give the child one message. That whatever is said in theory, in practice some kinds of conflict can only be resolved by breaking up. And for many who go into adulthood fearing this, the prospect of marital disharmony can be a very threatening one, and can lead people to shy away from commitment and the possibility of a partner's unfaithfulness or abandonment. The last thing they want is to leave themselves as exposed as adults as they were as children.

Child as Parent

Even though family breakup can be particularly traumatic, the issues surrounding a parent's marriage are often much more complex than whether or not the parents stay living together. There may be factors other than the separation itself which bring emotional repercussions at many different levels. Not infrequently depression and despondency can afflict a child who is party to its parents' unhappiness. And those feelings themselves can feed into later relationships.

Rachel's story is an interesting example. She was the older of two children and had lived through a particularly angry and bitter breakdown of her parents' marriage. She could not remember a time when there had not been rows or recriminations, and from the age of seven onwards would be woken by prolonged shouting and screaming and banging of doors. When she was thirteen her father left home for good, and her mother went through a period of financial hardship as she tried first to get maintenance from him, and then to find suitable work which would bring enough income for herself and two children. Constant anxiety about the health of Rachel's younger brother, who was severely asthmatic, made the situation worse.

During the whole of this time the only stable point in the mother's life was Rachel. At the age of nine the child had become the mother's confidante. She had sat up late worrying about her father's absence. She had carefully watched the people he spoke to whenever he drove her anywhere. She noted the number of evenings he worked late. Her anxiety over her mother's vulnerability turned into a fierce protectiveness towards her. But there was also an inbuilt helplessness, for she could not effect any reconciliation between father and mother, nor prevent her father from leaving home. Her mother then relied on Rachel for everything through the rest of the girl's teen years. All she needed to compensate for the rejection from her husband came from her daughter: companionship, affection, encouragement, emotional support. Now Rachel had gone to college, and although her mother had fully supported and encouraged her, she had no way of releasing her from the anxieties which the girl had carried for her those many years.

At eighteen, and away from home, Rachel felt she was missing out on life. She came to talk to me ostensibly to ask if there were ways she could learn to be more outgoing. She had some friends in her local young people's group at church and she was surrounded by people her age at university, but she felt very much 'out of everything'. Rachel's despondency was brought to a head when a popular and friendly girl in the same corridor at college had laughed at her in public and, in front of a dozen others, had told her to 'mellow out and lighten up a bit'. She felt humiliated and embarrassed.

As we talked she insisted she *was* depressing. She hardly ever found anything funny, and could not force laughter just to please other people. She liked being with people, but did not engage with them, and although she had nothing against their levity she never felt part of it. Consequently, young men in particular very soon lost interest, probably erroneously thinking her to be critical of them or standoffish. So she went through periods of disliking herself enormously for being such a miserable freak, and weaving fantasies about how it might be if she were different.

It was hardly surprising that Rachel felt uneasy with people her own age. For emotionally she belonged to a different decade. She was old. She had experienced very little childhood, and almost no nurturing. Over a period of years she had in effect lost both parents, and had instead become a parent to her mother. And so she could not now relate to those who were still childlike in their attitudes or enjoyment of life. Her route to change was to be a painful one. For it brought her into unexpected and very deep anger with her mother for the years of lost childhood and adolescence: for having been exposed to adult fears and worries, as well as having a distorted relationship with her father. It brought her too into seeking out her father to find out what kind of person he really was; then encountering more pain as her former fears and impressions about him were confirmed. Experiencing a new rejection from him she was brought again into the reality of what her mother had lived with. Yet once it passed these initial stages her journey was ultimately a positive one. For as she opened herself up to change, she gained confidence, and energy and made some deep, strong friendships. Two years after she had left college her Christian faith helped her to forgive first her mother and then eventually her father for the hurt and harm they had caused her. She was ultimately able to move into a new, freer maturity and a strong acceptance of her self-worth.

Child Abuse

At the root of many people's fear of intimacy, or anxieties within an intimate relationship, lies a history of a different kind of trauma from that of loss. A past dominated by child abuse leaves those who survive it with layers of negation, depression, anger, confusion and bewilderment which sometimes need many years of patient work to unravel, and leave behind. This can be the case even in those people who cannot recall the details of their abuse, or even that it happened. For there are those whose painful memories are 'buried alive in the unconscious'. Pat Collins comments: 'Remarkable as it may seem, there are . . . many men and women who are consciously unaware of the fact that they have suffered the trauma of being sexually abused as children. The extent to which people put hurts and painful feelings of this kind into cold storage is the extent to which their capacity to experience positive feelings will be frozen as well.'⁴ The experience of being repeatedly abused, either sexually, mentally or physically, outweighs most other negative experiences in the past of any child.

There are some striking reasons for this. The sheer *loneliness* of being an abused child stands out against the spontaneous and effortless way other children are able to communicate about their everyday lives. The child who knows it is abused stands instead in a conspiracy of silence. The silence is imposed often by the abusing parent or adult, especially in the case of sexual abuse, and is reinforced by the feelings of shame which confront the child. The confusion itself can bring bewilderment, as the whole basis for a child's understanding and morality is turned upside down. Those who should be caring are those who are violating, so the 'kind and the good' are all mixed up with the 'cruel and the bad' in the child's experience. There is simply nowhere to go and hide, for what should be the place of safety is also a place of terror.

I have worked for some years with the survivors of child sexual abuse and even though I hear similar responses time and time again they never fail to make an impression on me. The acceptance of guilt is one such response. I always find it extraordinary to hear yet another person say that they feel they were in some sense to blame for their abuse, although I am no longer surprised by this 'confession'. It has been said to me in so many circumstances, even from one speaker who had been sexually violated from the age of three. The reason for this is straightforward. Abusers regularly blame their victims for provoking the abuse. The child is accused of 'deliberately turning on' her abuser, or of being 'too attractive'. And in the child's mind this hits a mark. Why else would a father or a stepfather do this to her unless she herself were to blame? She must be the dirty one, the bad one. Then the parent who fails to protect the child, usually the mother, also leaves the child with confusion because the child often senses that there is some complicity in the abuse, but knows too that she is despised by her mother. This reinforces the guilt, and sense of being bad. And then there are often some memories of sexual stimulation sometimes being experienced as pleasurable, even though most survivors also report it to have been repugnant. One man spoke of being stricken by memories of 'pleasure' from the sex-play initiated by his babysitter over a seven-year period, even though it was mixed with distress, anxiety and tears. It had in fact prevented him from seeking help with the abuse for twenty years. Yet it is evident to anyone that a child can never be guilty of the sin of violation committed against her or him by an adult. It is so easy for an adult to manipulate guilt or compliance or even sexual excitement in a child, and guilt lies only with the manipulator and not the child. But it can take a long time in counselling before the survivor is able really to accept that, and a longer time still before this 'rational' understanding soaks through to the emotions.

The effects of child abuse have become familiar. Those who have been invaded as children may go through many kinds of body hatred; for the ongoing pain is so intensely connected with what has happened to their bodies. So the response is sometimes to cover it all up, to overeat, to wear heavy, shrouding clothes, anything which will make them look unattractive and undesirable and keep the pain out of view. The same drive is there when abused people become anorexic: one woman expressed her slow starvation as a 'wish to become invisible', not to exist at all. The pain could not be blotted out whilst her body remained to remind her of what she had been left with. Other ways of dealing with the past have been to become promiscuous, often accepting constant abuse, or to find oneself the victim of violence from a partner. For years to come the deep sense of defilement might be an almost inescapable part of identity.

For many who are its victims, child abuse can mean that the past is always present. Isolation and fear, depression and numbness, anger and bewilderment, overachievement and compensation have all been part of the stories of those who have been damaged or violated in childhood. And for many it is a long journey to wholeness. It can be a long time before real intimacy with others seems a possibility. Even the first step of breaking the silence can present enormous difficulties, especially for people who have found some way of coping up to now. Many do keep the terrible secret for years. It is not at all unusual to find women and men in middle or later years of life who are just beginning to recognize that they have not been healed from the emotional damage done to them decades before. Scars can heal, bruises can disappear, but the sense of self-worth is far more permanently seared. Even when some healing has taken place there might be new pain to work through at a later stage in life.

A woman came to me at the end of a public lecture I had given. She was smartly dressed, very direct and efficient in her manner. She wondered if she might arrange to meet me for a brief interview. I was able to see her straight away. She told me in a very matter-of-fact way that she had endured a childhood of incest and physical abuse inflicted on her by her stepfather from as long as she could remember. She had worked through it years ago. She had been in therapy, had learnt to experience herself as a strong achiever and went on to make an excellent career for herself. At this point she was a senior manager in her firm. She was known to be utterly reliable in everything. She felt good about her job, and was quite aware of what it had taken for her to reach this place in her life.

I listened at the remarkably calm way in which she was able to talk about the deep pain she had gone through during so many years. Just as I began to feel that she was one of the very few people whom I have met who has been able to leave all the hurt behind, the real reason for the conversation was disclosed. A new fear had emerged for her. She had met someone she cared for. In her late thirties she was considering the possibility of marriage. But she was afraid. In fact she was terrified. She was not sure whether she would be able to fully trust this man with all the decades of pain inside her. She was not sure she could ever trust any man not to violate her body once she was in a position of vulnerability. She was unsure how she could respond to lovemaking beyond the very early stages which they now enjoyed together. For even though rationally she believed he would be a good, gentle, and loving partner, emotionally she still felt like a small child: confused, anxious and afraid.

Although she now had to work through her inability to trust, this woman had already done a lot of work to eliminate the deeply negative sense of self which she had gained from her past. Even so, it did not prove to be immediately straightforward. She went back to counselling along with the man she wanted to marry. An unexpected crisis arose when he himself began to be frightened of his own sexual feelings. Thinking about her violation brought him face to face with the terror of his own potential as an abuser. He even became worried that this might have been what had attracted him to her. Over some weeks of sessions on his own with a careful Christian therapist he was able to work through these fears and get them in perspective. Through prayer and new reliance on the power of the Holy Spirit he was able to also let them go. Although it involved a good deal of painful work they eventually both felt confident enough to face the future together. They have since gone into a marriage which has strengthened and blessed them both. They are now even able to help some other couples by listening to their fears and anxieties.

This is a wonderfully reassuring story. In my experience it is also relatively rare. Some other couples take the effects of abuse right into their marriages, and suffer for years before they seek help in working it through. Other people never even reach that stage. Instead they experience long-term depression or more violation and a further negation of their self-respect. A few go from abuse to abuse right through adulthood. Even for those who are able to break the pattern, at times the journey is so painfully slow and full of anguish that only very small goals can be aimed at. With one young woman I know the sheer ability to get through a day without taking an overdose is itself a reason for thankfulness. For she has spent so much of her life in hospital casualty departments and rehabilitation centres that a day without a suicide attempt is a day when she knows God's grace is with her, and experiences God's love protecting her. For a middle-aged man I know it is progress if he can work through his feelings of anger today, and not let them turn into violence towards himself or others. It is a small victory if he can handle disagreement without smashing his fist through the window-pane. For other people I have met it is a sign of encouragement if their depression is not utterly overwhelming and there are periods which lighten the constant feeling of numbness or dread.

What is important, however, is that those who have been hurt so deeply should always be given hope. And sometimes this is the hardest thing to communicate. I have a story which describes how hard it can be. One friend who had been greatly abused as a child is still 'frozen' inside although she is now a professionally successful woman. She had come to the place where she felt she just could not go on. The struggle seemed pointless. When she spoke to me it was the end of the day. She was tired, and deeply depressed. She dreaded the night with its fitful waking and inevitable nightmares which left her drained and exhausted for work. I had been with her for two days and now felt utterly inadequate. I was wearied myself with the weight of her constant pain. With no more words to help, I held her hand and prayed, not for her healing, but for her rest. I asked God simply to give her *hope* so that somehow and from somewhere she could find the strength to go on.

Sometimes it is only God who can help. And often that help comes when we are at the very end of our resources. It came now. My friend told me afterwards that not only did she sleep that night, but this time her dream was a completely different one. In it she found a mangled kitten by the roadside. She picked it up, gave it warm milk, and bathed its wounds. Under her gentle care the kitten revived and even began to purr. In the dream she then walked with the still feeble animal tucked under her jacket until a friend stopped her, and stroking the kitten, asked its name. She heard herself draw a deep breath and say 'Its name is Hope', and woke with a deep experience of peace for the first time in her life. She believed that God had met her in her dream and given the sign she had been longing for. She would survive and the past would be healed.

Theology of Childhood

I have been looking at the way in which problems in the past affect people's search for intimacy, and how specific childhood experiences can make that search a particularly difficult one. At the level of everyday life many of these problems arise because of the lack of value, care and nurture which people have been given. But there is a deeper reason why these problems are so enormous. At the level of biblical understanding it is because God's norms for childhood have been violated.

We find these norms in the Christian Scriptures. There are many aspects about childhood which are precious and must be honoured. Yet when the abuse of a child occurs these qualities are almost always exploited, denied or trampled upon. Take for example the aspect of maturation. One obvious thing about a child is its *immaturity*. A child is a child. A child is not an adult. Both physically, mentally and emotionally a child has not grown up. St Paul himself makes a significant comment in his famous passage on love in a letter to the Corinthians. 'When I was a child', he writes, 'I spoke as a child, I thought as a child, I understood as a child'. It was not until adulthood that the 'childish things were put away'. Paul is saying this not with disapproval about a child's immaturity, but with a very matter-of-fact endorsement. It is perfectly in order to be a child.

Harm comes to a child, therefore, when its lack of maturation is not respected. When we demand adult behaviour, or load a child with adult responsibilities we are not respecting childhood. Children have different priorities, and different abilities. They cannot always remember what they should be doing, they cannot get their minds round tricky adult problems, they have much shorter concentration spans, they cannot cope with adult emotions. We do not accord them the same legal responsibility as adults. Most of all they do not have adult bodies, but their young bodies should be allowed to grow unhindered, and not abused sexually for the gratification of another.

A child is also *vulnerable*. That is why children are put into the care of those who are older. Jesus himself recognizes a child's vulnerability when he issues that spine-chilling warning in the Gospel of Matthew: 'If any one causes one of these little ones who believes in me to stumble, it would be better that that person be thrown into the sea with a millstone round his neck.' A child's vulnerability is there to be honoured, not destroyed. For many people who have been abused the turning-point comes when they recognize that their abuse has not gone unheeded by God. The terrifying question, 'But where was God when all this happened to me?' is never answered by the statement 'He was on the side of the abuser.' Instead, when people have been able to take God back into those years of abuse, and experience for the first time perhaps God's deep anger at what has happened to a child he loves, it can be the beginning of healing.

In his teachings to the disciples Jesus points to the *trust* of a child. He uses this as an example of our own trust towards God. A child is to lead the way in our own attitude of obedience and acceptance and trust of God's love and God's goodness towards us. Childhood is given great affirmation in the life of Christ. He not only urges us to be *childlike* rather than full of our adult vanity and self-sufficiency, but he also shows us how to relate to children with more respect and kindness. When the disciples are sending away the 'mothers of Salem' who have come to Jesus with their youngsters, Jesus intervenes. His ministry is not only for the adults. His time and energy is not too important to give to children, but he draws them close. The old Sunday school picture of Jesus with a child on his knee might be too sentimental and Victorian for our present tastes. But the truth behind is too important for us not to heed.

This draws us to another vital recognition. It is that children are people in their own right. A child is not on the way to becoming a human being but from the very beginning is *fully human*, with full dignity and worth. From the moment of creation a child has its own relationship with God, its own access to prayer, its own awareness of love and goodness. Both Scripture and our own experience teach us that the Holy Spirit speaks as directly to a child as to an adult, and even reveals to those who are young what is hidden from the mature and worldly-wise. This means that our relationship with any youngster, even our own child, is only ever that of carer and guardian. No one can *own* a child: not its family, the local authority, the state, the religious leaders. Each child is a creature of God, and although a child may be prevented from developing that relationship, no one can take it away.

Conclusion

Our ability to form intimate relationships today owes a great deal to the intimate relationships others formed with us in the past. We may be profoundly grateful that our parents loved us, and nourished us and surrounded us with care and a sense of well-being in our spirit. We may look back with joy and happy nostalgia, knowing how deeply we were prepared then for the intimate relationships we enjoy now. Or we may still be struggling with hurts from the past which have wounded not only us, but those with whom we are now trying to relate.

It can be helpful for all of us to think back over our childhood and remember those significant events which have left their marks on us; to ask for example what are our happiest memories, and our most frightening ones; what kind of relationship did we have with those who were closest to us; what was our first bereavement, and what impact did it have; what were the experiences of loss which we suffered most? Those who know the answers already to many of those questions will be those who know well some of the joys and hurts which they have gone through in their younger lives.

There is a danger if we begin to categorize those people without painful memories as 'normal' and those who are still suffering as 'abnormal', or even worse as 'emotional cripples'. The reality is that most of us are in some ways damaged, hurt or maimed, either at birth itself, or through circumstances during our lives. Far from shrinking from the truth or reaching out for easy labels we need to realize that this is a perfectly acceptable way of being human.

Once again, however, we must remember that the past does not have the final word. It can be ultimately put to rest in the forgiving and healing power of Jesus Christ. For just as Christ promises that the Holy Spirit of God will bring to our remembrance all those things which we should hold on to, the Holy Spirit can also ultimately heal us from the years of pain. All those damages and hurts which lie deep in our memories and prevent us from knowing freedom in our lives can die themselves as they are swallowed up in a greater love which speaks peace to the depths of our soul. Jesus told the crowds in the synagogue that he had come to bind up the broken-hearted and to set the captives free. And those who are still held captive by the past can have their wounds bound up and their spirits restored.

Our search for intimacy need not stop with a bang against the brick wall of childhood pain. It can eventually transcend the wall and grow into strength, maturity and freedom on the other side.

7

Gender Differences in Intimacy

Men must be somebody: women must find somebody.

Lerner

I grew up in a climate where you did not have to ask what was different about men and women. It was obvious. Men had just fought and won a war. They were strong, disciplined, able to handle responsibility. My father, uncles and grandfather all exuded this protective, masculine strength, at least to my childish mind. As a small girl I felt inordinately proud of my father's naval medals and of all the photographs of him in uniform. Some of my earliest memories were of big family gatherings after the men were demobbed from the services some years after the war had ended. There was singing and laughter and stories; such stories. To a youngster who had spent her infant years only with women it was magic, and just a little intimidating.

Years later I was to discover other things about men, even the men in my own family. I was to see uncertainty and pain. I was to glimpse vulnerability and deep dependency needs. I was to learn of many unresolved issues which did not evaporate in the decades of peace: issues of guilt over those who died; a sense that somehow they had been betrayed.

The love I had for these important men in my childhood did not, however, change with the realization that they had Achilles' heels. If anything it became stronger. For the admiration and respect born out of folklore and war legends was translated into a compassion rooted in their humanness. Although young, and unfamiliar with male emotions, I recognized something of their struggles and their unmet needs. I sensed too that the intense military training and discipline had left them stranded in civilian life. For here they were no longer required to act as though death did not matter and feelings did not count, so long as the enemy was defeated.

My father left the navy and moved inland to be with his new family. It cannot have been an easy transition, for the sea had been his life for so many years. His father and brother made the other choice. For his brother especially that choice was to have tragic consequences. Some years after returning to sea a terrible storm shipwrecked his vessel. A hero in peace time as in war he paid dearly for his gallantry, losing an arm whilst still at the ship's helm. After a long time in hospital in Norway he was pensioned off. For him it seemed the loss of everything: his dignity, his manhood, his identity. Land life seemed claustrophobic and empty. Oddly, perhaps, now that he was home all day he felt inadequate as a husband and as a father to his two small daughters. His depression worsened after my father's younger sister died after a hospital operation. Still in her early thirties she had struggled for years with a serious heart condition, and this time she did not recover. She had been devoted to her two brothers. Her unsaid goodbyes deeply affected each one of us who survived her.

One day, just a year later, I was on my way to take an examination at university when I had a message from my father that his brother too was dead. It had been a perfectly avoidable accident. It was as if my uncle simply did not care whether he lived or died. Once more the mourning was intense. My beloved grandfather especially was grief-stricken at this second loss, all the more since it was of his son and lifelong companion. The bond between them was closer than that with my grandmother. Grandad never recovered from the pain of separation and died himself the following year. For my father, who cared for his family intensely, these three deaths so close upon each other were devastating and a personal defeat.

Being aware of the juxtaposition of power and vulnerability in the lives of the men closest to me, the stereotypes of masculinity that I have read in so many books have always left me unimpressed. In my experience as in the experience of so many others, it has simply not been true that it is always men who are strong, logical and self-sufficient; or that women are weaker, more emotional and in greater need of protection. Indeed as I have gone through life I have met many men who are very emotionally dependent on others whilst many women I know are temperamentally strong as well as analytically competent. I have listened as publicly adequate men have privately crumbled without affirmation and constant support, yet have encountered women who battle alone against considerable odds.

It is certainly true that the women I have known best have been tough, resilient survivors; many of them capable, industrious women, able to cope with hard work, enforced single parenthood and all kinds of deprivation. Although I have heard many accolades given to men for their single-minded leadership skills, I have rarely seen the same admiration paid to women for their ability to develop so many different skills at the same time. My experience of women is that they are multifaceted, creative, able to turn their hands and their minds to many very different tasks, and yet often quite unaware of their own power and abilities.

It is also true that men I have known have been strong, emotionally perceptive, able to articulate memories of pain, remorse, close companionship and intense grief. I have watched men weep at the useless loss of lives, whether in war or in the mindless bombings of the many terrorist campaigns. I have listened to stories of tenderness and sacrifice, of love for children, of despair in loneliness. My memory is packed with carefully filed snapshots of unrelated scenes: a middle-aged Jewish man, cap in hand, standing by a gravestone for over an hour, talking and sharing things that were deeply on his mind with his father who, the gravestone told me, died five years before; an old church organist, lonely and bereaved, defiantly playing the 'Dambusters' march at the end of a Remembrance Day service and leaving in tears because his memories hurt too much; a rough, young 'delinquent', his face hard and defiant, suddenly remorseful and broken at the sight of a mewing tom-cat which he had unintentionally injured.

Real people are complex and have an uncanny knack of defying generalizations, particularly ones issued by those who live in theory and not in practice. Stereotypic pronouncements about sexual differences often fall far short of the mark. *Real men* cannot be summed up, catalogued under certain dominant characteristics, whilst *real women* are put under others. The amount of overlap is enormous, as I have discovered in my own marriage as well as in my parents' relationship. Both men and women are capable of endurance, bravery, logical thought, intuitive behaviour, decision-making, prayer, nurturance and deep spirituality.

Both women and men have dependency needs, fear of exposure, longings for affirmation, acceptance and warmth. Both men and women struggle with emotions: each can know anger, resentment, frustration, remorse, hatred, joy, forgiveness and love. We often hear the comment that women and men are the opposite sex. Yet we are more like each other than like anything else in creation.

Image of God as Male and Female

This should not surprise us, for if women and men are together the *image of God* we would expect them to share common characteristics. A biblical understanding starts from an acceptance of those commonalities: as the image of God men and women both fully share the ability to love, to initiate, to think. They share all the deep aspects of being human. This is established in the earliest biblical literature. In the creation story in Genesis, men and women are involved as equals in the three sets of relationships which are presented there: with the world, with God and with each other. Our relationship with the rest of creation is to be one of stewardship, respect, honour and care, for together as male and female we are the guardians of God's world. Our relationship with God is to be marked by obedience and dependence, trust and openness, for we are not to lay claim to any human autonomy. Our relationship with each other is to be one of identification and support, of distinctiveness and union, for we mirror one another in our humanness. The likeness between the sexes, in our imaging God, undergirds everything else about us. Adam's cry when Eve is disclosed to him: 'Bone of my bones, flesh of my flesh' does not draw our attention to the centrality of fundamental differences between women and men. It is the greatest shout of recognition and completeness that literature has ever recorded.

The tired debate about 'gender roles and the Bible' is premised almost entirely upon the assumption that patterns of public, male –female hierarchy that we have seen in so many societies through the ages must have some biological base. And biology must then be reinforced by Scripture. 'Otherwise,' the question is posed, 'how could these patterns have existed this long?' In a short step that rhetorical question then leads to another one. 'So why should we change things now?' And in spite of the weariness of the debate the arguments return for yet another hearing year after year. In a

recent book which runs to 556 pages one writer's enthusiasm for
keeping the old *status quo* intact leads him to somewhat wild and
bizarre generalizations:

> Should there be 'an end to all distinctions based on sex', as the
> unisex proponents would have it? Or should parents shape the
> sexual identities of their boys to masculinity and of their girls to
> femininity? If we took a vote in America, I suppose the results
> would be like these:
>   Is sex a meaningful distinction for human identity and roles?
>   All those in favour? 90% (Those Americans who favour
> Christian values)
>   All those opposed? 1% (Members of the National Organiza-
> tion of Women)
>   All those abstaining? 9.9% (some folks always fail to vote)[1]

If that is how research is carried out, no wonder some absurd
ideas result!

The main problem, of course, is that into each one of the concepts usually used in this debate are loaded so many assumptions.
In this reference, for example, there is an assumption that *sex* and
gender are the same thing – which as almost any sociological or
anthropological study will show is of course not so. *Sex* is to do
with our anatomy, physiology, chromosomes, and the biological
characteristics of being male or female, whereas *gender* refers
to the social roles and expectations of men and women. The
relationship between the two is often very complex and changes
over time, culture and circumstances. But there is nothing in
Scripture which bases any roles in the difference in sex organs!
Then there is the assumption that we all know what is meant by
masculinity and *femininity* and that these are universal biological
attributes. But they are gender characteristics and vary widely
from society to society: the hand-holding and fondling behaviour
of young Bangwa men I referred to in chapter 4 would be seen as
perfectly 'masculine' in that culture, but in American society there
would be quite another name for it. A third assumption is that
only 'unisex proponents' want to end 'sex' distinctions between
men and women, but so many of these so-called 'sex distinctions'
are patterns of discrimination, labelling, power relationships and
fear, and are the quite legitimate concern of many professional

bodies as well as of committed Christians. The final and most worrying assumption is that these authors inevitably speak for the Bible, Christianity and God. So they insist that those people who have 'Christian values' must also reinforce old stereotypes and act in a generally mindless way (which apparently accounts for 90% of the American population!). I am delighted to declare that this assumption also is ungrounded.

I believe there is nothing in a biblical account of maleness and femaleness which would lead us to some of the absurdities about 'sex roles' which some people posit. Sex is recognized as given by God, as a powerful gift to us for intimacy, and procreation, and as a potential source of pain and conflict, unfaithfulness and sin. There is nothing mentioned in the biblical account at all about 'masculinity' and 'femininity'. Indeed, it is questionable whether the biblical writers would have had any use for these concepts for they are words coined solely in contemporary societies. In fact very little is said in Scripture about *gender characteristics* at all, although there is a good deal written about how we should treat one another in Christian fellowship: namely with dignity and respect, submitting to one another out of reverence for Christ, honouring the weaker members, not seeking our own interests, but having the humility of Christ as our example. The Bible does address *particular* relationships between women and men, for example the relationship of husbands and wives. But the passages which focus on this have to be taken as a whole and not out of the context in which they were given. The problem is often that they have been made to *define the fundamental differences between male and female*, in such a way that a great chasm opens up between the sexes, and profound misunderstandings are reinforced rather than examined. The result is that the Bible can be used to justify what it was never intended for.

There are so many sad and alarming examples of this. Consider the following. One writer tells us that men have a (biological) *need* for 'a sense of accomplishment and achievement in goals', and then goes on to show how St Paul organized relationships with these 'biological needs' of men in mind:

> I believe the admonition in Ephesians 5:28–32 for husbands to love their wives and wives to respect their husbands reflects a deep, important need of each sex. Men, who are by nature more

assertive, who arrange their social organization hierarchically, and who seek to elevate their level of control and respect, can find fulfillment and daily stress relief through the admiration of a wife who respects her husband.[2]

Here, men's so-called *needs* are laid at the door of nature or biology (rather than as a result of the way in which patriarchal societies have organized work, power and status). There is a naïve identification of the modern capitalist ethos in the US with the early church, and then the Bible is interpreted as being a justification of the patterns which are dear to the heart of this American male! On the other hand women's *needs* (again apparently biological) are interpreted for women, and they are told that these needs coincide with the requirements of propping up male status. Cynics can surely be forgiven for suspecting that self-interest and special pleading are being passed off here as science and theology!

Biology and Culture

Although we must dismiss this kind of arguing as facile, we must not of course reject every case for the importance of male-female differences. For there clearly are biological differences between women and men. Even on first glance this fact must be evident. What is more, there are enough serious studies which have investigated the effects of different hormone levels, anatomy, limbic systems, and the use of brain hemispheres in women and men for the results to be significant. The conclusion regularly drawn is that variations in each of these areas do influence to some extent the way in which men and women behave or function. There are *some* biological or physiological reasons for the greater aptitude for languages amongst girls, and the greater manifestation of numerical skills amongst boys. There are *some* reasons why most women are more nurturant, and men more 'disconnected'.

Yet, as many of those who carry out this research readily concede, it is easy to overrate the findings or use them to explain what they cannot explain. Studies attempting to relate differences in cerebral organization to the relative absence of women in engineering, for example, have proved inconclusive. What we know of the differences between men and women's 'brain hemispheres' simply does not account for the size of the discrepancies which actually exist in work patterns in society. They might indicate that it is likely there will be more men than women in engineering and technology. But if the difference in hemisphere use were transposed directly into society it would at most suggest that engineers would occur in the ratio of 60 per cent men: 40 per cent women, rather than 90 per cent men: 10 per cent women which is closer to what we have at present. Similarly, the volumes of research on the impact of testosterone levels in men still do not explain why in Britain men are far more likely than women to be surgeons and consultants, even when women form half of all entrants to the medical profession. Biology takes us only so far. As Mary Stewart Van Leeuwan in her excellent book *Gender and Grace* insists, 'Something else must be at work.'[3]

That 'something else' to which she points is the whole pattern of *learning how to be men and women* – the cultural expectations which are loaded on to us within the society in which we live and grow up, and that process of socialization embraces every area of our lives. Everyone conspires to be part of it; so our parents, our peers, our schools, our newspapers, our soap operas, even our psychologists interpret for us our gender identity and help us to develop into acceptable men and women. Not surprisingly over time these become our own perceptions and experiences and the differences which are there in embryo become consolidated into daily routines and ways of seeing reality.

Gender Culture

When we look at some of those observed differences between men and women the first thing that strikes home is that they are not at the level of basic human needs and characteristics. They are much more at the level of culture, expression of emotion, and communication. That is why so many books on women's needs, women's biology and women's psychology written by men often miss the point: women and men's experiences are different because their social contexts differ, and the expectations we have of them differ.

This means that aspects central to the way we relate to others – sensitivity, empathy, and dependency, for example – are likely to be experienced in contrasting ways by women and men. This makes the search for intimacy a more complex one. It means that sometimes we need to learn more than we think about another person. We need to understand something about *gender culture*, about how we develop the ability to listen, to share, to work together. We need to recognize how much each of us has been culturalized by our upbringing and role expectations of others. In a tongue-in-cheek account of men and women's relationship problems, the *Lake Woebegon Days* author, Garrison Keillor, thinks he has put his finger on the main issue:

> Girls had it better from the beginning. Don't kid yourself. They were allowed to play in the house where the books were and the adults, and boys were sent outside like livestock. Boys were noisy and rough and girls were nice so they got to stay and we had to go. Boys ran in the yard with toy guns going *kksshh-kksshh*, fighting wars for made-up reasons and arguing about who was dead while girls stayed inside and played with dolls, creating complex family groups and learning to solve problems through negotiation and role-playing. Which gender is better equipped to live an adult life, would you guess? Is there any doubt about this? Is it even close?[4]

This amusing scenario makes a very serious point. It is that women have been given different agendas from men in Western culture. They have indeed been allowed simply *to be*, whereas men have usually been encouraged *to be doing* and, as Keillor points out, this often goes back to childhood. Over several years I used to stand at the junior school gate watching the children play whilst waiting to take one of my own sons home. I always smiled at the way the girls would regularly be clustered in twos or in small groups, talking together, sharing together and sorting out who were their 'best friends'. Friendships were often made, kept or broken by conversations, especially the sharing of secrets. Often two girls would run to a third with the question, 'Do you want to know a secret?' and the new bond would be cemented in the intimacy of the confiding. The boys on the other hand were much more likely to be in larger groups, hurling themselves around the playground after a football, or shouting noisily at people who got in their way. The talk between them was less likely to be about intimacies of secret-sharing than verbal display: telling stories about themselves or competing over the successes of rival football teams. They would jostle for status, with the acknowledged leader of the group making his position felt until there was a strong challenger backed by others. The odd boys who were left out of all this activity and display seemed at a loose end, and only occasionally would one link up with another boy, or join any of the girls. Not being active or accepted as one of the crowd was to court dismissal.

The focus on activity rather than on closeness is an important part of male gender identity in Western capitalist society. This is true whichever 'time zone' a man belongs to. Michael Ignatieff, a social historian, has suggested that people in our society are separated by time zones divided into 'those who spend money to save time and those who spend time to save money'. Roy McCloughry explains:

> A busy executive races down the motorway in his BMW talking into his mobile telephone, portable computer and fax on the seat beside him. He has all the accoutrements of wealth but he has convinced himself that he has no time. A mile away a man in a string vest stands smoking a cigarette on the twelfth-floor balcony of a high-rise block of flats. He is trying to fill his. If he had money he could go and do things, but he has no money. There are two days before his social security cheque arrives. He has all the time in the world.[5]

The point is that whichever 'zone' a man finds himself in, his life and worth is still defined by *time*, by *activity*. (And until relatively recently a woman's worth was defined by her success in marrying such a man.) Yet this definition is not good news for the development of intimacy. Being busy, having a full diary or a full address book is no guarantee of having good relationships. Indeed the opposite is more likely to be the case. When life is measured out by digital figures anything which takes time has to be justified, and *wasting time* can be viewed with dismay. So intimacy is squeezed into a context which is surrounded by the stopwatches and pressures of 'real time'. Friends or even a spouse can feel that they become just like business acquaintances, having to be booked into the diary for a dinner out, or even a dinner in. People do not appreciate being subject to the Filofax, to be fitted in around more important things in a person's life. Yet even when a man has *enforced* time through unemployment, redundancy or disability he is likely to shrink from intimacy because he has nothing to say. Since his worth is still defined by time and activity he can easily feel devalued and worthless, without the confidence necessary to be able to open up to another. 'There is no point to intimacy because life is not going anywhere.'[6]

The expectations and evaluations which our society imposes upon men and women can therefore have powerful implications for the development of intimacy in our lives. Only when we recognize the force they have and the way we can become trapped within them can we begin to free ourselves from their grip. For gender culture is not a given which must fix us for ever. It is something which we ourselves can redeem before God, so that our lives and our relationships more fully honour the image that we bear.

Gender and Emotions

It is almost trite now to observe that women have been given more 'emotional scope' than men. Yet it remains an important fact. As they have grown up in North European, Australian or American societies, women have been allowed a range of emotional expressions which have been discouraged in men. They have been expected to cry more, to express sadness, or disappointment, to feel miserable or admit to depression. This last point in itself is interesting. For although statistics indicate that men on the whole suffer more depression than women they are less likely to give it that name. For the word 'depression' is stigmatizing. If it is to be acceptable in modern masculine gender culture it is much more likely to be labelled as 'stress'. (It is also interesting to note that the way people 'work at' overcoming stress also perpetuates the idea of activity.)

Although as I have tried to show earlier both women and men have deep emotional 'dependency' needs which connect them to other people, these needs are rarely attributed to both sexes. A whole culture of women's emotional fragility and need for emotional protection has long been part of Western mythology. The same patriarchal systems which have reinforced dependencies in women have refused them to men, with the result that until recently for a man to confess such needs has been seen as a sign of weakness, or folly. Lillian Rubin observes the effect this can have on a man: 'He's not without an inner emotional life . . . But ask him to express his sadness, his fear, his dependency – all those feelings that would expose his vulnerability to himself or to another – and he's likely to close down as if under some compulsion to protect himself.'[7] Kimmel explains the reason: 'Why would a man give away information that would make him vulnerable among his competitors in games, education or the workplace?'[8] So a man is allowed by society to have sexual needs or needs for comfort, but he has not had permission to be emotionally needy.

The problem is that intimacy requires vulnerability. It depends on our ability to be real about ourselves and to be able to let other people into the places in our lives which we have not got fully sorted out. It requires us to have some skills at relationships, to be willing at least to attempt to communicate what we feel and try to explore why we feel those things. My appreciation of a well-known Christian male preacher leapt high when he shared with me and two fellow leaders the details of an incident where he had let down someone who had relied on him. His regret was that he had made too hasty a promise, and found he could not keep it. Reflecting on this with us, his friends, he felt his weakness was that he needed not only to be liked but also to be seen to be omnicompetent.

This man took a considerable risk in his disclosure. Any one of us could have used it against him, not least the men in the group who anywhere else would have been his 'rivals'. But our friendship and his honesty before God meant he was unafraid to show us what he was like, and admit where he needed to grow more. Yet this is a rare occurrence in my experience. It is rare also according to many studies on the subject, especially those carried out in the United States. For they regularly show that though men might have a large number of contacts, relatively few of them have close personal male friends with whom they share self-disclosure in any depth. One piece of research reported that 'when the nature of intimacy as self-disclosure was explained to men, 87 per cent of them had to admit they had never experienced such intimacy with anyone'.[9] Two psychologists, Douvan and Adleson, conclude from their work that, far from being open and candid, adult male 'friendship' in America is full of avoidance and caution. They describe such 'friendship' in strong terms: it is 'a mutual flight against boredom, a pact against isolation with an amendment against intimacy. Those things which are crucial to personal integrity, such as a person's history, values or work are studiously excluded from the interaction.'[10]

Surveys which have focused specifically on married men also come up with interesting findings. In several such studies married men and women are asked to name their best friends. It is significant that many men name only their wives.[11] The reasons for this might vary. One explanation might be that given the focus on time, many men simply pour their energies into the relationship which is the most central and important in their lives. Another could be that men limit their confiding and closeness to the one person they feel they can trust, for whilst it might be safe for a man to be vulnerable with his wife, it feels less far safe to be vulnerable with another man. Whatever the reason Stuart Miller spells out the conclusions. 'Men may have wives, they may even have women friends but their relationships with other men are generally characterised by thinness, insincerity, and even chronic wariness.'[12]

Significantly, in the same studies women have often been able to name three or four other women whom they would regard as close friends. In these relationships the acknowledgement of feelings and emotion, of anxieties and self-doubt are usually commonplace and unselfconscious, as everyday as putting on the kettle. Women it seems have fewer apprehensions about their openness being used against them. The same explanations could be given for why women outnumber men in church congregations in every age group. They are more prepared to admit their interdependence with other people, are usually more practised in the art of sharing, and have far less to lose in acknowledging their need of God.

I have an interesting story which illustrates the difference in how men and women approach emotional areas. Some years ago I was invited to speak about marriage to a group of largely itinerant Christian workers working within a 'faith outreach'. What became evident as the day progressed was that many couples were having marriage problems, but were unsure how to sort them out. Having spoken to the group as a whole about the pressures on marriage today I was then asked to spend time first with the women and then with the men separately.

When I joined the women's group we sat in a circle, and faced one another. After a few minutes of awkwardness several of the more outgoing women offered me comments about their lives which the others were able to share. Within a very short time we all began to talk and I listened to the struggles they faced trying to live out the Christian faith in a way which had integrity. We talked of the considerable pressures imposed by low income and their husbands' jobs. We talked about money difficulties, problems with schooling, problems with adolescents. We talked about the wedge between fathers and children, about the way many of the husbands were so work-involved that the family took a very back seat. Some of the women had little self-confidence, feeling unimportant, as if they did not matter. Some of them were very worried about their children. A large number shared the sadness they experienced at hardly ever going out with their husband or having a real holiday away from the work. Several of the women could not remember when they had last received a birthday present. The conversation was not bitter, nor complaining. It was characterized more by the weight of anxiety, loneliness and suffering. It was motivated by the desire to make things better. As we talked, many wept, others comforted them, and we all drew together in a time of prayer. After a long time with those women I felt I had been blessed both spiritually and in terms of human encounter. Although they were aware that Christian service could be far more joyful than they were experiencing, their central commitment was to serving God, whatever that required of them.

After tea I was invited into the men's group, and the contrast could not have been greater. The men all sat in rows facing one direction, with considerable more distance between each other. I was led up to the front of the hall like a public speaker, and ushered on to a small platform. Everyone sat attentively waiting for me to begin. As I had no particular agenda I asked what they wished to discuss with me. With courtesy and a matter-of-factness several of them raised a hand and made some suggestions. Each item revolved around theology. They told me they wanted me to give a short input on the theology of headship, of divorce, and other issues, to be followed by discussion. I did as requested and we had a cerebral and highly animated conversation on many finer points of pastoral doctrine. During a brief lull in the flow of debate I asked if I could make an observation. They said I could. So I told them that in the women's group we had sat around together and shared deep personal things that were on our hearts, but when I joined them, the men, they kept the subject very academic and asked me to be 'Teacher'. I wanted to know why. Silence fell and they studiously avoided looking at me or at each other. After what seemed like an age a man at the back bravely stood up. Not answering my question he asked simply, 'Could you tell us what our wives said, please?'

I have thought a good deal about those two encounters and my observations have been reinforced in other contexts many times since then. It is almost as if the women were more emotionally schooled than the men. Women are especially trained in sharing pain, in articulating things that hurt and which they know other women will either share or understand. This is even more evident in other cultures. I have often been struck by pictures on television of groups of mourning women in South Africa, Bosnia, or Greece. Each woman expresses personal grief, yet their lament is essentially *communal*. Their tears are on behalf of each other. Sharing together the suffering, and hearing their own pain echoed in the cries of the others brings its own ointment and healing. Anthropologists such as Joel Sherzer have studied this process of 'tuneful weeping', and found similar patterns in far-flung societies. It is very much less evident within men's relationships.[13]

Although in the Middle East, and many other parts of the world, men's culture is much more demonstrative and direct,[14] in northern societies it would seem that men are reluctant to share what hurts or troubles them with others, especially with other men. Some go out of their way to avoid it. Many would rather insist they have no problems, even when it is evident to close observers that they are struggling. On their own and within all-male groups it seems that many men have not developed the means of easily getting in touch with a crucial area of life which is readily available to most women. This does not necessarily mean that the men who fall into this category are *unwilling* to have this faculty developed. When men do face relationship problems they can show the same concern as women to understand their emotional lives better, even if they do not express it the same way. The men I spoke to at that conference illustrated this point well. Although they simply did not know how to discuss their emotions together like the women, once they had prompted me to start them off, they were not in the slightest degree antagonistic to the process. I was not only able to open up some of the problem areas of their marriages, I was able to outline and identify with their wives' role of 'emotional managers', interpreting fathers to their children, and the children to each other.

The sociologist Kimmel believes that a kind of emotional liberation often comes for men through the women they relate to, and this can be especially so if those women themselves are easy and expressive. 'In traditional male-female relationships, men experience their emotions vicariously through women. Many men have learned to depend on women to help them express their emotions, indeed to express their emotions for them.'[15] It may simply be because the women are often more practised in this art that men feel at ease with the process. Or it may be because women are not in the same masculine competition that men will allow themselves to acknowledge their insecurities and weaknesses, and to learn from them the language of vulnerability. What is striking is how those men who have learnt this language are often better able to cope after the death of their wives than those who have maintained an emotional 'closedness'. They can also be a source of strength and healing to others.

Sometimes of course a woman is unable or unwilling to perform this mediating role, for not all women find they can handle or express their own emotions, let alone cope with those of others. Sometimes a man resents the intrusion, refusing to be 'interpreted', feeling often misrepresented and misunderstood. He may reject the implication that he cannot assess himself and needs to be told what he is like by another person. He may indeed also respond very negatively to the seemingly impossible task of fulfilling all the requirements that a woman may have of him. For not only is he now to be strong, wise and competent; he must also be empathetic, and emotionally in tune. Garrison Keillor outlines the problems this brings for men. Still tongue-in-cheek he describes the 'guy who women consider Acceptable':

the man who can bake a cherry pie, go play basketball, come home, make melon balls and whip up a great soufflé, converse easily about intimate matters, participate in recreational weeping, laugh, hug, be vulnerable, be passionate in a skilful way, and then next day go off to work and lift them bales into that barge and tote it.[16]

Yet although Keillor can poke gentle fun, the move towards a greater emotional involvement is important for men. For it is not their maleness which is thereby eroded, it is the crippling power of patriarchal stereotypes. A 'biblical masculinity', to use a phrase much beloved by some Americans, is not one which places the man ten feet above contradiction. It is one which emulates the qualities which Christ himself manifested. Those qualities – openness, compassion, vulnerability, emotional awareness, and empathy with others – are available to each one of us who want to be Christ's disciples. For in the end they are not about being male or female. They are part of our very nature as human beings.

Gender and Communication

'Even if they grow up in the same neighbourhood, or on the same block, or in the same house, girls and boys grow up in different worlds of words.'[17] Sociolinguist Deborah Tannen identifies the importance of these two word-worlds in adult interactions and relationships. Her widely read work points us to the different styles, sense of status, assumptions, agendas, goals and 'metamessages' which men and women bring to the whole process of communication.

Her work and that of others[18] has greatly elucidated my own observations. For many years I used to lead summer school seminars for Open University students. The seminars would involve both men and women, often in equal numbers, who were at the same early stage in their university career, and had met each other for the first time that week. It always fascinated me how marked was the difference between the discussion styles of the women and men. One year I kept a timetable of 'gender participation', noting who reported back for each group, how they began the presentation, how long each person spoke, and so on. The results were sensational, not least because they were usually unrelated to ability in the subject.

Looking at six different groups, the men spoke more often than the women and took longer over what they said. On average the men's combined contributions occupied more than 73 per cent of the time, even when they were outnumbered in the group by women. When the men spoke the style would usually be direct, informative, often lengthy, and fairly authoritative. Men also were four times more likely to interrupt other speakers, especially if the other speaker was a women, and generally were given little resistance when they did so. By contrast, fewer women took part and their contributions would often begin with an apology such as 'This is probably not a very good point, but . . .' or 'I may not have understood this very well, but I think . . .' and then often a very succinct point would be competently delivered. Their presentations were on average very much shorter, yet even then they were likely be interrupted or corrected during them. They would also be more likely to appeal to someone else in the group for help in expressing a particular point.

What made the exercise so interesting for me was that when I asked each group at the end of a 'timed' session who they thought had spoken more, and who had spoken longer, most of them would agree that it had been about the same. When I read to them the results they would be inevitably surprised, which indicated to me that this situation was perceived as normal, acceptable and equal!

In any public arena, unless she has the expertise through specific training or unless she has learnt to be assertive, a woman is far less likely to venture her opinions on to untried territory than a man. For the fear is that she will be dismissed, or even worse, disliked. And those few women who regularly did speak at length incurred the impatience of the group far more than when a man acted in this way. It was often to the presence of such a woman that men in the group would occasionally point as evidence that my calculations must be faulty.

But the greater male participation was also related to the *style* of communication which was more normal in this situation. It was a style of abstraction and reporting. My own observations that on average men communicate much more *factually* than women have been born out by the work of many linguists. What is now well documented is that the majority of conversations initiated by men are largely about giving and receiving information, imparting instructions, planning agendas, reporting events. Men's talk is direct, sometimes confrontational or open to debate, and usually purposeful. In women's conversation, however, there is less focus on factuality or on receiving information than on establishing connections with others. So not only does the talk between women move more quickly on to personal stories or illustrations, it is more inclusive and less direct. A woman who is listening to another will most likely be punctuating the flow of conversation by sounds designed to encourage or denote acceptance, sympathy, understanding. Unlike that between men, disagreement or confrontation is not usually part of the relationship, for 'women are more likely to be indirect and try to reach agreement by negotiation'.[19] All of this is present whenever women and men get together. And whereas for most men the seminar room does not require such a big jump in style, for many women there needs to be a process of unlearning past ways of communicating and adopting new ones before they can become comfortable or proficient.

Problems can occur simply because of these different styles of communication. All too often men and women simply misread one another. Men can interpret women's niceness or their attempts at negotiation and indirectness as weak alongside male decisiveness. They can mistakenly assume that such a woman is unsure of herself and cannot make up her mind about what she wants. This is why many men are often nonplussed by a woman manager who does not simply instruct them, or act autocratically, but attempts to incorporate other views in the decision-making process. Before it is admired, it is often perceived as 'messy' or even 'time-wasting'.

It is not only relationships in work situations which are affected by these differences. They can be even more pronounced in close relationships. Back in the seminar room some men rejected my calculation of their participation in communication on the indisputable grounds that 'everybody knows that women talk more than men'! And of course they had a point. For in the context of a close relationship, or within the home, it has been shown that women not only initiate most of the conversation, they also are more likely to miss it when it is absent. In studies which ask people to list reasons for divorce, women put lack of communication high on their list, yet this is much less regularly mentioned by men. This does not only suggest that many married men lapse into long periods of silence; it also indicates that women experience men's style of communication to be lacking in intimacy.

A couple I know, late into a third pregnancy, were not getting on too well. Then came a row which utterly confused the husband and left his wife feeling irritated and patronized. He had arrived home, and had asked his wife how her day had been. She began to tell him about her severe backache and how it had been an uncomfortable day with intense heartburn. He listened attentively throughout, and finally remarked with concern: 'You ought to tell the doctor.' When she left the room he picked up the mail and began opening his letters.

When they saw me a week later he could not understood why this response had made her so angry. He had been listening, and had given her his undivided attention. He had understood that she did not feel well, took her backache and heartburn seriously, and was being as helpful as he could in advising her what to do. As another woman it took me no time to realize what had gone wrong. She was not asking him to *do*, to move into problem-solving mode. She did not want advice. She could work out for herself what she needed to tell the doctor. She had been pregnant twice before. She simply wanted empathy and understanding. So whereas *he* felt he was taking her condition very seriously, and was being very considerate towards her, *she* felt she was being fobbed off, her feelings dismissed. What her sharing of the day's discomforts needed in response was not gratuitous advice but a long hug, lots of sympathy and words of appreciation and encouragement. Yet it was only with a third person present that he was able to see where he had gone wrong, and she was able to admit how much she needed his comfort and support!

This story brings up two other points of difference. The first is that *advice* is offered far more by men than by women. There are a number of reasons why. Sometimes offering advice is part of a deliberate ploy to establish status ('You're not quite competent. Let me help you to get that right . . .'). More regularly, however, it is an unconscious assumption *of* status, an unconscious but none the less firm belief that to be male means to be in a position of advising women, and of needing to offer such advice. With most men this is an understandable error. For it is a deep assumption of much of our culture, and comes out in work relationships, social situations and advertising. I am always struck how even in areas where they are unequivocally more competent than men (such as in doing the family wash), television advertisements still portray women as in need of male instruction (for example, which washing powder they should use!). The fact that this nonsense still sells the product indicates the extent to which women themselves have bought into the myth.

The second point illustrated by the story is also a key one. It is that many women do find it very *hard to own up* to what they actually do want. A woman is often reluctant to say clearly what she wants because she feels that if a man loves her he should *know* this, intuitively. But requirements of telepathy are not ones which most men can fulfil! Consequently, the less she owns up to her feelings, the more likely she is to live her life according to what other people want. This can be made worse if on those few occasions when she has tentatively opened up her own wishes for negotiation, a list of arguments have been immediately put forward against them, and she has immediately backed down again. Years later she can find herself bitter and resentful towards that other, and angry with herself for not having been more assertive.

But women have also been reluctant to speak out clearly because to them it has not seemed right. To be direct about one's personal wishes can run counter to all the ideas about women's role as negotiators or appeasers in family situations. Very often in Christian circles this is reinforced implicitly in teaching about the sexes. If women are told that their deep God-given needs are to take a back seat whilst they always look after others, they can feel both awkward and guilty if in actual experience they find they want something for themselves. Trying to resolve the dilemma can lead to very manipulative relationships, whereby women have to 'pretend' they are going along with something for another person when they are carefully creating a situation in which they covertly get their own way. What makes this process even more absurd is that the whole teaching of the New Testament urges us towards honesty and openness, and to a mutual recognition of each other's needs. 'Speaking the truth in love,' says St Paul, 'may you grow into Christ who is the head.'

I want to add a brief postscript on what Tannen calls 'meta-messages', for an awareness of these is crucial if we are going to progress in our understanding of gender communication. These are the codes and nuances which lie beneath the actual sentences uttered and give clues as to how what is said should be interpreted. Some women approach a conversation with an expectation of understanding and a grasp of meaning which seems extraordinary and often far-fetched for many men. They are often accused of 'reading things in'. But many women have been trained, almost unconsciously, from their earliest years to listen beyond the words that are spoken, to the meaning that is intended. Consequently, when they listen and talk they are relating not only to the linguistic sense of the conversation, but to the complex agenda which directs what is going on at a different level. Frequently, this means that women and men can come away from an evening with others with quite different perceptions of what was being communicated. 'You never let me direct the conversation in my way,' complains an irritated husband to his wife after eating with a group of friends. 'Why did you stop me when I started to ask about his new job?' She returns in exasperation: 'Because it was obvious that they had just been rowing about that before we came!' From the husband's perception nothing whatsoever was obvious. Yet beneath the normal pleasantries the woman had heard her friend's despondency about the changes she was facing, accurately surmised its cause and decided that a dinner party was not the time to bring it out into the open.

The coupling of a direct, informative style with a listening for metamessages can produce some interesting interactions. We need to learn to listen to each other, and then also to listen to what each hears from the other. No wonder many people find communication both demanding and complicated within intimate relationships. It is summed up in the amusing snippet I came across some time ago:

A man came home with wet fish to be cooked for supper.
Wife: 'Where did you get this fish?'
Husband: 'From the supermarket.'
Two weeks later his wife brought some fish to cook for
    supper.
Husband: 'Where did you get this fish?'
Wife: 'Why, what's wrong with it?'

Conclusion

So many of the gender stereotypes which have influenced the way we have understood men and women have harmed our relationships. They have been damaging because they have placed enormous wedges between us, and then built social policy, educational programmes and even church structures on these assumed differences. Within intimate relationships the damage has been even greater, as stereotypes of masculinity have prevented men from relating to so many areas of their emotional lives, and stereotypes of femininity have prevented women from being able to say directly what they want from those they love.

But the stereotypes have been dangerous for other reasons too. They have so often reduced the differences between men and women to biology, and then generalized broadly from inconclusive evidence. They have failed, therefore, to note the enormous influence which is contributed by the cultures we live in, whether those cultures are national, social, economic, gendered or verbal. In fact there is a complex interplay between so many aspects of life – the biotic, the rational, the emotional, the historical, the social, the economic, the ethical, the aesthetic, the legal – and each of these play into our experience of gender and our lives as they are lived out together. Whether any single characteristic in an individual man or a woman is due more to biology (sex) or to social, historical, cultural, and moral factors (gender) can never be fully resolved. For we cannot study a 'control group' of people who have never grown up in a social context. I believe the jury will probably stay out a very long time on this verdict until the case is finally adjourned.

The greatest problem, however, has come when the perceived differences between men and women have been made 'ontological', that is, built into the very foundation of the universe. They have been read back into what is understood as the order of creation, laid down by God, with dire warnings issued for those who might be trying to overturn them. And this stifles the possibility of real growth. It puts in jeopardy the task of looking afresh at our gender relationship to see what we might have missed there to which the Spirit of God is pointing us.

Our differences as men and women are part of the richness of responding, as the image of God, to our age and culture. But we need to be sure that we do not set in concrete that which God is asking us to demolish and rebuild; we need to be confident that we do not deny those deep aspects of our humanness which God is asking us to recover. God has made us male and female for our enrichment and for our mutual interdependence. But beneath all the characteristics of sex and gender lie a deeper set of characteristics still. It is when we focus on our humanness, on our intrinsic relatedness to each other as the image of God that so many of these differences of biology, culture, aesthetics and community can begin to assume a truer perspective.

8

Friendship and Intimacy

Without friends no one would choose to live, even though he had all other goods.

Aristotle

I was delighted when I first read what the book of Ecclesiasticus had to say about the value of friendship:

Faithful friends are a sturdy shelter, whoever has found
  one has found a treasure.
Faithful friends are beyond price. No amount can balance
  their worth.
Faithful friends are the elixir of life, and those who fear
  the Lord will find them.
Whoever fears the Lord will make true friends, for as
  people are themselves, so are their friends also.[1]

The images are powerful: *priceless, protective, intoxicating, immeasurable, faithful*. That such extravagant language should be poured out in praise of a relationship which is so neglected in modern Western society suggests that we have some rethinking to do. For the Bible makes it clear that intimacy between friends is one of the richest ways of knowing *shalom* – that deep sense of God's peace and well-being. Friendship is one of God's gentlest gifts to us, so basic, and ordinary, yet the very 'elixir of life'.

Like many others I have discovered the truth of what that ancient writer wrote in my own experience. For friends have always been very important in my life, even though the nature of my friendships has changed with age and circumstances. When I was single and a university student my closest friends were those with whom I shared significant aspects of my daily life. Initially they were simply companions, those with whom I spent time. But with some the relationship would go deeper for we felt especially drawn towards each other and at home in each other's company. As those student years went on strong bonds developed between us. Friends were people who trusted me enough to disclose their hearts to me, and to whom in return I confided my own longings. Our communication together was open and safe, and a conversation could last for hours. Yet the friendships were cemented in the everydayness of life – the mutual enjoyment of the view as we walked down the hill to lectures, an exhilarating afternoon swim in the sea, an evening time of prayer together, laughter or reflection over a late night drink – these were the stuff our relationships were nourished by. Years later I realized what a privilege it had been to share so much time with people whose lives had touched mine so closely, and whose love for me had so enriched my being.

Later, after I was married with children, Alan and I shared many friendships in common, and several of them focused around the family. As well as incorporating our university friends, now scattered, they were often with those whose families were at a similar stage to ours, and who therefore shared child-related concerns. Other parents struggled with us to find time to have dinner together, to swap nightmarish stories of teething infants and incessant tiredness. Other mothers in the neighbourhood shared with me the varied experiences of being a woman and a mother. Our lives were domestic and busy: we shared preschool rotas, some had jobs outside the home, and many of us found activities we could enjoy together whilst our children were safe around us. We tore up old sheets for Mother Teresa, wrote letters to our MP about child pornography, read and disagreed over feminism. Single friends during this period were also precious. One in particular entered our lives just after our first child was born. As newcomers to the area she brought us an invitation to attend her church, which we did to the enrichment of all our lives. Our relationship grew deep and when we moved from the area she persisted faithfully in letter-writing and visiting even when we were too tired to actively reciprocate. As a result, she has seen the whole family through its many stages of growth, travelling across continents to be with us. We have loved her in sickness and in health, and been loved in return. She knows us at our best and our worst, and for me in particular, her friendship is a vital part of life.

Now, friends are largely those I work among, those with whom I share important things in life, those I have got to know well during travel and lecturing trips. Good relationships develop from shared interests or from being thrown together with congenial people in common concerns. Of course, old friends who stretch back over half a lifetime remain particularly significant. Yet we have to struggle to find time to keep those older vital friendships alive and nourished. For very often nothing within the normal routine draws us together. In a busy demanding existence there might be no good reason to set aside relaxed time for travelling and meeting, and every reason not to, except for the one fact that we want to be friends.

Many people could tell similar stories of changing friendship patterns and of those which have weathered the years. Yet it is also true in our contemporary culture as a whole that friendship is one of the most neglected and devalued relationships. And it is interesting that even though people are searching for greater intimacy with others they rarely see this as being a search for deeper friendships. It is more likely to be for some more exclusive relationship, often a sexual one. It is sad that in busy lives friends are those who generally put up with fifth best. They are the ones who receive the fag-ends of our time when all the essential duties are performed. They are those still in line after time has been given to spouses, or lovers, children, work, or one's own pursuits.

Cultural Pressures on Friendship

Many cultural changes have contributed to this devaluation. The privatization of the home, for example, gives us the myth of self-sufficiency, where we surround ourselves with all we want and where other people can present an intrusion into the autonomy of our own lives. It also soaks up our time. An average of thirty hours a week spent in front of a television screen easily drains away creative energy, and when added to the domestic routine of meals, work, sleep, chores and DIY it leaves the average person little time to give to friendships. The result is that people begin to live vicariously through television characters, where a daily dose of gossip from soap operas lulls us into the notion that we are enjoying real relationships. The tabloid newspapers readily perpetuate the myth, caring little about the blurring of fantasy and reality, for stories about television personalities sell papers much more than the analysis of news. These vicarious relationships have one major attraction. They are undemanding. People on a screen do not require reciprocation. They make no request, issue no ultimatum, are unbothered whether we remember birthdays, return phone calls, or do our share of the washing-up; they never disagree with us, or challenge our own autonomy. The result is that when we tear ourselves away from celluloid friendships to those with real people we can feel sadly ill-equipped to build something that will grow and last.

The changes in population mobility have also affected the way we relate to others. I live on a street in a theological college campus where more than one third of my neighbours changes each year. People we have come to regard as friends suddenly all leave. Immaculate gardens where we shared our barbecues become overgrown and disregarded. New curtains go up in the empty windows of homes we once visited regularly. Children who played football with our children quietly disappear and are replaced by younger ones. Not surprisingly over many years of this regular upheaval we find ourselves increasingly reluctant to put down any emotional roots with people who are literally here today and gone tomorrow. Yet in spite of our hesitancy other people want to know us, and we find ourselves drawn again into relationships, to pay the cost when the next removal van comes.

Misconceptions of Friendship

The transience of contemporary life, the demands on our time, and the substitutes to real companionship have all left their mark on the way we relate to others. But these alone do not account for the considerable gap between the potential and actuality of friendships. 'Few sing the praises of friendship,' writes Olthius, 'because few have experienced its height.'[2] It is probable that few have even sought its height. Many people hold misconceptions of what friendship is actually about which means they do not invest time and energy in it. Such misconceptions can become dominant.

Take the notion, for example, that friendship is about being single and being young. It involves knocking around with the lads, establishing group rules and in-language, with bantering rivalry.

Or it is having a laugh with the girls, sharing women's talk and doing some of the things that later become crowded out by the responsibilities of careers and babies. In this view friendship means youthful camaraderie, being reckless about the future, not getting too tied down. Friendship belongs to the immature adolescence which we have to grow out of. For when we become men and women we put away childish things. Such attitudes as these get friendship off to a bad start from which it often never recovers.

Friendship, Singleness and Marriage

Another idea is that friendship is merely a prelude to marriage. The married or cohabiting state is seen as the 'normal' one, with friendship as a poor and temporary substitute, distinctly inferior to sexual partnering. We carry this implication around even by the language we accept. Two people declare publicly that they are 'just good friends', and we accept this as a denial of a deeper relationship. We suspect they are probably lying. We are disappointed if it is true. For being 'just good friends' is something negative, indicating their affection is *only* friendship, nothing deeper like romance. It means that they are not after all contemplating marriage, or having an affair. And as far as many others are concerned, this is tantamount to having no relationship at all.

Friendship clearly needs to be defended against this negative image It affects same-sex friendships badly. For someone who finds a partner, the friend can now become a person of the past, as if matrimony and close friendship are somehow incompatible. The marriage supersedes the friendship, either ruthlessly demoting it or making it entirely redundant. So it is a common cry from single people I know, both women and men, that the marriage of their friends often brings double misery. Not only can they feel themselves on the outside of a new all-consuming relationship but also their own special affinity is now relegated or discarded. The sense of isolation increases when the new partners seem more inclined to spend time with other pairs who can speak a common language of couple-talk, and old single friends only become interesting again when they too find a mate. Not surprisingly where the vast majority of the population marries at least once those who do remain single can end up feeling status-less.

This comes out in an observation made by a recently married woman:

> I married at thirty-nine and yet I felt that people finally viewed me as an adult, as more mature, as somehow more legitimate when I married. I resented this implication that my life had just begun, that I had fulfilled my heart's deepest wish. I, in contrast, felt I had had a wonderfully rich and fulfilling life as a single.[3]

Courtship and marriage bring new loyalties and a new intensity of relationship for many people, but it is not the only significant way to live. And when the commitment to marriage takes place at the expense of all other relationships then not only does it increase the loneliness of those around, it also puts unnecessary emotional pressure on the couple themselves. It says something about friendship that is too trivial, and something about marriage that is too demanding. It requires that marriage becomes the central relationship which must provide everything we need to grow as human beings, and that what we do not find in marriage we should not seek elsewhere.

This view has many adherents, not least within the Christian church. The central concern has been to protect marriage, even more so as the breakdown rate has continued to increase. Consequently, close relationships outside marriage are seen as a massive potential threat: at best a form of neglect of the married partner, at worst a statement that marriage as an institution is inadequate. Indeed the reason why some friends are dropped after marriage is that they are perceived to present a question mark over the unity of the new relationship. There must be no room for other intimacies, no space for divided loyalties.

This is even more the case in friendships between people of different sexes. Our sex-crazed culture suggests than any form of cross-sex intimacy must inevitably lead to the bedroom. And so a deep fear of sexuality is often projected which presents it as so all-engulfing that it will contaminate any relationship unless regulated firmly by marriage. Consequently, any unmarried woman who maintains a close contact with a married man friend is seen as suspect, and possibly even promiscuous. There are anxieties expressed towards his wife, and about the trustworthiness of the husband. The unmarried friend can easily be seen as 'the other woman', even when the friendship is innocent of any kind of unfaithfulness. Equally doubtful are friendships between people married to different partners. The fear is always that the relationship could intensify and compete with the marriages. Therefore people are often advised that the safest thing is to maintain only superficial relationships with others outside marriage, and to look to one's partner for all the friendship needed.

Unfortunately, not only is this unrealistic, it is also pernicious. Even more, it is a poor interpretation of biblical teaching, which does not see friendship as only for the unmarried. What is particularly true in biblical literature is that there is a less all-encompassing view of sex. Instead, close relationships between friends are spoken of highly, and all intimate relationships are not reduced to sexual ones.

Of course there are dangers when patterns of intimacy develop between people. Love is always a risky business. But the dangers come not from the closeness of friends but from the blurring of boundaries. Friendship and marriages can support and enrich each other, when the two are not confused. A married man can be good friends with another woman provided they both know that the relationship is friendship and not marriage. A married woman can enjoy the friendship of another man as long as it does not intrude into the specific intimacies of her closeness with her husband. Ironically, it is often when people have few friends outside their marriage that the relationship comes under greater strain, and is therefore more open to threat. Sexual temptations are much more likely to occur when there is loneliness and stress within marriage for then another relationship can quickly become distorted. It can indeed take on an intense, or romantic dimension, where fantasy, temptation and feelings of guilt can further endanger a strained marriage. Cross-sex friendship is about openness and support, not about forming a close attachment with a rival to one's jealous spouse. In that case, the marriage itself probably needs some help and attention first.

What in fact has become more and more evident today is not only that single people can suffer stress when cut off from close supportive relationships, but that this is also true of marriages. The decline of extended family leisure where both singles and marrieds in the family would spend time with other close relatives has intensified the problem. Yet if it were acknowledged from the start that friendships offer strong and legitimate bondings which add to rather than threaten the stability of marriage, then married partners would have fewer emotional burdens to bear alone and those who are single would not be excluded from the companionship of close, married friends.

Married partners can, of course, also be friends to each other, and indeed friendship and companionship within marriage become more important as the years go on. Stale marriages are those without companionship. Friendship is vital both within and outside marriage. But what needs to be acknowledged from the outset is that they are two distinct relationships, but both valid and vital.

Friends and Neighbours

Another confusion is to identify friendship with neighbourliness. For, as with marriage, the two overlap. Because they live near to us, and because of the time constraints of our lives, neighbours can easily be those outside the immediate family with whom we have most regular contact. In traditional neighbourhoods the person next door is the one who provides routine tasks, watering house plants or feeding pets whilst we are away, and is the one to whom we turn in an emergency. Good neighbours who care about our well-being contribute to the stability of our lives, and the mutual concerns we share – the safety of the common stairs in the flat, the level of noise in the area, the standard of the local school – draw us together in many forms of mutual support. And sometimes a deeper bonding results, especially when we discover common interests or have compatible personalities.

Yet neighbourliness is not the same as friendship, which is something I discovered in a very down-to-earth way as a child in Yorkshire. When I was a young girl my parents' neighbours and friends were easily distinguishable. Friends, both single and married, were people who knew a lot about my parents' pasts, often telling me stories at their expense. They had access to our home at any time. They were the ones my parents chose to spend time with, sometimes even going out together. I called them 'aunt' or 'uncle' and often found it hard to distinguish them from my multitude of blood relations. On the other hand neighbours were a more regular feature of life but far less familial.

They were the ones who would take in the washing if it rained whilst we were out. They might call to see if my mother wanted anything from the shops whilst they ran their own errands, or they would 'see after the children' if my mother was called away to a sick relative. It was our neighbour who talked over the fence or came into a kitchen for a cup of tea. Yet curiously, the relationships remained formal ones, with respect and distance built in. First names were not part of the common vocabulary. My aunt lived next door to her good neighbour for thirty years, yet referred to her and addressed her as 'Mrs Brown' to the day she died!

Of course social mores change, but it is still possible to be a good neighbour without being (in the sense in which I am using it) a friend. The concept of neighbourliness which underlies most of the discussions in the Western world is at root a Jewish-Christian concept. And from this perspective the underlying norms of the two relationships are different. Being neighbourly involves us in the practical loving of our neighbour as we love ourselves. And there is a wealth of biblical material on this, for neighbour-love is that which underlines justice, welfare, the provision of housing, supplying food-aid and not exploiting the poor as well as making good relationships. Passages in the early books of the Bible illustrate how central this was. For example, if a neighbour's ox or ass was found wandering the person finding it was required to protect it from injury and take it back. Or when fields were harvested the workers were not to go to the very edges of the field, or harvest the crop twice, but ensure that something was left for poorer neighbours to glean. Being a neighbour had very concrete, earthy requirements, spelled out in careful detail. And the principles hold today. They involve caring for the lives of our neighbours, being reliable and trustworthy, doing nothing which would cause harm or injury, or give offence. They also involve not coveting things that our neighbour has, for that means putting ourselves first in the relationship as well as opening ourselves up to temptation. They might even involve, as Jesus showed in the parable of the Good Samaritan, being prepared to go out of our way in order to seek the welfare of our neighbour, and to break down the factors which often cause barriers between people: race, status, class, religious differences. For the concept of 'neighbour' is ultimately all-embracing. There is to be no one outside its scope.

Neighbour love includes everyone, which is why in the end loving our neighbour cannot be identified as friendship.

Being neighbourly draws us into seeking the well-being of others and acting for justice on their behalf. But it does not also mean we must spend time developing a deep and intimate relationship with our neighbours, sharing with them the hopes and fears of our hearts. We only do that if our neighbour is also our friend.

Friendship and Fellowship

A misconception prevalent in Christian circles is that fellowship is friendship. Church provides us with friends. Yet although there is an overlap the two relationships are different, and failing to distinguish them can lead to considerable frustration.

What is at the heart of fellowship is the mutual acceptance of one another as children of the same God. The New Testament letters to the early churches are still central today in understanding how Christian believers should relate to each other. For example, they are to show sisterly and brotherly love, to nourish and enrich one another in the Christian faith. They are to remind one another of Christ's teachings, and the central beliefs of the faith. They are not to show favouritism to people who have status or wealth, and are not to put problems in the way of other people's faith. They are to make allowances for other people's weakness; we are not to stand in judgement over them. The emphasis is on acceptance, growth, love, support, working together, demonstrated in St Paul's image of the body, where every organ functions together, and no part is inferior to another. Fellowship or sisterhood implies sharing, supporting and loving. It can be the means whereby people are taken out of ourselves to a new spiritual sense of reality, as in worship. It can be the place where people begin to understand more about God, about themselves and relating to others. But it is still not the same as friendship.

This may come as something of a relief! If you are a member of a church you can probably bring to mind quite a few staunch and committed Christians with whom you have no immediate desire to form a close, intimate bonding. This should not surprise us. We do not choose our fellow and sister believers; we do not relate to them because we find them amiable and congenial, or even because we share many other things in common. Rather, there are likely to be many people who share our central beliefs with whom we are nevertheless personally incompatible. I can think of a few such people not a hundred miles from my home! So if we suffer the assumption that every Christian ought to be our friend then we will end up frustrated and with a very bad conscience. For, often, not many of them are. We may even dislike some of them. And what we need to recognize is that such a state of affairs is quite normal, for emotional preferences of this kind are often beyond our control. So rather than agonizing about *why* we feel less than warm to other Christians (or denying that we do), a more crucial question is how we deal with negative attitudes. If we feed and water them so that they get stronger, firmer, and more fully formed then we may be heading for some sleepless nights, and if dislike becomes the central, directing feature of the relationship our feelings of guilt may well be justified. Learning to accept people with whom we are incompatible is one of the marks of Christian maturity.

But there is a more obvious reason why we need to reject the idea that we must be the friend of every Christian. There are far too many of them. We can meet no more than a tiny percentage, and if we did much of our time would be taken in trying to understand each other's language and customs. Even in our local congregations, let alone in the church world wide, believers are too numerous for us to call all of them friends in the fullest sense of the word. This in no way prevents us from being in fellowship with other believers. We can still financially support or pray for those whom we do not know, even if they live half a world away, and honour those we find difficult in our own congregations. For there are things deeper than personal preferences which unite Christians, and which will last into eternity. But we cannot call them all friends without changing the meaning of friendship.

Because fellowship and friendship have often been confused, people are unsure what church relationships are about. There has quite rightly been a greater emphasis on moving beyond superficialities and getting to know fellow- and sister-believers in a deeper and more open way. But if the developing of personal friendship directs church life, we not only feel guilt-ridden when we fail, but also devalue the worship aspect of our lives together. Rather than trying to turn the community of believers into a con-genial social club, the focus of fellowship is the living and working out of faith together, the hearing and doing of the Word of God.

Fellowship, then, is not the same as friendship. It is centrally based on sisterly and brotherly love, and grows through mutual support and encouragement. Christians are urged to accept each another, to spread the gospel together, to build up the body of Christ with one another. And fellowship always points beyond itself to the Christ who is the head of the body. So the relationship is only meaningful amongst those who are of the 'household of faith', who share the same fundamental beliefs and religious commitments. What is more, it involves no choice. As with our neighbours we are required to love our fellow-believers whoever they are. The fact that so many of us may seem unlovable is not an excuse for ignoring that.

One final point also needs to be mentioned. It is that fellowship is not superior to friendship. When we split 'spiritual' off from 'natural' forms of love, and identify the 'spiritual' with God and church life whilst clumsily relegating friendship to the 'natural' we create bad theology. Such dualism ignores the fact that for the Christian there is no area of life which is excluded from the kingdom of God. Friendship – just as much as fellowship, neighbourliness, marriage or parenthood – is a great gift from God to human beings to be richly enjoyed.

Norms of Friendship

So what is this thing I have been calling friendship? By now it will be evident that it is complex and distinctive. It is not camaraderie, not marriage, not neighbourliness, nor fellowship. It is a relationship built on affinity and good will. But from a Christian point of view friendship still has a structure and underlying norms. Openness, equality, faithfulness, inclusiveness, honesty and commitment are central to its meaning. Friendship is between equals, and is entered into freely. It is inclusive, often involving more than two people. It rests on mutual commitment and honesty. It grows through open communication. It shows concern and care. It relies on faithfulness. It is founded on trust. Each of these aspects are vital if there is ever to be intimacy in friendship. For where any of these qualities are lacking, then the friendship will be prevented from growing into a relationship which is sustaining and deep. We will look at these characteristics therefore in more detail.

Choice

We choose our friends. And this distinguishes friendship from both fellowship and neighbourliness. For although we simply accept our brothers and sisters and love our neighbours, our friends are personally selected. By its nature friendship is preferential and founded on congeniality. This means we both choose those who are to be our friends, and by implication, those who are not. Yet this is not elitist. It means simply that there will only be a few people who know us very deeply, for true friendship needs both commitment and time. It is only when we find those with whom we can enter into a close relationship that we want to commit precious hours of our lives to them.

Being preferential in our choice of friendship is very different, however, from forming an insider group. C. S. Lewis warns us graphically of the dangers of the 'Inner Ring'. It manipulates those who would belong and inflates the privileges of belonging. But it is very seductive, for

> at all periods between infancy and extreme old age, one of the most dominant elements is the desire to be inside the local Ring and the terror of being left outside . . . We hope, no doubt, for tangible profits from every Inner Ring we penetrate: power, money, liberty to break rules, avoidance of routine duties, evasion of discipline. But all these would not satisfy us if we did not get in addition the delicious sense of secret intimacy.[4]

Yet the creation of such an inner-ring clique is counter-productive to real intimacy. It inhibits true friendship precisely because it is so caught up with its own self-importance. The exclusive circle of supposed intimates closes us off from wider relationships and we can find ourselves caught in a powerful political structure, which leaves us without freedom. Other potential friends are now defined as outsiders for everyone outside the circle must be reminded frequently that he or she is not in it. But belonging to such an inner ring can become dangerously constricting, and quickly stale:

> Once the first novelty is worn off the members of this circle will be no more interesting than your old friends. Why should they

be? You were not looking for virtue or kindness, or loyalty or humour or learning or wit. You merely wanted to be 'in'. And that is a pleasure that cannot last. As soon as your new associates have been staled to you by custom, you will be looking for another Ring.[5]

The cultivation of an insider group ultimately robs relationships of choice, requiring conformity from its members. In its most powerful form it becomes all-consuming and all-controlling. By contrast the friendship which is based on truly personal choice results in relationships which are open and congenial, not closed in and exclusive.

When choice is one of the key characteristics it follows that friends need not share the same faith commitment or belief system. Instead, strong friendship can develop between those whose beliefs are very different. Friends can share intimacies and disclose their longings to others who might even reject the faith that sustains them. For what binds friends together is not fundamentally a common commitment to God or view of the world, but a mutual commitment of troth to one another. Of course, this idea itself has biblical foundations. Such troth is possible because of the nature of our shared humanity, where we all are made in the image of God. Consequently we each understand experientially what it is to be human, and share ourselves openly even if the basis for this humanness is not agreed upon. Needless to say, a shared faith can deeply enrich any relationship and bring close friends even closer. But deep friendship can exist even between people who see the world very differently.

Equality

Friends are equals. Real intimacy, in any relationship, depends on an acknowledgement of equality. In fact it can only exist where there is mutuality and reciprocation, and where patterns of dominance and subordination are not exercised. That is why it is very difficult to talk of intimacy existing between people whose relationship is a hierarchical one. We can see this historically in the way the fundamental lack of equality between men and women made cross-sex friendships unusual in certain periods. The ancient Greeks, for instance, wrote much about trust and love, and eulogized about friendship; but it was almost always male friendship, for women were not deemed to have the rationality to be equal. Similar attitudes were carried into the medieval church. Those who thought, along with Thomas Aquinas, that women were 'misbegotten men' were hardly likely to cultivate deep friendship with such ontologically inferior persons. And those men who have stereotypic attitudes towards women, rather than seeing them as real people, will find friendship with them difficult. They might also discover that true intimacy eludes them. Only those who know themselves as equals discover the wealth of mutual enrichment.

Equality of relationship must be upheld irrespective of age, gender, class, status or racial divisions. For wherever superiority or rank are allowed to operate then the bonding of friendship is limited. Pulling rank or status is death to friendship, as is the cultivation of a relationship not for the sake of the friend, but with an eye to other benefits it might bring. Dazzled by the success or status of others, some go to lengths to associate with high-flyers, for getting on equal terms with the stars enhances their own standing.

Kevin was like this. Unused to much self-reflection and something of a failure professionally he liked always to be around the great and the good. In fact he would go out of his way to be invited to functions where he could associate with people he felt were his 'own kind'. Contriving to be seated next to someone of public note he would, by the end of the meal, have shared a 'confidence', obtained an address to send his companion some interesting article, ascertained to what other event he might obtain an invitation, and established himself in some concrete way in that person's consciousness. The relationship would be one of several that he would then work on whenever the opportunity arose over the next few months. It was very satisfying to be able to drop the names of these friends into any conversation especially when they helped him to cultivate even wider acceptance.

The point is not that Kevin was wrong in wanting friends, but that he did not understand friendship. Nor could he have faced it if he had known. For the friendships he tried to form always rested in the end on things incidental to the relationship: influence, reflected glory, access to the 'right' people. They were not relationships of equality. They never involved him in any kind of exposure, for that is what he feared most. They provided him with a smokescreen of success that he could hide behind.

People develop such relationships for many kinds of reason: material benefits, insider information, high visibility, promotion at work. 'Social climbing' has been around for generations and still operates today. But the so-called friendships formed on this ladder are rarely intimate. Instead they remain functional and emotionally barren.

This does not mean that friends need to come from similar backgrounds, have the same IQ, or earn similar salaries. Because friendship moves outside normal authority structures its potential is enormous; deep friendships can exist between those from widely different social, professional and economic settings. Young and old may also become friends, and often do with considerable success. What is necessary, though, is that these differences are not carried into the relationship itself. Within friendship these can only be externals and never the focus. We need to be, as C.S. Lewis puts it 'on neutral ground, freed from our contexts'.[6] We need to be allowed to exercise our freedom towards each other, and to respect each other as equals in the relationship.

Honesty and Open Communication

Friends are those who may be honest with each other. Communication between friends needs to be open. In a mature friendship which has a proved track record of trust and commitment, there are few 'no-go' areas. There is the possibility of discussing anything that matters, of 'trying out' ideas, or sharing personal whims or dreams. Open communication does not mean, however, that friends need to talk a lot. Sometimes friendships are formed between two people who are by inclination quiet and untalkative, and yet who enjoy each other's company and know each other well. Even very articulate friends may not always want to talk; they can nourish a closeness which learns to share quietness together and not be afraid of silences. Non-verbal language also can communicate acceptance and trust of each other and reinforce the feeling of mutual well-being.

Yet self-disclosure most often does come through conversation. Sharing incidents in the past, learning a vocabulary of feeling, being able to speak the truth in love are all part of developing the language of intimacy. A true friend is one whose needs for sharing or silence you can respect, and who will receive your own confidences in trust.

Creating a safe environment for self-disclosure does not necessarily happen quickly. I was surprised recently when a friend I had known for many years told me hesitantly and tentatively something she had never disclosed before. It was nothing dramatic or earth-shaking, yet for her it was a very profound act of sharing. And I would have never known nor guessed this secret otherwise. In a curious kind of way that disclosure has become a milestone in our friendship. For something close to the very heart and identity of my friend is now part of my knowledge also.

Having the openness in our communication to be able to show yet more of who we are and what matters to us is a deep underlying aspect of friendship. Yet self-disclosure can happen and there may still be no friendship. Two single women I know of offer an interesting example. One of them, Pauline, talks about herself very openly to Celia, the other. She shares how people have always hurt and misunderstood her. She confides her thwarted ambitions, agonizes over her vulnerabilities. Her insecurity makes her yearn for a confidante who will give her time and listen. So Celia listens. But she shares little. She does not unburden herself to Pauline. Two reasons lie behind Celia's reluctance. The first is that she does not trust that what she says will be treated as confidential. The other is that she doubts if Pauline will be interested. And on each point she is probably right. For Celia's own needs do not form part of the relationship. It is founded instead entirely on Pauline's dependency; on her past hurts and present needs. What binds the two women is Pauline's desire be found interesting and her need for affirmation. So there is communication, but no intimacy. There is disclosure but no mutuality.

I had a most curious experience of this myself in Los Angeles. I had been speaking at a theological seminary, and went for a walk to clear my head in downtown Pasadena. Waiting at a red light to cross the road I became aware of a young woman at my side, trying to get my attention. 'Hi!' she announced, 'I'm Karen. What's your name?' Trying hard not to grin at this very un-English encounter I reciprocated with the requested information, with the result that for the next thirty minutes I had a walking companion who shared much of her life story with me. During the time it took to walk round the town I discovered that she worked in a local store during the vacation which she disliked intensely, was at college the rest of the year, and lived in a flat with a girlfriend who upset her because she was so untidy. She had left her own home because of a poor relationship with her father, who criticized her day and night and gave her little freedom to live as an adult, even though she was now twenty-three and doing well at college. People in her year were too 'cliquey', so she was intending to move away from the area as soon as it was feasible, and maybe travel to the east coast of America, although she worried about her mother and did not really want to leave her behind. In addition to these many complex details about her personal history I heard a lot about her emotions: how she felt about parents, marriage, brothers, flatmates, anger, hurt, pain, betrayal, travel, the president, and God. When, quite exhausted from information overload, I concluded our walk, she smiled brightly and with enormous warmth said how nice it had been to get to know me, for she did not have many friends.

It was both an amusing and sad incident: amusing because I needed to say virtually nothing to keep her happy, and had been chosen for this intense communication on the flimsy grounds of apparently having a 'sympathetic face'; sad, because in spite of the buoyancy of this chatterbox companion, she was manifestly lonely, and in danger. I was only a passing visitor, yet I was glad that this time she had offloaded on to me, and not to someone who might have abused or violated that trust.

The intimacy of true friendship eventually builds up communication which is open, honest, reciprocal, trusting and safe. Friends are those who can speak the truth to one another, not with the motive of point scoring or making jibes, but because the friend needs to hear. But the truth can sometimes be painful, which is why so often we shrink from confronting it, both in ourselves and in others. We never like to hear bad news about ourselves. It can be even more uncomfortable to have a fault pointed out by a friend than by someone whose opinion we value less. Yet when a friend has the freedom to speak this kind of truth to us then it can be a time of facing up to many things. 'Faithful are the wounds of a friend,' said the wise Solomon in the book of Proverbs, 'but the kisses of an enemy are deceitful.'[7] We are taught by our culture to be more ready to accept the kisses of an enemy, because they come so often with what we want. We are so used to being massaged with flattery with no longer any attempt at subtlety, for our culture knows that this is how to make people shop, buy or vote. And so when we can spend so much of our time in agreeable self-delusion it is a rude intrusion to hear a voice which confirms our nagging fear that reality might be different. Yet to hide from intimacy, because it might wound, prevents us from discovering the healing which can follow.

Faithfulness and Commitment

All I have said so far points to the centrality of commitment. For just as much as in marriage, at the heart of a friendship is the concept of troth: the open giving and receiving of one another in commitment and faithfulness. This is often a hard concept for contemporary society. Commitment in marriage is difficult enough, even with all the legal and familial apparatus to reinforce it. So to suggest that a free relationship like friendship is binding in some way is to go against that deep individualism where the need to live authentic unfettered lives, free from the constraints of other people, is deeply engrained in the ethos of the late twentieth century. It is to reject the contemporary climate of moral autonomy which tells us we should be free to make decisions as we wish, to relate to whomever we wish, and to come and go at will.

Yet from the Christian perspective I am outlining, friendship does not allow this kind of autonomy. As a relationship of commitment it rests on faithfulness to the friend. Whether we are single or married, friendship involves a commitment to mutuality and reciprocation, with the assurance that there will be no betrayal, and that things disclosed in confidence will be safe. The knowledge that we have about others gives us great potential power, for in a relationship where much has been shared, much is at risk.

Patrick discovered this in a painful way after his father died suddenly, leaving the estate in a messy condition. Patrick was single and had expected to continue in the family home but his sister wanted to realize her own assets. Unwilling to wait a year until he could buy her out, she pressed Patrick into the sale of the house and to the proceeds being split. The combination of bereavement, loss of home and the bitter family quarrel left Patrick severely depressed and he plunged himself into work as compensation. He confided his misery to Terry, a close friend and colleague, who had known problems himself surrounding his divorce. The new situation strengthened the friendship between the two and helped them both adjust to loss. A few months later the firm made its appraisals for promotion, and Patrick was clearly the favoured candidate for a higher post. In a moment of envy during the interviewing process Terry mentioned his friend's distress over the recent family row and suggested some instability. Patrick was not promoted. Reading the assessment form he knew why, and felt the betrayal by his friend was as severe a blow as the loss of advancement. He could not bring it up with Terry, who ignored the subject. Consequently, it was never cleared between them and within a short time their relationship died.

Faithfulness can be very demanding. It can go against self-interest and sometimes may require self-denial and even sacrifice. The trouble is that human beings do not find self-denial easy. Nor is it easy to admit it when we have betrayed someone's trust. To come to that person to ask for forgiveness can leave us raw and exposed. For it amounts to an admission of the very last thing we want to know about ourselves. It involves dropping the case for our defence, even when we have constructed a convincing one, and being ready instead to plead 'guilty'. Even more than that, it involves throwing ourselves on the mercy of another fallible human being who is also vulnerable and may not be prepared to forgive. No wonder that if that is the price of faithfulness and trust, many shrink from this kind of commitment.

Our society itself has become one in which faithfulness has a low premium. During some research on domestic abuse some years back I became involved with several wives of clergymen who shared with me their very distressing experiences of domestic abuse. I referred to this in a small footnote in a publication, and within days I was bombarded by newspaper journalists, television producers and programme researchers. Would I please let them have the names (and preferably addresses and phone numbers) of some abused clergy wives? The camera people could black out the women's faces, the voices would be disguised and it would be over in an hour. All they had to do was to be interviewed in the confidentiality of my office, just sharing their stories with me, the camera crew, and twelve million viewers. I was both stirred and angry at the media's insatiable greed for the sensational. In order to notch up a score on the ratings war they were quite happy to ask that I betray my faithfulness to vulnerable women who had kept silent for many years.

Of all the aspects of friendship it is faithfulness that is focused on so frequently in both the Hebrew Scriptures and the New Testament. In the Gospels, Christ himself experienced unfaithfulness in his friends: Judas who betrayed him to the unjust authorities, and Peter, who denied ever having known him. James and John wanted public recognition from him, while Thomas doubted his credibility. Even the closest friends who went to watch with him whilst he prayed in Gethsemane fell asleep, leaving him to struggle with the fear of death and alienation alone. With no one to share those moments of darkness and terror the isolation must have been intense.

It is interesting that the women who followed Christ illustrate the faithfulness of friendship in sharp contrast to many of the men. Not only did women support his ministry financially, but they provided constant hospitality and love. Some of them left their homes, their comfortable lives and their families to travel with him from Galilee to Jerusalem. They watched the ordeal of his public humiliation. They stayed close at hand throughout the horror of the execution. They followed the procession from the cross to note the place of burial. Without a care for the authorities they went to embalm his body on the third day. It is not surprising that to this kind of loyal commitment should be entrusted the greatest message of all time, that there is hope beyond the grave, resurrection for the dead, for Christ himself is risen.

Singleness, Friendship and Physical Intimacy

It has always struck me as odd that bodily intimacy is seen as crucial in marriage but as having no place between single friends. Our obsessive culture has few categories for physical expression between people and, by and large friendship is not one of them. We have been taught to assume that – unless they are married – any man and woman together are having an affair, two men who are very friendly are homosexual, two women who have their arms around each other are lesbian. And if we have no proof of that then we apply to word 'latent' to their condition. 'He doesn't get on very well with women,' a friend told me of a young man in her study group. 'I think he must be a latent homosexual.' Maybe, but unlikely, for many homosexual men relate very well to women. More likely he has problems with shyness, self-confidence, abrasiveness, fear of rejection, loneliness, and so on.

The trouble is that the labels come out so easily, and are used so glibly as though the whole kernel of our identity can be summed up in one word. More than once I have been asked to 'declare myself' in a discussion with others. Am I bisexual, heterosexual, or lesbian? Am I sexually active or celibate? Am I homophobic or sexually open? But of course the categories themselves are dangerously limiting. They are designed to suggest that the fundamental definition of our human personhood is an essentially sexual one. Therefore if we are not able to agree to a sexual label for ourselves it follows that we are either confused, or living a denial. Depending on which side of the debate is speaking, we might be seen as latently homosexual and needing therapy, or covertly gay and needing to 'come out'. Indeed the gay community has itself encouraged and sponsored naming to establish the importance of recognition, hoping to show that sexual politics underlies society. However, the end effect is to reduce very complex and varied human experiences to those which can be summed up in one sexual label.

This climate makes it difficult to approach bodily intimacy in friendship. It can often be the last thing about which friends themselves talk to each other. Instead, self-consciousness, embarrassment, or fear of being misunderstood can act as powerful deterrents. Where physical contact of almost any kind is seen as a prelude to something 'sexual' it can lead those who are friends into physical frigidity towards each other.

This prevalent cultural fear of showing real bodily affection can be disguised by all kinds of idioms. I was interested at the body language communicated by American men in a Mid-West macho gathering. There was much heartiness, punching, rugged handshakes, and arm-slapping. It was a noisy, friendly, physical scene, and the men clearly were proud of their close 'buddy' relationships with each other. But I noticed that they also required a good deal of physical space around them. And even when they had shaken hands, or gripped someone's shoulder they would move back into this space, so that everything was kept at a safe distance. This contrasts so much with what is often observed of heterosexual men in the Middle East, where they will often walk together holding hands.[8] (It reminds me of a conversation I once witnessed between an American and an Arab. The Arab needed physical proximity to speak to someone; the American needed personal space, so it virtually ended up with the Arab pursuing the American round the room as each tried to find the right distance for the conversation!) Idioms of body behaviour vary enormously with culture. But whether they be hearty back slapping, fatherly shoulder-holding, or debutantish air-kissing, there is nothing in these mannerisms themselves that communicates intimacy.

The presence of these conventions does, however, say something which is important. It is that human beings need some means of communicating their feelings physically to other people. Other cultures seem to recognize this almost intuitively, and have a much wider range of physical expression than our own. But the fact that we do not regularly see men linking arms or holding hands to walk down the street does not tell us that they need no physical intimacy with each other. It says more about the taboos of the culture in which we live.

In fact most people have deep needs of physical intimacy. Needs of touch, closeness and bodily affirmation lie very deep in our psyche. The task seems to be to find an appropriate physical expression of this for friendship. For people vary. Those affectionate people who like to hug and kiss others can often bring a greater sense of self-esteem to people they are with simply through their affection. They are warm, spontaneous and tender; their problem is less one of knowing how to show bodily warmth to another, than when and to whom. Other people feel very uneasy when their personal space is intruded upon. Rather than invite closeness and touch, they feel their autonomy invaded by another's attempt at closeness. This indeed can be the case for all kinds of reasons. As we saw in an earlier chapter those who have received little bodily affection in the past, or have been physically or sexually violated find it hard to trust another in this area. Yet the intimacy of friendship can over the years provide a safe place for even this kind of healing. Faithful and committed friends, who long for our well-being, can also be trusted to love our bodies in a way that helps to restore them. When people who are hurt and in emotional pain can experience the physical warmth and nurture of a friend and allow them close enough to hear their heartbeat, then healing is beginning. And those just unused to receiving physical affection can find great pleasure in the simple touch of another's hand on theirs, another's arm round their tired shoulders. There can indeed be a safe and open context in which both to give and receive bodily affection. It can be part of the intimacy of friendship.

Conclusion

Friendship offers a great, largely untapped resource for meeting some of our deep needs for intimacy. It is demanding, time-consuming and often sacrificial, but so is any human relationship which moves beyond superficiality. True friendship is not simply a casual take-me-or-leave-me arrangement, but one where there is real trust, disclosure and commitment. The norms of friendship are spelled out clearly within a Christian view of relationships, yet these norms are important whatever the belief system of the friends. They are to do with our fundamental humanness, our relationality, the way in which we all image God. It is possible, therefore, for those right outside the Christian faith to enjoy a Christian structure to their friendships because that is what true friendship is all about. Deep friendship takes us into a closer encounter with who we are, and shows us a glimpse of who we might be. Even hardened sceptics have talked of friendship bringing them closer to believing in God. For when we are brought face to face with the deep, lasting and faithful love of a friend we experience something which cannot be ultimately explained or understood in any other terms.

9

Marriage and Intimacy

*Marriage is to human relations what monotheism is to theology.
It is a decision to put all the eggs in one basket, to go for broke,
to bet all of the marbles.*

Mike Mason

The disillusion with marriage amongst many contemporary critics
has to be put into perspective. In spite of increased breakdown,
cohabitation and the strength of the homosexual lobby it is still
the case that 90 per cent of the population marry at some time,
and that most of them will stay married to one partner for life.

Over thousands of years and across millions of culture groups
marriage has offered human beings a powerful way of drawing close
to each other. Widely divergent cultures have developed their own
patterns of legalizing the bond between a man and a woman, and
despite the many specific contexts there are marked similarities
underlying them. This means that whatever the particular *shape* it
takes, something recognizable as marriage exists in virtually every
society.

For good reason, then, marriage has been widely accepted as the
area of life which caters most fully for the personal and emotional
needs of people. It was affirmed in the earliest chapters of the Bible
as the most clearly defined way of meeting deep human need for
companionship, and love. It was endorsed in the New Testament
as the right context for sexual intimacy. St Paul, often wrongly
lambasted as a male chauvinist, is eloquent on the closeness
and mutuality of marital sex. The physical bonding, the close
companionship, the mutual respect and sacrificial care of a woman
and a man is one of the deepest areas of human experience.

Marriage today can still fulfil these biblical aspirations. In the
security of a committed relationship people can grow sexually,

emotionally, intellectually and spiritually. Couples can provide close friendship for each other where they develop greater self-confidence. For marriage offers people a stable base for true interdependence, where they can experience both closeness with the other, and time to be alone. It offers a relationship of profound mutual hospitality, where someone else is allowed into the most personal areas of life, without defence and without reservation. A good marriage is in fact the relationship where we risk all. We leave our ego exposed and vulnerable, ready to be cut down to size, and humbled before that other. This means that the other has such enormous power over us, to build or to break, and so the process has to be mutual, or we could neither bear the responsibility, nor risk the terrible cost.

Therefore, even at the end of the twentieth century, in spite of the multitude of pressures which pull in an opposite direction, marriage remains a magnet which draws so many of us into its field. Why else would the most unlikely people dress up in silly clothes, and amidst the showing-off of tiny bridesmaids and confetti thrown by elderly aunts give everything away to each other in promises made for life? For what other reason would two otherwise sensible people willingly endure lengthy, embarrassing speeches about their childish quirks, and commit themselves to public spectacle and humiliation by grinning friends? A wedding is not just a perfunctory ritual. There is something so powerful about the idea of a committed union between a woman and a man that we cannot easily turn away from it. And the magnet still attracts even when people have been hurt, or humiliated or treated abominably by a previous partner. Amongst those who suffer considerable unhappiness in their first relationships there are a large number who return to marriage for another try. It is as if many know, almost instinctively, that it is not marriage but human sin which has let them down. Very public marital failures do not seem to have dented the optimism which year after year ordinary people exhibit in coming together to plight their troth, and the cynical attack on monogamy voiced by many in our culture is not evidently shared by millions of other people.[1]

Interestingly, it is not shared either by the authors of the first comprehensive survey of sexual behaviour in Britain published in 1994. I noted earlier the findings of this research on changes in sexual attitudes and lifestyles over the past forty years. We might therefore expect this study to challenge the future of marriage as an exclusive, lifelong union. Yet the four authors maintain that their findings 'give little support to the assertion that marriage is losing its importance in Britain'. Their conclusion was 'Once entered into [marriage] is certainly viewed by the majority of the population as an exclusive relationship for both men and women alike.'[2]

They found in fact that permissive attitudes to sex changed greatly when they were put in the light of a marriage relationship. Here commitment was seen to be important. More than 84 per cent of all women and 79 per cent of all men felt that extramarital sex was 'always wrong' or 'almost always wrong'. And young people from sixteen to twenty-four showed the same attitude towards adultery as those who were thirty or forty years older: categoric disapproval (81.5 per cent of men and 84 per cent of women in their teens and twenties said it was wrong, compared with 82 per cent of men and 87 per cent of women in their fifties). The fact that many men and women could not always practise what they believed and did leave their partners for others was not seen as a reason for watering down the importance of marital faithfulness.[3]

This constant return to the pull and the commitment of marriage is surely an unmistakable demonstration of the search for intimacy. In the act of loving and giving two people experience a union which is greater than themselves, a yearning which takes them out of the boundaries of their own self-delineated existence. When we receive love which feeds our bodies and touches our souls every part of our being is affected. There is a new warmth and generosity of spirit; the experience of feeling utterly valued and infinitely important. The very world changes with the discovery of requited love, the amazement of the reality of that Other. The boundaries of the self shift: I become inclusive of the one I love. The Other is not me, yet speaks to me and for me out of the depth of our being together. The playful dichotomy of being separate yet communal is there at the very centre of a love relationship: two people are corporate together: two personalities, but one flesh, one heart, one soul, one love. 'This is a great mystery,' whispered St Paul. 'It is like the mystery of Christ and the church.'[4]

Yet of course the cynics are partly right. Within any marriage the first experience of joy and mystery is never enough. There are many pitfalls ahead. The messiness of daily life, the struggle with temperamental differences, the build-up of frustrated ambition, or just plain self-centredness sit smugly in wait for us along the journey. It will call for more than the early intoxication of the Mystery of the Other to keep us together in the dark times. But this is not because there is something intrinsically wrong with marriage. It is rather because what we understand as love will affect and determine how our marriage grows. And we can easily get love wrong. We can treat it as though it were power or duty, social custom, feeling, sex, or habit and miss the uniqueness of its strength. Instead of knowing a love that grows, enriches and enables us, we can be left with a counterfeit. But a lie, a half-love or a crumbling substitute all too often bring bondage not blessing.[5]

Culture, Marriage and the Bible

It is part of the feminist claim that the patriarchal structure of society inevitably shapes marriage, and to some extent this is true. All marital patterns take place within a cultural and historical context which influences them. But the concept of marriage must not be *reduced* simply to a patriarchal relationship which subdues women, for at its heart it is independent of patriarchy.

We can demonstrate this even in early biblical culture. In the Old Testament marriage was part of the extended familial pattern of relationships, including not just the union of two people but the joining of families, the outworking of kinship networks, the commitment to a continuation of the generational line. Patterns such as polygamy and bride-price show how much marriage was tied up with patriarchy. Jacob, for example, had to work for fourteen years for his father-in-law and accept an extra wife before he got the bride of his choice. In the book of Ruth marriage is even tied up with redemption: the kinsman-redeemer had to protect the needs of the vulnerable members of the extended family, even to the provision of an heir for a dead male relative. Yet even here there is much more to marriage than patriarchy. Although intertwined with the community and family as the seat of God's blessing, it is nevertheless a relationship which has its own intimacy and mutual respect. Wives are certainly not presented as weak or powerless. Ruth takes her own initiative and effectively chooses her future life partner. Hannah, much loved by her empathetic husband, nevertheless rejects his solace and brings her own prayers

to God for her longed-for child. The wives of the patriarchs –
Sarah, Rebecca, Rachel – are strong, perceptive and wise women,
often more closely in tune with God than are their spouses. And
in the book of Proverbs the picture of the 'good wife' points to an
active, public figure, who holds her own against the merchants,
buying fields and held in respect by all. (It is significant that in
Jewish families today that passage is often read in honour of the
wife at the beginning of family Sabbath celebrations.[6])

The strength, commitment and intimacy of marriage provide
powerful metaphors in Old Testament prophecy. Isaiah likens it
to God's love for his people: 'For your Maker is your husband
. . . he is called the God of the whole earth.' God's compassion
is poignant: 'The Lord will call you back as if you were a wife
deserted and distressed in spirit . . .' (Isaiah 54:5–6 NIV) In the
book of Hosea marriage is used to illustrate the unfaithfulness of
God's people; Israel pictured as an adulterous wife goes easily
with other lovers. Far more than being defined by patriarchy, the
marriage relationship is founded on faithfulness.

The New Testament contains even deeper insights into marriage.
St Paul's central teachings on marriage are not a reinforcement
of patriarchal relationships. In the growing church there is no
emphasis at all on marriage within the context of male family
line, rather on marriage within 'the household of faith'. Belief
and commitment to Jesus Christ is now to provide the bedrock of
marital choice, rather than obedience to parents or extended family
loyalty. Marriage and faith are to go together. If someone marries
outside the faith there might well be conflict of loyalties, and a
strain put on wholehearted commitment to God's service. It could
even lead to loss of belief. So where a Christian convert is married
to someone who does not accept the faith their relationship is
actually given different consideration from a marriage between two
Christians. In Jesus' famous teaching in the Gospel of Matthew,
divorce is not to be permitted, except on grounds of adultery. In
reinforcing this St Paul adds that if an *unbelieving* spouse wishes
to leave the marriage this is to be accepted, although the believing
partner is urged not to seek a separation but to love and honour
the other, so demonstrating the grace of God.[7]

St Paul's teaching gives little attention to the various 'roles' of
marriage which later exegetes have wanted to read into his letters.
No suggestions are made concerning who should do 'productive'

work or who should work at home, nor who should be engaged in child care and who should lay down the law. There is certainly no declaration at all as to who should make any 'final decision'. Indeed the model of marriage which that particular idea presupposes – the model of debate, assertion of hierarchical authority and the inevitable rightness of male will – seems foreign to St Paul. Instead, his focus is on union and unity. He picks up the 'one flesh' idea of the Old Testament and develops it in a graphic and reciprocal way. In marriage, says the apostle, neither husband nor wife own their own bodies any more. Instead, 'authority' passes to the other. The often neglected point is that for St Paul this process is *entirely mutual*. There is no autonomy of the male or subordination of the female but full interdependence; on marriage men give up their sexual independence as fully and as completely as women.[8] St Paul's model for Christian marriage is not a pyramidical structure of gender relationships but mutual love, submission, respect, giving and sexual union, where the 'marriage bed should be kept pure'.[9] As with all Christian relationships, it is to be one of prayer and humility, 'looking to one another's interests, not your own'.[10]

Marriage in the New Testament is therefore not male-dominant but mutual, exclusive, faithful and intimate. Nor is it the sole focus of intimacy, for intimacy was there in the friendship amongst the disciples and within the early church. The marital bond should never serve as an excuse for excluding those who are not married, for all are called into relationships of hospitality, and brotherly-sisterly love.

Culture, Marriage and Today

This Christian commitment to marriage has been embedded in Western society for centuries. A high view of fidelity, of the centrality of love, and of the separation of marriage from economic or political structures have been at the basis of the institution, at least for the majority of the population. Today, I believe, we are moving even closer towards a biblical vision as we try to leave behind the patriarchy in society which has so often accompanied marriage. In the closing of the cultural and economic gap between men and women, couples are more able to realize the mutuality and reciprocity in their marriages together. By stripping from the relationship some of the baggage of former years which obscured what marriage meant, the focus sharpens more on intimacy, love and bonding than on functions people perform.

In other obvious ways, however, our culture has moved away from New Testament norms of society. The consequences are sad. It would not be an exaggeration, for example, to suggest that in spite of even the most lavish and detailed wedding preparation every marriage in Britain and America today potentially gets off to a bad start. That is because the very *meaning* of what those two people are doing is fundamentally out of step with the ethos of contemporary society. In our prevailing climate of *individualism*, marriage is a statement of *community*. Inevitably, this must mean that those coming to marriage in our present era need to unlearn some of the deepest attitudes and ideas that they have absorbed all their lives so far. For when a whole generation has been not only invited to pursue self-interest, but been penalized when it has failed to do so, it is difficult indeed to now abandon what is so familiar for an unknown way of life. Coming to marriage from a diet of undiluted individualism leaves people with the need to empty their shelves and restock them with ingredients which must look risky and highly doubtful.

The disillusion with contemporary marriage is thus understandable but misplaced. The problems which play into the lives of couples are not in the underlying institution itself, but in the way in which marriages have been shaped and structured by prevailing and conflicting social ideas. The extraordinary truth is that despite enormous social and moral changes the resilience of marriage remains. Far from being despised as an outmoded institution, marriage today is expected to provide greater meaning for people in society, and a higher than ever level of closeness and intimacy.

Roles

The move from marriage as a structural, functional unit to one which should yield high levels of emotional satisfaction certainly does not suggest disenchantment with marriage. It rather indicates that there are now staggering expectations of the quality of relationship it must provide. The focus is no longer on traditional husband-wife breadwinner-homemaker *roles*, but the quality of life together. Jack Dominian described this shift a decade ago:

Currently there is a desire to move beyond economic sustaining and the undertaking of the traditional roles of husband and wife. Emotional sustaining is emerging to be just as important. In the intimate world of contemporary marriage, couples want increasingly to be understood in the depths of their being. They want their partner to feel and appreciate how they experience life and to respond accurately to their moods, feelings and emotions. Ideally, men and women, but particularly the latter, want their partner to be in tune with their inner world, sometimes without saying anything.[11]

If this is true, it has not occurred by accident. It is linked to a greater shift in the importance given to women's perspectives and experiences in marriage. Jessie Bernard once observed that in every marital union there are two marriages: his and hers.[12] Women and men experience marriage in different ways, and whereas previously marriage might have been defined along 'male' lines that is now no longer the case. This obviously brings new criteria of success or failure. The survival of marriage is much more dependent on the depth of its intimacy and personal commitment than ever before. For many women in particular a marriage which fails to meet these requirements is inadequate, whatever the level of economic stability, or smooth organization of roles and duties.

Yet the shift from traditional gender roles brings new challenges. Greater flexibility means more pressures. Without the fixed patterns of the past, everyday life can be very complex. Timetables have to be negotiated, disputes over responsibilities have to be settled, agreement needs to be reached over where to go on holiday, who takes time off with the children, what to do when there is a clash of interests. Marriage has always been open to stress, for it is a demanding and intensely disruptive relationship. It disturbs our ego, it takes us quickly out of our depth. But today those stresses multiply because of the external demands of society. An inbuilt lack of time, strains of commuting, debt, unemployment, isolation, immobility or redundancy along with struggles over bringing up children in a climate of uncertainty, add to the strains on any marriage. No wonder some couples are caught up in constant wrangling and collision.

The 'emotional sustaining' of which Dominian speaks is not therefore automatically assured simply because there is fluidity of roles. There has also to be the readiness to switch off from external pressure, to make time for one another, and give communication a high priority. A more creative relationship and personal satisfaction for both partners can only be found when there is real encounter with each other. When a marriage is sustained on a deeper commitment to the other than to the self, the intimacy which results can take the strain and face the difficulties without despair.

Cohabitation

Mae West might be called the prophet of cohabitation when she said, 'Marriage is a great institution but I'm not ready for an institution yet.' In fact since the mid-eighties at least half of all couples who live together have not felt ready for this institution. Some have become ready and gone on to marry each other, or someone else; yet others have stayed permanently unready, finding new partners outside marriage. The popularity of cohabitation is evident. It seems to combine maximum opportunity for relationship with minimum need for formalities. In an age of individualism and consumerism cohabitation provides choice and freedom with 'no strings attached', or on a trial basis.

In reality, however, the relaxed, easy image is somewhat different. Quite frequently one of the couple is more committed to the relationship than the other, and this can lead to pain and anxiety especially where there is infidelity. Jealousy is not confined to marriage! Cohabiting men are statistically far more likely than all married and older single men to be having sex with more than one partner.[13] Then, when one of the couple wants to start a family there can be pressure on the other to marry, or a sense of insecurity if children arrive without some certainty of commitment. The idea that cohabitation bypasses the restrictions of marriage and produces a greater chance of happiness is a cultural myth. Where commitment is absent satisfaction is usually short-lived.[14] As almost all contemporary research suggests, cohabitation does not produce stronger relationships, freer relationships, or more mature relationships in the future. As in North America, premarital cohabitation in Britain is now associated with an increased likelihood of divorce. Of couples marrried in the early 1980s, those who lived together before marriage were fifty per cent more likely to have divorced after five years.[15]

This has many implications. The naïve view of cohabitation as 'marriage preparation' needs to be modified and a fuller picture given through education or training programmes. The church also needs to expand its ministry to couples including to those who cohabit. If love and understanding can be shown more than censure to those who have set up home with each other outside marriage there is always the possibility of growth. For they will need as much, if not more, help with their relationship as those who do not cohabit first. Those who have shied away from marriage because of the messiness of family breakdown, or because they are afraid to risk the consequences of failure, need a place where they can share their own problems with others. And if those living together are not already married to other people there is always greater hope for their relationship. To help cohabiting couples towards more trust and commitment, to a covenantal love where they can be faithfully committed to each other, is indeed helping them to find marriage.

Stability

Most kinds of relationships are less stable than they once were. Couples are not held together as much by class, economic security or religion as before, and the extended family plays a smaller role in supporting young couples. With the widespread pattern of separation and divorce, most people in society will have experienced the breakup of marriages of relatives and friends if not of their own. This climate of marital instability is unsettling for children, and seeing another couple's failure at reconciliation can also affect adults. Particularly if their own relationships are floundering it can weaken their confidence. They can quickly feel adrift and insecure about the future, and increasingly anxious about whether their marriage can get through the next few years. Many who once would never have contemplated divorce can find themselves faced with this as a real possibility.

Shifts in stability makes us address the question of what kind of future we want to see for marriage in our society, and they force us to give more recognition to the pressures which couples face. Very much more can be done to provide support and resources which will help people both to get ready for marriage and keep going through stressful stages of a relationship. Better economic help for families, more support for young couples from within the church can all lead to a new surge of hope within individual marriages. Very often it simply needs a helper to 'unpack' those all-encompassing and over-arching marital problems, so they are brought down to size where they can be addressed one by one. In so many instances, when such help is given, especially for couples in their first few months of married life, the fear is taken out of anxieties, and there is encouragement to persevere.

Two conclusions might be drawn from all this. Changes in society do add more tensions or problems to a relationship as central as marriage, but they cannot by themselves deal it a death blow. They might in fact bring greater enrichment for couples as new styles of cooperation deepen their lives together. Whatever the changes, if marriage meets part of the intricate needs of our humanness which God has breathed into the very creation for our bonding and enrichment, people will continue to find that it holds promise and fulfilment for their own lives.

The second conclusion is that the quality of a marriage does not depend on having the 'right' social structure or arrangement; it can still be strong and viable whatever the social context. A marriage can operate within patriarchy or within individualism, and still bring blessing to those who understand and live inside what it really means. The institution of marriage can be devalued through exploitation, or commercialized romanticism, but still be real for those who know its own truth and power. For if marriage is essentially about the loving and committed union of two people nothing outside can destroy it.

Defined by Troth

What defines marriages is *troth*: the covenantal commitment of love expressed in those age-old words, 'for better for worse, for richer for poorer, in sickness and in health, until death parts us'. And when this love lives within the marriage it relativizes any social context. This should alert us to the dangers of patronizing 'old model' relationships, dismissing them as role-bound and not much concerned with intimacy. Yet what seems nearer the truth is that a generation or two ago intimacy was experienced in a different fashion and many such marriages knew a high level of contentment and satisfaction. Beneath the predictability of marital routines was often an intimacy that our own individualist culture has lost sight of, which was deep and lasting. For some couples it was built into and defined by the very roles themselves, and a comfortable, taken-for-grantedness did not automatically mean emotional deprivation.

One incident from my childhood stays with me as a graphic illustration of this. I remember as a girl going with my cousin to the home of her friend. We were talking with the girl and her mother when the father came in, weary and dusty from the late shift. There was no embrace, or show of affection, just an abrupt nod of greeting, and a tired smile. His meal was already waiting in the oven, but before she put it on the table his wife took the towel which had been warming in front of the fire and went upstairs with him. I discovered from her daughter that it was a regular routine: she scrubbed his back whilst he washed away the dirt of the day. Then she would come downstairs and set out the meal whilst he put on clean, warm clothing which she had already aired. There was no discussion about it, no request made, but the wife's concern for the immediacy of his needs, and his own dependence on that love and care spoke very clearly of the significant relationship between them. Of course it could be construed as typically patriarchal, a product of a male-dominated society, which demeaned the woman, treating her as a servant. But that would only be half the explanation. It was also deeply intimate. It was something to do with knowing and being known in ordinary, bodily details. It was about the humility of acknowledging physical need, and accepting help.

This would not be seen as a good model for marriage today, and indeed that level and type of interdependence is at variance with the deep individualism in our culture. But the main reason why it would be spurned in many circles is because of its apparent negation of the woman, and the central focus of the needs of the man.

It was interesting, therefore, to discover many years later what had become of them. A year before the husband was due to retire, his wife was diagnosed as having cancer, and had extensive surgery. He immediately gave up his job, and with some help first from their married daughter, cared for his wife through the post-operational phase. She actually made a very good recovery and for the next three years they broke the routines of a lifetime. The husband took on the household cleaning, shopping, washing, serving, ironing, and eventually also all the cooking, leaving her to handle only easy personal tasks. By conserving her strength they were able to go out regularly and even to take on some ambitious travelling, which included a first trip abroad for the wife. They went everywhere together, and were visibly contented companions, both clearly enjoying their new lifestyle. Then, four years later, cancer cells once again began to invade her body and, other than for visits to the hospital, the woman became housebound. The husband nursed his wife completely for the remaining ten months of her life, and took a long time to adjust to her death. I found it very illuminating to hear the way in which his care was described by two people of his own generation. I was told that he was 'as good and conscientious as any wife could have been', and that 'nothing was ever too much trouble for him'. What also was singled out for high praise was the fact that he 'never once left her on her own, but stayed there to do everything for her'.

We cannot rush to draw conclusions about the long-term quality of a relationship simply from the way people slot into particular social structures at a certain stage in life. There are not set formulas for the development of real intimacy. For there is nothing which comes close to the freedom and unpredictability which is at the heart of marriage. In the end it is the uniqueness of love, the tenacity of commitment, the recklessness of promise and the deep acceptance of each other which will direct the lives of those who live within it.

Dealing with Marriage Problems

Although the contemporary pressures on marriage make the possibility of wreckage very easy, with most cases of failure the factors that caused final break have been around for a long time. 'Marriage isn't a word,' says the cynic, 'it's a sentence.' Often, marriages go stale, partners get bored, and some couples find the level of animosity builds up to an intolerable level as the years go on. So they often search around for some satisfactory explanation as to why their relationship has not worked. Sometimes when one of the couple is particularly unhappy that person will locate the problem back into the very beginning of the marriage. And the diagnosis comes, 'We are incompatible; we should never have married in the first place.'

Incompatibility: I married the Wrong Person
There is a devastating finality to this conclusion. For if there is something deeply wrong in the very combination of two people, where a clash of personality itself cuts them off from each other, there seems to be no hope for the future. Yet people do often marry those with whom they are temperamentally at variance. The early risers frequently end up with the 'night owls', the gregarious with the solitaries, the methodical with the disorganized, the foolhardy with the anxious, the talkative with the silent! There is no end to the contrary permutations which human temperaments can allow. People can also be wrongly matched because they marry others too much like themselves. Two people who both enjoy listening rather than talking can end up with little communication or self-disclosure. Two people who are both impatient and do not suffer fools gladly will have problems tolerating one another's foibles and those of their children. And when neither partner has any sense of time or forward planning, life together can soon become random and chaotic.

What is interesting is how people like these come to marry each other in the first place. It is probably because no one asks them to take an aptitude test or fill in a personality question-naire! They have not spent enough time on the psychiatrist's couch. It may be the haste and folly of romance. But it is also probably something to do with love. For love has an annoying tendency to block out those niggling tell-tale doubts, that criti-cal assessment that everyone around us can make, those clear evidences that frankly we are not suited. Love seizes us at our most irrational point and turns us into near-sighted opti-mists. And so people come and promise to love, honour and cherish each other until death do them part when the voice of cold reason would tell them: this relationship is going to take years off your life; run now, avoid this marriage like the plague!

The curious thing is that so many marriages actually cope. Some even thrive on incompatibility. Through the irritating habits and annoying tendencies of each other, people grow in awareness of their own and some can begin to laugh at them and let them go. In the times of frustration and disagreement, they learn about how to love and how to care deeply for another. In the disappointments and failures they discover that some things are more important than the tidiness of a self-organized existence. The amazing power of marriage to take two utterly distinct, utterly different human beings and make and mould them into one union, must surely be one of the clearest indications that there is a God! And not just any old god, but a God of great humour and playfulness; a God who sees through the ridiculousness of our human individual idiosyncrasies, and invites us to taste of community.

It is probably not surprising that around 85 per cent of married couples feel at some time that they married the wrong person. It is the explanation to which we turn when marriage has gone sour, or we are locked into stalemate, or where the relationship is tottering under acrimony and resentment. And because that diagnosis allows space for face-saving retreat we are unwilling to give it up for the struggle of trying to keep the relationship open. So often we simply do not want to be challenged, moulded, changed, reassessed. We do not want to give up our 'solution' or capitulate to another viewpoint for the sake of that irritating, demanding, disappointing person who is our consort. Yet, if we put this self-fulfilling explanation on hold and work at relating together, there is always a possibility of redeeming the partnership, and reclaiming lost ground. For it is never simply 'incompatibility' which ends a marriage. If it were there would be almost no marriages in the first place. It is a breakdown in love. And that needs a much deeper diagnosis.

Self-Interest

Far more than incompatibility, the preoccupation with oneself puts enormous strain on love. The shift from a commitment to self to a commitment to the marriage is a difficult one to negotiate today, not predominantly because of differing personality characteristics, but because of the influence of the pervasive ideology of our culture. Some couples can never make that shift; many of those marriages which founder in the first few months come unstuck on this issue.

One couple I got to know, Shirley and Michael, demonstrated this precisely. Shirley was sure there was nothing incompatible between her being married and pursuing her career to the full. Michael disagreed. He did not consider modifying his own career demands but assumed that sooner or later Shirley would come round to his way of thinking. However, he increasingly grew to resent the commitment his wife had to her job, her colleagues and her leisure needs. He also resented having to do what he regarded as an unreasonable proportion of the domestic chores. Both partners made strong demands on the relationship as the place where they ought to be able to relax and get away from the pressures of work, yet neither of them was prepared to give way in areas which involved some sense of sacrifice. Shirley claimed the right to change any arrangement with Michael if something important came up at work. Michael went out late with colleagues if he felt like it. Increasingly they quarrelled about their involvement in housework, about control of money, and about visits to parents. When, because of recession, Shirley was given the choice of moving to a new area with her job or accepting redundancy, Michael became irritated and impatient. He refused to consider moving, because of the implications on his own work future. He argued that now was an ideal time to start a family. Shirley felt that a family would trap her into dependency on a man who thought only of himself. Michael felt if anyone thought of herself it was Shirley. Within a few weeks Shirley moved on her own and only months later the marriage broke up.

Called in to listen to the couple on a number of occasions I was struck by the difficulty each had of hearing the needs and the longings of the other. Everything was a matter of negotiation, of weighing what he wanted over against what she wanted, and if the scales did not balance there was an insoluble problem. I listened carefully to the way they spoke. They had no 'we' language; they talked only of 'I' (or more regularly of '*you*', where the pronoun was inevitably pronounced accusingly). They seemed incapable of even conceptualizing such notions as 'how this might affect *us*', or 'what *we* should do about *our* dilemma'.

Many of their conversations sounded as if they were two individuals who happened to be living at the same address; any concession to the other was interpreted as giving in and showing weakness, or else as credit for magnanimity which brought a better bargaining position later. When I queried the sheer level of their inability to be vulnerable with each other, they admitted it was out of step with reality as they knew it, so unthinkable that neither could take such a risk. Even though it meant sacrificing their marriage and going through the trauma of breakdown it seemed less painful than giving away too much of their own self-will.

Learning the language of community, even where the community is just two people, is essential in marriage. For the words themselves belie the reality beneath, that neither person has a monopoly on reasonableness and that each needs the other. Being able to admit to what one wants, and to be willing to have those wants challenged by another is a risky endeavour. For it exposes one's insecurities and selfishness, as much as one's lofty ideals and longings. But without such mutual exposure and sensitivity there can never be community, and without community marriage is at best a list of individually negotiated contracts. It is only in the learning to give that I can learn to love, and when I learn that, it is so infinitely more satisfying than having my own way.

Disappointment

Sometimes people come to marriage with very high ideals. They have seen the poor relationships of parents or relatives and are determined to make theirs better. Far from being caught up in individualism they are totally committed to being in union. They do not want to have separate lives, but to do everything together, to share a oneness which is more than bodily satisfaction. They see theirs as a marriage of intimacy, not just regularity. They want a unity which is reciprocal and symmetrical, where the needs of the one are reflected in the understanding of the other. They do not need close friendships outside marriage, for they are utterly absorbed in one another. In the initial stages of being deeply in love they have little doubt that their marriage will re-establish the norm for what all marriages should be.

When, however, marriage fails to live up to these high expectations there can be an enormous sense of disappointment and confusion. The disappointment can frequently begin within the first few weeks and be accompanied by bewilderment and perplexity. Background issues which were never clarified in the early days of dreams and passion now become real problems when they crop up with regularity. Inability to make the other *understand*, or frustration at little acts of thoughtlessness all can compound the sense that the marriage is not working.

Given the wide sweep of different backgrounds and temperaments it should not surprise us that even committed couples come adrift in their hopes for the marriage. Sometimes there are different levels of satisfaction involved. For one of the partners the longings for a particular kind of intimacy or enrichment can be very deep and its absence can signal great frustration. For the other who is content with things as they are, the partner's disappointment brings perpetual discouragement, resulting in a desperation to know what more can be done to make that person happy.

The first ideal which usually needs to be abandoned is that of 'telepathy'. Understanding requires self-disclosure, not the power of mind-reading. So the sense of being let down has to be *communicated* to one another in a 'safe area' where the couple can agree to listen without allocating blame. When disappointments can be shared without the fear of rows or further deterioration of the relationship, each can begin to hear the pain and sense of defeat of the other. In this context the couple can begin to examine the layers of frustration or fear and recognize the attitudes which have dominated the relationship: demands which the other is required to meet, ideals of communication, romance, thoughtfulness and so on which the other is required to live up to. And with the identifying of those things can come the will and even the strength to let them go, and move on to firmer ground.

Disappointment within marriage has one very clear answer: acceptance. The issue of acceptance is the core spiritual issue which lies at the heart of every marriage. For we are all failures. We are all disappointments. No one person can be all that another dreamed of. And so often we have to let go of our ideal of what a husband or wife should be like, and give ourselves in love instead to the one we actually have. We sometimes have to die to the hopes and ambitions on which we tried to build our lives, die to ideas and dreams of how we wanted to be happy, how we thought we should be loved. But these are painful deaths. They can leave us desolate and exposed. That is why it is often only possible to die these deaths when they are 'simultaneously huge acts of trusts in something beyond myself that I believe holds my life with care'. So say two authors who help people through this process of letting go. For it could be that God's purpose for me is far bigger than my own. Perhaps 'what God wants to do in me cannot be accomplished in the marriage of my dreams. Perhaps it can be accomplished only in the marriage I am actually in.'[16]

Rows

Most people who live at close quarters with each other have rows at some time during their relationship. For such closeness highlights the ways two people are both similar and different, and these are each a potential cause of friction.

It is not uncommon to come across a couple for whom argument is a normal part of conversation. They disagree verbally, contradict each other, and rarely come to a point of agreement on an issue, yet they do not see this as anything particularly serious. They might hurl abuse (or even objects!) at one another but would show surprise if someone suggested they had problems in their marriage. For another couple, however, this kind of scenario would be devastating. It would be an indication of the utmost defeat, that they had grown to detest each other and were close to the end of their relationship. Attitudes towards conflict, and what is understood to be a row vary greatly, influenced as they are by earlier family patterns. In noisy, demonstrative families people speak their minds openly, arguing and often raising their voices as a matter of course. In more restrained households there is a distaste shown towards such emotional display, and feelings are best kept to oneself. Rows within marriage therefore need to be 'read', especially by the couple themselves. What distinguishes a mild disagreement from a serious quarrel can be confusing for people from different backgrounds.

The anatomy of a row is complex, and there are endless reasons why they take place. They can be triggered off by circumstances, attitudes or moods. They may be the result of long-term differences, or short-term immediate pressures. Tiredness, irritability, misunderstanding or anxiety may produce them. They can be the means of clearing the air, and letting the lid off feelings which have to come out before peace can be resumed. They may simmer on for days or weeks creating an atmosphere of misery and hardness. They can depressively define the very relationship, playing through continued disrespect day after day in well-worn clichés and debilitating non-involvement. It is not the *presence* of conflict in a marriage so much as the *kind* of rows that take place which divides a healthy from a damaged relationship.

Most rows flare up because something is done or said which offends the other. But where the same row crops up again and again then it is more defeating. There can be the sense of not being listened to, of needs not being heard or met. If this situation is allowed to continue without the frustration being addressed and no attempt made to resolve the issue, there is already the beginning of a long-term sore which will only fester until the wound is cleaned and healed. That is probably why New Testament writers urge that it be resolved as soon as possible in an attitude of openness and forgiveness. 'Be angry, but don't sin,' says St Paul, and he also adds, 'Don't let the sun go down on your anger.' That is blatantly practical advice, for taking a row to bed is essentially a prescription for a very poor night's sleep.

The problem is that many couples let rows drag on until well after dark. A typical bedtime scenario is where the angry partner wants to 'have it out' and the other wants to sleep. So one is seething with fury and the other clamps down on the argument, refusing (often piously) to be drawn into a row. But silence, in the face of another's pent up feelings, is a powerful weapon. If it is used now it will not be welcomed. Rather than quelling the storm it will more likely produce a hurricane, and the final devastation could be far worse than if the rumblings had been dealt with hours before.

Facing the conflict and dealing with the offence is the only way to heal the hurt and repair the damage of a row. And talking over a disagreement takes time. In pressured lives it is all too easy to retort angrily and chalk up the score rather than to work through the heat to the source of what went wrong. But the response instead requires patience, readiness to listen, and to hold back our judgement for a while. Hearing the claims of the other, and facing up to our own part in the row can be a painful process, for it is a blow to most people to find that they are in the wrong. Yet it is also a healing process, for through it we learn more about how to live together in a relationship of deeper sharing and trust.

Lack of Disclosure

I have talked of marriage as the potential place of great openness. But sadly for some people the reality is very different; it is the very place where they are least able to reveal their feelings. Consequently, they feel stifled in a relationship where they know little sharing and little freedom. 'I don't feel free to be the person I really am,' confided a long-married woman to me recently, 'because I know my husband would dislike me.'

Ironically, it is often because people have too much invested in a marriage rather than too little that they cannot take the risk of disclosure. There is the fear of disapproval because it feels very close to rejection. The greater its weight, the more distant the relationship can become. When a man cuts into the flow of his wife's animated conversation and tells her impatiently that she always repeats herself, she is likely to find less and less that she can talk to him about. She may also find her self-confidence ebbing away. But she is not likely, as a result, to develop the sort of conversation patterns of which he approves. For what often happens is that disapproval fails in changing the other; it only produces a subdued wariness about doing or saying the things the other does not like. Unless the other chooses to change because the partner's assessment is right, this aspect of that person's life simply goes 'underground'; staying a key part of her but no longer shared or disclosed. And if that 'underground' part is close to someone's very identity, the gap between a couple can become a chasm. People who are afraid of opening up to their partners begin to find that it is easier to reveal their innermost selves with strangers.

Intimacy makes us vulnerable, and people so often do what is expected, or what is approved of rather than disclose where they have been hurt or misunderstood. A man who feels humiliated by his wife's scorn of him will not readily share his feelings again. To safeguard against vulnerability he may minimise self-disclosure, and stay emotionally comfortable by playing well-defined roles. People reduce risks by avoiding conflict, especially conflict which drags up painful memories. Yet holding back on reality, or masking it with some face-saving device might save a situation now, but if it is repeated in the long term it can do much damage. One woman said, 'I built up feelings of anger and resentment at him all along, from way back in the beginning. There were things he did that made me mad, but I never told him.'[17]

At its least damaging this lack of openness can lead to boredom in the relationship, where what matters to one person can never be explored together, and where communication becomes routine and superficial. So many marriages in their middle years flounder simply out of neglect, where yawning boredom with each other and with the weekly routine stifles any stimulation and excitement which once might have been in the relationship. Worse, there might be a living out of two different lives: the joint life which is cautious, full of avoidance, and empty, and the private emotional life which is resentful, defeated or escapist. In a disturbing analysis of marital loneliness one psychologist describes an alarming escapism syndrome which sometimes goes along with the sense of being trapped. He calls it the 'death fantasy' and sees it as a product of long-term anger towards a partner, usually from a wife to her husband. 'One woman struggled with a husband who refused to discuss their marital troubles. She admitted that she secretly wished that her husband's plane would crash during one of his business trips.'[18] In his analysis this wish was alarmingly common.

Hurt, disapproval, avoidance or rejection take away marital freedom. They leave a partner trapped in a relationship which feels empty and draining, saps self-confidence, and brings despair and loneliness rather than well-being. In response to such emptiness one partner, or both, might become excessively work-oriented, getting from their jobs the satisfaction and well-being which is absent from marriage. For some it is a short step from finding a substitute in work to finding substitutes in other relationships. The syndrome of the man whose 'wife does not understand' him has been played out for decades in bars, restaurants and hotel bedrooms; to be joined in recent years by the woman whose husband treats her with disdain. But overwork, substitute relationships and unfaithfulness are never the real answer to isolation within marriage. That answer can only be in sorrow and forgiveness for the past, and the willingness to reopen hearts to one another. Without that pain of self-disclosure there will never be *shalom* in the relationship, but with it the Holy Spirit of God can bring new life out of even the deadest and bleakest marriage.

Intimacy and Marriage

If it is true that marriage can provide relationships of warmth, closeness and intimacy even in the context of contemporary social disintegration of community, how does this happen? I believe three issues deeply embedded in the New Testament teaching on marriage point us to an answer.

The first is that marriage is about norms and principles and cannot be redefined at whim as a free, unstructured arrangement. It is about 'leaving and cleaving': leaving parents and making a new union with a life partner. It is about faithfulness, honesty, sexual exclusiveness and trust. It is about promises which people make to each other; not so that we can be held in bondage to rules, but to create the climate of security and peace which are essential for any relationship to grow. Marriage vows are significant, not only in giving us an opportunity to state our intentions, but in defining for us what lies at the heart of this relationship we are now entering. Mike Mason makes the perceptive point: 'The decisive finality of vows was intended to free people so that they need not see their life's energies being drained away in endless courting rituals, in the constant hunger for sexual fulfilment, and in a continual search for "meaningful relationships".'[19]

The second is that marriage is also about closeness and enjoyment, sharing with each other the gift of time, and the excitement of passion. But this second is not separate from the first. Intimacy and warmth within a marriage grow from the stability and security of the relationship. For both are characterized by love. That is why New Testament letters talk about the marital structure of submission and love and then move straight on to the details of how this love should be developed. St Paul's advice to husbands would not be out of place in any contemporary counselling manual. Love your wives as you love your own bodies, he suggests. And indeed this is fine advice. If the detailed daily care which we all give our personal bodily needs was spent on our marriage partner, the level of intimacy would soar away. It is interesting too that Paul gives this advice to the men. It is almost as if he has heard the complaint of many women today, that they come a long way down in their husband's attention, and in his allocation of time and priorities.

The third is that marriage is about growth. It is never a static relationship, but develops through phases. It has to separate from parents, form a new unit, and rework old relationships from a married base. It has to negotiate the connection between marriage and work, making sure that marital intimacy always is given time. It has to honour the needs of one another, recognizing too that needs change over the years. All the developments which take place over a lifetime – parenting, ageing, unemployment, illness, bereavement – are potential points of growth as well as stress. There can be confidence as early stages of the relationship grow into something which is yet deeper and more sustaining. But the right conditions for growth are essential. The relationship must be given warmth, nourishment and space to breathe. If it is choked by control, crushed by judgement, or stunted by neglect it will be a struggle to survive. Mature marriages are those which have grown, where the love and understanding of each other has been grounded on the bedrock of commitment and acceptance.

Conclusion

Marriage is neither a social accident, nor a deliberate product of a patriarchal society. It is part of the very lifeblood of our humanness: given to us both in God's created order for our lives, and in God's redemptive provision for our healing. Characterized by love, faithfulness and commitment, marriage provides a powerful and inimitable structure for the expression and growth of intimacy in our society.

Yet marriage is under pressure, both from the emptiness of a fragmenting society and from the restlessness of the human heart. That pressure cannot be relieved by declaring this to be an outmoded institution, ready to be replaced by less constricting relationships. It can only be countered by entering much more deeply into the fullness of what marriage offers us, and understanding the power it can give our lives and our society. Marriage is essentially an act of troth – of open, giving trust. It is the utter invasion of privacy, the unrelenting exposure of one to another. Its fulfilment lies in the time, care, respect and love two people are prepared to give each other. Its strength lies in its origins beyond ourselves.

10

Sexual Intimacy

*For a joyous moment we pass beyond fear, lower our barriers,
open our hearts, meet, touch, join and are fulfilled.*

James Olthius

An important part of the intimacy of marriage is sexual intimacy.
But this is also the area where our culture invades relationships
most of all. We have not been allowed to be innocent about sex.
In a climate of loneliness and skin hunger, sex has been paraded
naked through the streets as the answer to our personal problems.
Yet the sex we have seen there is not real sex. It is a commodity. It
is a performance rating. It is a public display, humiliation even, of
one of the most sensitive areas of human life served up for profit.
Cut off from its roots in trothful love it is tarted up for consumption
in ever more bizarre and twisted ways.

Linked with this is our society's deep ambivalence about the
body. In recent years we have seen an explosion of interest in
body health, fat-free foods, multi-gyms, safe sunbeds and annual
mass marathons. But at the same time we have become increasingly
neurotic and negative about the body. The fear of ageing, of
being fat, of dying underlines the urgency which persuades even
nine-year-olds to diet. The messages are confused. Magazines,
fashion shows, gymnastic and athletics coverage all tell us we love
the body. Anorexia clinics, video nasties and rape centres point to
a very different conclusion.

So when a couple comes to bed, it is hard for them to come
on their own. They bring the sexual baggage of the culture, as
well as of their own past. They bring all they have seen of other
people's lovemaking, all they have had drilled into them about
foreplay, erogenous zones, penetration, multiple orgasms; all they
have fantasized about seduction. Some of them bring memories of

good or bad lovers, experiences of being abused, patterns of sexual obsession and pornographic images. And all the false messages which have been drummed in their ears often harm the gentle mechanisms of love and patience and self-giving. For when real sexual intimacy takes place it is unique. It is an act of precious giving and receiving between two people who blot out the world and touch each other in the closeness of union. It is so different from the desperate lovemaking where 'people are driven into each other's arms in fear and trembling, [and] embrace each other in despair and loneliness'.[1] It is different too from the messages which have invited them to seek autonomous, self-interested sex; to see others as merely a means to their own erotic pleasure.

If we reject the unique, interpersonal basis of our sexuality we open the door to discouragement and narcissism. There is a great chasm between the continuity of acceptance which lies behind the long-term, loving commitment to one partner, and the transient sex where people pick up and drop the bodies of other people as their fancy takes them. As one psychologist observes, 'in the process of such rapid change we offer recognition at one moment and rejection at the next'.[2] There are many costs to meet, and the price is high. Another psychologist spells it out: 'When we isolate physical genital sexuality from its rightful place in personal human contact, it becomes a god we serve by concentrating on getting bigger and better orgasms. We become driven by the demon of sex even as we seek the goddess of sex, and then there is nothing human about sex at all.'[3]

Sex and the Church

The confusion of our culture has left a great opportunity for the Christian religion to help re-establish the wonderful humanness of sex. Sadly in the past there has not been much evidence of an enthusiastic grasping of this opportunity. Rather, much of Christian tradition has shown embarrassment about the fact that sex is there at all! Whatever view they meant to pass on to us, there is no doubt that the message actually conveyed is that sex is probably God's 'Greatest Mistake'. Among Christian writers, from the early church fathers to Martin Luther onward, sexual pleasure has been given a bad reputation, even within marriage. It has left its mark on Catholic and Orthodox doctrine in particular. Mary the mother of Christ had herself to be the product of an immaculate conception rather than good, straightforward copulation. She had also to remain a perpetual virgin after the birth of Jesus, rather than a woman who then had normal sex and several other children. Historical libraries are littered with stern pronouncements. St Jerome insisted that 'he who too ardently loves his wife is an adulterer'. Confessors' manuals from the medieval church stated that sexual intercourse was not to be performed on Sundays, Wednesdays, Fridays and some holidays. It should be performed in one position only, and never during penance.[4]

Inevitably the church's unease with sex has rebounded mostly on women. They were the ones made to feel guilty since clearly they were the ones 'to blame'. Although the stereotypes changed from women as 'base, carnal and licentious' (medieval period) to women as 'the fount of all purity' (Victorian period) they were nevertheless still identified with the 'problem' of sex. Either they were sexually dangerous and needed to be ruled by men so that chaos would not break out, or they were morally superior and needed to be protected. So in one century we see the persecution of thousands of ordinary women accused of being witches, and causing among other things male impotence. In another century we see the subjugation of women who were too pure to be allowed to vote in the messy business of politics. 'Poison the woman and you poison the fount of all virtue.' Despite the early suffragists' endearing slogans ('Votes for women and chastity for men') the double standard of Victorian sexual morality persisted until safe contraception could hide the evidence of a woman's misdemeanours. Men could be forgiven their sexual improprieties, but women, never. They had to safeguard the morals of the whole of civilization.

Even though these attitudes have been purveyed by societies in collusion with the church they are all a far cry, of course, from the biblical picture of marriage and sexuality. The Bible celebrates human sexuality. The New Testament endorses its joyful mutuality. Warnings about the addictive nature of obsession and abuse come in the context of the recognition that sex is powerful and demanding, close to our very identity as persons, and a reciprocal source of joy and pleasure. Furthermore, marital intimacy is unashamedly erotic. The language used in the Bible to describe it is often direct and uncompromising. That is probably why the public reading of Scripture has been carefully controlled in some church traditions. The lectionary kindly edits the Word of God for us, leaving out those passages which are too rude or too graphic for our sensitive ears. Even the *Songs of Songs*, that wonderfully sensual love song, has been carefully 'spiritualized' for us by centuries of Christian preachers. We have been invited to read it and think of it as God's love for the church. But how we can read the erotic *Song of Songs* and think of the church has always been a mystery to me! It takes a considerable feat of imagination to reflect on the congregation at Cockfosters when I read the lines:

> Let him kiss me with the kisses of his mouth.
> Your love is more delightful than wine.
> Turn, my lover, and be like a gazelle
> or like a young stag on the rugged hills.

The Bible and the Body

A biblical view of sexuality does not need to find a 'way out' of accepting the erotic. It takes seriously the fact that we are *bodily* creatures whose flesh is to be neither worshipped nor belittled, but respected and loved. For this is the way God has made us, and this is how God came to live among us. One of the central Christian doctrines, the incarnation, is itself an endorsement of our sexual humanity. For Jesus had a body, Jesus was a body, Jesus touched the bodies of others, the disease-ridden and deformed as well as the beautiful. He was kissed, stroked, and anointed in return, even by a woman of doubtful sexual reputation. Jesus' body needed food, drink, sleep, comfort and exercise, and when he washed or swam he was probably naked. Nothing could be more convincing of the ultimate honour of human sinews, skin and bone than the reality of Emmanuel, God bodily with us.

God has provided marriage as a special place where we can celebrate the body. It is the place where we may be fully naked to each other at our most vulnerable, our most exposed. Humans alone have the choice of whether or not to be undressed with another. Unlike all the rest of creation human beings *uncover* to make love: we take off our protective clothing and disclose who we are. Our nakedness with each other recalls the nakedness we all have before God. And we begin to get a real glimpse of how the one flesh of marriage can indeed be like the mystery of Christ and the church. Before the face of our creator there is no place to hide, no covering to put on, no concealment of who we are. In the imagery of the Bible it is only the church, the bride of Christ, that can welcome this utter visibility because the bride knows that the sin which defiles and disfigures has been forgiven by Christ's redeeming love. And marriage echoes that exposure, where husband and wife do not retreat from each other's gaze but accept one other in the sanctuary of troth.

To be naked with each other is more than an act of physical uncovering, however. For the heart must be naked along with the body. If we say with our bodies what we do not believe with our hearts then we are telling a lie. And when this lie is told, we cannot retract it. We can only redeem it by naming it for what it was, and asking forgiveness. For the bodily statement 'I love you' must ring true with our whole will and mind if the language is not to be devalued or the coinage counterfeit. Mike Mason makes a similar point: 'Exposure of the body in a personal encounter is like the telling of one's deepest secret: afterwards there is no going back, no pretending that the secret is still one's own or that the other does not know it. It is in effect the very last step in human relations, and therefore never one to be taken lightly.'[5]

Sexual intercourse does not, therefore, of itself establish intimacy. It presupposes and then deepens it. The paradox of giving away one's sexuality to another, is the paradox of then not having it to give away. For we have passed on the guardianship to the other, and receive in return that other freely given. The risk is overwhelming. We are emptied of all bargaining power. It is only within the context of trust and the assurance of commitment that such intimacy can grow in peace, unhurried, unchoked, and with the security of acceptance.

Without a celebration of the body sexual intimacy is not possible. There may still be sex, there may still be copulation, but the intimacy of two lovers who gaze in excitement and wonderment at one another's flesh will be absent. Yet that celebration itself can only take place within boundaries of trust and commitment. Intimacy grows from the knowledge that here is safety, here is love, here we will not be betrayed. The old biblical word 'troth' still expresses most succinctly the kernel of the marriage relationship. For Olthius it is the key to unlocking the meaning of sexual intimacy. Troth and sex go together, bound up with each other in celebration of committed love: 'Troth without eros and sexual union is thin, burdensome and unexciting. Eros and sex without troth is capricious and fleeting.'[6]

Approaching sexuality with a biblical outlook therefore gives us both a vital framework from which we can understand its meaning, and important categories whereby we can assess the health or sickness of a relationship. We recognize that sex was not a grotesque error on the part of a creator who ran out of ideas. But it is a purposeful structure breathed into creation by a God who wanted us to draw close to each other, and see a little of what it means to be united as male and female in God's image. Sexual love is not inferior to 'spiritual love', for God did not produce a hierarchy of components within our human selves, but created us as whole beings. A couple in marriage is called to worship God as much by their trothful, erotic sex as by their prayers for each other. All that God has given to us can enrich our well-being and enjoyment. And when sex becomes disengaged from our personal and committed lives together then the whole relationship is in trouble. When there is unfaithfulness or sexual deceit, then before the marriage can ever grow again there must be repentance, forgiveness and healing.

The biblical text itself has inspired many to write and explore the themes of love and sexuality. Phyllis Trible compares the story in Genesis with the Song of Songs. For her, Genesis 2–3 is a love story which has turned sour. Beauty and intimacy has ended in defeat and destruction. Sin, lies and judgement take the joy and harmony of the Garden of Eden into the sorrow of recrimination and exile. So the Song of Songs redeems this tragedy. Once again the one-flesh union of sexuality is extolled and the man and woman enter another garden to treat each other with deep tenderness and loving respect.[7] It is a picture in microcosm of the themes of creation, fall and redemption, and how these affect even the most intimate of our relationships. Calvin Seerveld's book *The Greatest Song* retells the love story putting it to music, and contrasting the voice of the beloved with the voice of the seducer. The biblical message about sex points always to its power, its emotional depths, and its rightful place within a context of troth.

Within a Christian framework, therefore, sex means naked

commitment: it expresses covenantal love between two people. Intercourse is a symbol of the total availability of love for that other person with whom we are inextricably bound. Once we have offered ourselves bodily and emotionally, in full exposure and vulnerability there is in principle nothing more of ourselves left to offer. Instead sex becomes the route to deeper knowledge of the other, to exploration, acceptance and the self-giving of love.

Unpacking Sexual Baggage

It does not take a social scientist to observe that many people in our culture do not live in the sexual intimacy I have been describing. All too often the patterns are of despair and anxiety rather than growth and joy. Yet the reasons behind this do not always point to lack of commitment. Couples who love and value each other can still find problems within their sexual relationship which baffle them, and leave them defeated. The sexual baggage which they bring into their relationship can be burdensome and oppressive. Attitudes of parents can leave their own unspoken fears, or areas of sensitivity. The idea that sex is dirty, repulsive, silly or boring can have been transmitted over many years without our realizing how much we have taken in. Fears of being overweight, of body smells, of growing unattractive, or over-sensitivity about some aspect of appearance can all be triggered and reinforced by inadvertent comments.

Years of sexual fantasizing can also affect marital intimacy, whether that fantasizing has been triggered by pornography or masturbation. Where patterns have become obsessive and addictive a man can find them hard to leave behind in his lovemaking with a real woman. A woman can be affected by fantasies even where they have not been fed by pornography. Forty years ago, in the Kinsey report, *Sexual Behaviour in the Human Female*, about two thirds of women said they had fantasies during sex. This was taken up by Nancy Friday in the 1970s and Sheila Kitzinger in the 1980s who examined the sexual fantasies women have. They discovered that many of them revolve around images which are predominant in society. Whereas male fantasies during sex are often about domination, women's fantasies are about being dominated, being overpowered or 'conquered'. Some women therefore become *voyeurs* in their own lovemaking, looking on at imaginary seduction scenes, or playing through the innocent virgin being persuaded by the man of the world. Sometimes, women can only become sexually aroused and reach orgasm by imagining a situation which recalls the fears and excitement whispered about in early stages of their lives. Kitzinger comments: 'Many women find themselves in a double-bind between fantasies which are sexually arousing and their awareness that such fantasies exist as a sick parody of relations between men and women in our society.' In holding on to such images of domination they realize they are 'accepting roles that are scripted by men'.[8]

The problems of 'disconnected sex' can be difficult, and can spoil the closeness and openness which binds a couple together. Sharing the problem is the first step. Then, for a man, there might have to be a conscious commitment to allowing care and respect for his wife to dictate the lovemaking, even if it means initially losing some of the excitement which went along with old patterns of thoughts and images. For a woman there might need to be a deeper love and appreciation for her own body and a willingness to say what pleases her in lovemaking, and what she enjoys. It is important for each partner to help to release the other from a fantasy life, to be fully present and take deliberate initiative in sex. That way the focus returns to the real person, and the act becomes one of mutual involvement.

Gender and Sexual Intimacy

Even in the area of sexual fantasies it is evident that there are marked differences in the way women and men approach sex. Sometimes the important differences are hidden under layers of stereotypes. Roy McCloughry quotes the report of a magazine survey (*Gentleman's Quarterly*, July 1991) that men think about sex an average of fifteen times a day, and comments wryly: 'It's a wonder the "average man" has enough time to read the magazine.'[9] Yet the very male-female differences which make marital sex so exciting in the first place can also add to its frustrations. Sometimes problems can arise because of different gender patterns of sexual response.

It is evident that many men experience initial sexual attraction in a more heightened way than women, and they are also more likely to act on it. This has implications not only for heterosexual but also for homosexual behaviour. Casual sex not only has a much bigger part in homosexual than in heterosexual activity,[10] it also is more prevalent amongst male homosexuals than amongst lesbians. 'The gay scene doesn't have equal significance for male and female; the sexual marketplace character of gay pubs and clubs holds less appeal for the latter than it does for the former . . . It would be very rare for a woman to cruise the street or public toilets in search of a partner for sex; not so a man . . . Gay men are far more likely than gay women to begin potential sexual relationships with a casual encounter.'[11] Not only does this have continuing implications for the spread of HIV, it also means that those men who try to create a climate for a '*Christian*' homosexual lifestyle of monogamous lifelong relationships are battling against a very powerful tide.

Some homosexual men reject a celibate lifestyle because they argue it is not possible to enjoy intimacy and closeness with another without sexual expression. This assumption is found amongst heterosexual men also and suggests another important point. Because of the way in which men have often been denied emotional closeness in other areas, for some of them sex is the only route available to emotional warmth and expression. Consequently, because they experience sex as the main path to tenderness, in the lives of many men deep feelings are themselves often *sexualized*. It is important to remember this when we consider the different patterns which lie behind destructive sexual aberrations. Men who become involved in incest or paedophilic behaviour, for example, are not *always* those who are uncaringly abusing a child for their own self-gratification. It could also be a perversion of genuine warmth and love which, through an inability of the man to make adult responses and respect boundaries, has become sexually focused. Within marriage itself, where a man finds it difficult to be demonstrative or emotionally in tune with his wife, sex can be the way in which he expresses all his affection and love for her. For men more than women, sexual attraction, affection, protectiveness, and feelings of gratitude, are often entangled together.

For most women it is different. Differentiation is much easier, because they have traditionally been allowed a wider range of emotional responses and expressions. For them also emotional closeness is usually a prerequisite to full sexual enjoyment. In one study of more than 90,000 women, 72 per cent reported that they actually preferred cuddling to sex.[12] More than half of these women were under 39, and had not grown up in a culture of sexual constraint. In Shere Hite's famous study of 4,500 women, 98 per cent said they wanted more emotional intimacy with the men in their lives, which for them meant more communication about personal thoughts and feelings.[13] This is because for women the quality of sexual love is also related to the level of connectedness which exists in general in the relationship: the support of attentive listening, the warmth of a regular hug, the recognition that they are noticed by their partner and matter to them.

And herein lies a problem. Many women need emotional warmth and affection before they can commit themselves sexually, whereas many men feel they need sex before they can let go of other inhibitions and draw close. *Sensuality* means different things for the two partners. For the husband it is supremely identified with erotic attraction and the joy of being at one with his wife's body, luxuriating in her closeness; for the wife, sensuality is there first in the non-erotic touching, loving companionship and without this, sex is experienced as abrupt or even abusive.

The meaning of sexual love is established by the whole context of the relationship, never as an isolated act of penetration. Yet for the husband, arousal might come readily as a response to his wife's body as she undresses in the bedroom. He loves her, she is beautiful and desirable and here is an opportunity for him to show it. For the wife, however, arousal is much more related to what has been happening between the couple over the last few hours. If no attention and interest has been shown her all evening she may well experience his sudden amorous overtures now as offensive and demeaning. She does not just want to be a 'turn-on'. She wants to be a person. Unless these emotions are shared, the question of sex can quickly turn into a battleground with neither partner understanding how the other feels.

It is possible within the same marriage, therefore, for a husband and wife to have very different barometers as to when things are wrong. Jack and Moira's story is a good illustration. Moira was struggling with lack of self-esteem coupled with a sense of monotony and isolation in their marriage. They had few friends, rarely went out together, and watching television occupied most of their evenings. She felt the marriage was dying and pleaded with Jack to 'do something about it'. Jack felt there was no problem except in Moira's head. They had each other, good health, a comfortable house, and a nice garden. Their sex life was regular, Jack had no interest in any other woman and he was quite content. And because Moira continued to have sex with him he could not accept that she really thought there was anything wrong with the relationship, otherwise why would she want to sleep with him? For Moira, however, the sex was by now unimportant, but she felt it was all that was left of the relationship. She had gone through one period before when, to make her point, she had refused to have sex, but this had only made Jack irritable and confused. She felt too defeated to try this again and was not confident that anything would be achieved. And so their marriage stuck at stalemate until Jack's own brother went through an unexpected and bitter separation. The whole close-knit family went into shock and a level of questioning began which they had never experienced before. Recognizing the familiarity of his sister-in-law's angry complaints and suddenly hearing for the first time his own wife's dissatisfaction, Jack swiftly agreed to seek help for his marriage.

Being aware, even in sexual relationships, that husbands and wives are different does not mean we need to fall back on tired gender stereotypes, but rather that each partner needs to listen to the other and not assume one can speak for both. It is also important to recognize that sex is not always the best thermometer to test the temperature of a marriage relationship. Only when sex takes place in the context of good communication can both wife and husband be sure they are loving each other in a way that nourishes them.

Sex as Communication

Sexual intimacy is a very deep form of communication. It communicates feelings and attitudes about oneself and the other person. It gives messages to the other person about how they are loved, desired and valued which can be taken and understood even when they are accompanied by few words. The messages are given through body language which is sometimes tentative, stammering, hesitant, confident or assured. And although the language is universal the dialect is unique to that couple. Just as a child learns its mother tongue and its regional accent over many years, so a couple learn their own language of love through years of listening and repeating back to one another, trying out new forms of expression. There are always new words to put in the vocabulary and new phrases to explore, so that even impediment or disability is no real handicap to this communication.

The stages of lovemaking – from preparation to arousal to climax to pleasant exhaustion – are all part of the intimate communication between two people. Each act of making love is a new conversation, one which wonderfully repeats the old, whilst adding something of today. When sex is good it speaks the language of affirmation and worth into the situation of the moment: whether in celebration, reconciliation, drawing close in grief, or blotting out fear. That is why one doctor talks of the power of the sex act as deep therapy. 'When you are feeling good, the unconditional acceptance and self-affirming exhilaration that sex provides can keep your spirits high. When you are feeling down and lacking in self-esteem sex "becomes more than a reassurance, it becomes an urgent therapy, perhaps one of the most powerful forms of treatment the spouses can carry out for one another."'[14]

So when we make love what we communicate is as important as how we communicate it. If we send signals of lust, irritation or self-interest, they will be there in the very heart of our lovemaking. But if instead we communicate patience, love, gentleness, and the vital importance of that other person, the act will have a more satisfying message. 'Every time we make love and find each other's bodies stimulating and pleasurable we affirm the sexual significance of each other, and through the sexual dimension our personhood.'[15] And as people grow older or infirm and the sex act itself becomes infrequent or disappears, that message of love remains. For at the heart of it is not mere copulation but the continuity of acceptance, encouragement and value.

At the profoundest level sexual intimacy communicates the deep interdependence of male and female throughout creation. And since we are male and female in God's image our union and our difference stem from the same source. Working this out creatively in loving and lovemaking is one of the great challenges of marriage.

Surviving Unfaithfulness

Although our culture shows increasing tolerance towards premarital sex, it also shows, as we have seen, strong disapproval towards adultery. Yet many people are unfaithful to their spouses and it is important to look at some of the causes and effects of this. Very often the seeds of adultery have often been sown long before the fruit is harvested. The factors which lead people into an affair are often little to do with sex itself: unresolved conflict, a desire to 'get back at' a spouse, loneliness, absence from home, infatuation, low self-esteem or just plain boredom. Although by the time adultery takes place the sexual attraction has been fanned into desire, the motivation behind it may be complex.

Although all forms of adultery involve sexual betrayal they vary in seriousness. There are affairs, often initiated more by the man, which are casual relationships and have no permanent existence. They might take place during absences from home or periods of loneliness or the unavailability of a wife through illness or pregnancy. Here temptation, or need for sexual comfort, might lead someone into an adulterous liaison which could spoil his marriage. Yet this is very far from the intention. For this man loves his wife, albeit inadequately, and has no desire to end his marriage. He simply wants something in addition. If faced with a choice there is no doubt which he would choose, but there sometimes is a doubt about his ability to maintain a faithful relationship under stress.

Although this might not be a central threat to the marriage, the sense of betrayal is likely to be very deep for the partner whose trust has been violated. The ability to forgive will also depend on how much remorse is shown for the act itself, and how strong is the promise to be faithful from now on. Making a clean breast of an affair, and having a firm commitment that it will never be repeated, are much more likely to lead to reconciliation and forgiveness than hiding it until discovered, and making little effort to change. The fear of infidelity can itself put strain on any relationship. For where there is no trust, there is no real intimacy either.

However great the pain from a casual act of adultery, other kinds of affair may undermine the marriage in a much more destructive way. For they grow out of a relationship which is already in trouble, and which may have been getting worse over a number of years. People who feel continually ignored, undermined or misunderstood are swift to notice the difference when someone else takes more than a passing interest in them. Some affairs are started deliberately as a desperate bid for attention, either trying to bolster up one's own low sense of worth or to rebuke for not caring enough. Some begin out of bitterness, when the relationship has deteriorated to the extent that adultery is used as a form of punishment. In this situation, says Lewis Smedes, the person who initiates the new relationship 'is not falling in love with a third person, he is falling in anger against his spouse'.[16]

Boredom is also high on the list of factors which trigger infidelity. The excitement of a chase and possible conquest, or the lure of new romance can seem compelling when put alongside a humdrum daily existence. There are those, however, who go after new partners simply because they are not capable of sustaining one relationship to the depths of intimacy it requires. Many who 'cheat' their spouse may think they are looking for a more exciting relationship, but may in reality be afraid of faithfulness because it is too adult and demanding. 'Instead of growing into maturity with one partner, they go over and over the same ground in each new liaison.'[17]

Although adultery can indeed be a devastating blow to a marriage, it need not destroy it. When there is some recognition of the pain this has caused, and some attempt at understanding the reasons for unfaithfulness by the spouse who has been hurt, the way is open to reconciliation. Forgiveness may be difficult, and many couples will need help to work through the aftermath of adultery. Usually the break with a third person is not clean-cut, even when that is the intention. The sense of loss, the memories of pleasure, and sometimes the remorse that this person has also been hurt may trigger a sense of longing to go back and pick up the affair again. Then there is the anger from the one who betrayed, which will have to be expressed, even if that threatens to drive a deeper wedge between the couple. So many emotions will need to be brought to the surface: jealousy, denial, blame, along with much heart-searching, if the marriage stands a chance of survival. Anything less minimizes the significance of what has happened, and stores up longing, resentment or bitterness to the point where, like a terminal disease, it eats away at all the healthy parts too. Most of all, with the ending of the affair will have to come a rekindling of the marriage relationship; not just a repetition of the situation which led to infidelity in the first place, but a new commitment to each other, and a new beginning to love.

Singleness, Sexuality and Chastity

Attitudes which harm real sexual intimacy may be a long time in developing. As singleness is no longer equated with chastity, and the age of first sexual experience gets younger, it means that for many more people problems with sex begin earlier. It is interesting for instance that a high proportion of those interviewed in the report on *Sexual Behaviour in Britain* who had sex under 16, felt they had sex 'too early'. Nearly 60 per cent of the girls, although only a quarter of the boys thought they should have waited longer. What was also significant were the different reasons given by girls and boys for having intercourse. It makes sad reading. Nearly 40 per cent of the girls felt they were in love, when the boys patently were not (only 6 per cent). For the boys the dominant factors were curiosity, natural course of the relationship, peer influence, being carried away, and deliberately wanting to lose their virginity. And 6.7 per cent of the girls and 3.6 per cent of the boys admitted to being drunk at the time.

The figures give in bald statistical terms an indication of the pain and regret which follows some people into later relationships. Something of deep personal value was given, but treated as commonplace. The likelihood is that those who are 'in love' get hurt, and can end up feeling used in someone's else quest for curiosity or peer approval. The damage this does to a sense of self-worth is hidden under the doubtful image of premarital sex as healthy and fun. What is more, the promiscuity which often follows from experiences of under-age sex robs many people of personal security, leaving them exposed to an increased level of sexually transmitted diseases, and unsure about themselves and the value of their relationships. It is perhaps not surprising that an American research project discovered that sexually experienced girls of 16 were more likely to report feeling lonely, and six times more likely to have attempted suicide than inexperienced girls in their class.[18]

The shift away from the valuing of chastity for single people has been gradual and reinforced by changing social factors. More reliable and available contraception has taken the fear of pregnancy away from young women, whereas fears of sexually transmitted diseases, though far more life-threatening, have not acted as anything like the same kind of deterrence. In both areas, however, the risks are considerable. In the 1980s the conception rate amongst girls under 16 rose by around 25 per cent, and the abortion rate by 30 per cent. On a longer time-scale, the risk from cervical cancer, HIV and other diseases multiplies. It is curious that at a time when there are more risks than ever from uncommitted sex it is now seen as an inevitable part of life. The television and advertising media have themselves shown a voyeuristic obsession with sex, offering a diet saturated with adultery, and premarital affairs, and reinforcing the idea that sexual involvement is a norm for relationships. When little positive is said about sex in any other context it is not surprising that this ethos becomes dominant. In response, much sex education puts the focus on 'safe sex' and birth control, and a discussion of chastity is effectively banished as something which no longer has any relevance.[19] Thus the myth is conveyed that it is impossible to remain single and chaste – a product, says Jack Dominian, of all these current attitudes where 'society takes the view that restraint is not possible and indeed bombards the young person with sexual titillation and condoms'.[20] It is even the case, as Trevor Stammers wryly observes in his excellent practical guide to sexual intimacy, that 'many popular books on sex quote from the Bible or refer to its teachings, usually in order to assure readers that they can safely ignore it'.[21] This has led in turn to well-meaning people within the church publicly 'giving permission' to youngsters to enjoy sexual relationships on the grounds that God has created the sex drive, and God does not want to spoil anyone's fun.[22]

The task of encouraging premarital chastity is therefore largely seen as a failed pastime of a bygone era, yet it is a much needed activity today. It is not yet clear what kind of future will be possible for those who begin their sexual experience very early, and go through life with many sexual partners, for this is the first whole generation which has been exposed to the ranges of disease and psychological effects this way of life entails. But we do know that it is a violation of sexual integrity which, when regularly repeated, is much harder to replace as a way of life. For the truth about intimacy is one which is learned through chastity and not promiscuity. It is a truth about utter vulnerability and disarmament which cannot be found in casual sex, however temporarily exciting it may be. For any sexual relationships which has built-in reservations is part of what Henri Nouwen calls 'the taking structure': 'It means "I want you now, but not tomorrow. I want something from you, but I don't want *you*."' For Nouwen, 'Love is limitless. Only when men and women give themselves to each other in total surrender, that is with their whole person for their whole life, can their encounter bear full fruits.'[23]

The irony is that the task of articulating this has been left largely to churches and religious groups, when their own record of communicating about sexuality has been less than impressive. Those who communicate it best within the church are those who live inside the 'giving structure' of love in their own relationships. People who have chosen to commit themselves in faithfulness to their partners and have worked through issues in their own relationships can often help others in the journey towards sexual troth. But at a more public level there are also some recent successes. The excellent sex education course *Make Love Last*, sponsored in 1994 by Care in Education, has had influence far beyond the church constituency. Graphic, incisive and funny, it has been taken up by schools all over Britain, who are anxious themselves to find new ways of speaking to young people about sex. Even the 1995 poster campaign, *Christians make the best lovers*, caught the imagination of the media, and put a number of discussions on the agenda. What is very clear is that the task of reaching a whole generation with a message which will bring hope for their own future has never been more urgent. If we want our adolescents to know good health and good relationships in the years to come we need to offer them far more than a slot machine full of condoms.

There is one more issue to consider. In an atmosphere of sexual neurosis, those who choose celibacy on the simple grounds that intercourse belongs to marriage can find themselves increasingly isolated. Especially as they move through their twenties and into their thirties and forties that sense of being out of step with the majority can become very strong. There can be the dilemma of coping with sexual feelings themselves, and of doing so in a climate which offers scorn, not admiration for those who opt for abstinence. There may also be the problem of being rejected by friends who feel differently, or of being pressurized to turn a friendship into a sexual involvement. Simply recognizing, as many do, that problems are not resolved by capitulating to pressure does not make it necessarily any easier to resist. Then, casual remarks from insensitive people ('but you're an attractive person, you ought to be able to find someone') can completely miss the mark and bring increased frustration. People who have struggled to accept singleness and celibacy for this period in their lives require to be recognized as normal human beings and not pitied as sexual freaks. The misery of being unnecessarily isolated can be much greater than that of not having a sexual partner.

Those who are chaste by conviction are in fact a threat to all who market sex as something which we must bow before. For they are often living testimonies to the fact that human intimacy is not dependent on sexual intercourse for its meaning or power. They also know the truth that we are much more in control of the way we relate to others than our culture is prepared to acknowledge. And in this they have the witness of history. As Jack Dominian wisely points out: 'For myself and for millions of my own generation who observed the rule of premarital chastity, the idea that instincts are so overwhelming that they cannot be contained is novel.'[24]

Christian sexual morality which underlines chastity is not easy to live by. It is demanding and sometimes costly in a society where so many areas of life have become sexualized. It involves breaking away from the impatience of a whole culture. But that is no good reason for not giving it a try. For when we turn our back on the voice that says 'I must have what I want and have it now', we can enter willingly into a framework of peaceful waiting which has the very love of God at its centre.

Conclusion

Christian norms of sexual exclusiveness, erotic love and faithful and unconditional relationships lie at the heart of human sexuality. A celebration of our bodiliness and the excitement of union is something which infuses the creation and takes us from one generation into another. Sexual intimacy is a powerful and exquisite gift from the creator, which takes our aloneness and our vulnerability and turns them to completeness with another.

Yet as with all gifts it is possible to snatch or grab at sexual love, and make it serve the demands of our own self-interest. Whether in conquest or manipulation, accumulation of partners or in simply passing the time, sex can be emptied of its depth and treated as a commodity. Even within committed relationships sex can become an empty ritual or a rationed 'duty', distorted by impatience or selfishness, spoiled by poor communication or inability to listen. But whenever any of these replace the trothful loving union which God offers to men and women we are no longer living in the fullness of our birthright. Sexual intimacy is always more than mere orgasm.

It is important to remember, however, that only one aspect of our sexuality is expressed in sexual intercourse. We also express it in warmth and touch, in closeness and care for the other persons who are dear to us. If in our lives there is no sexual union with another, perhaps because we have accepted celibacy, or gone through bereavement, illness or divorce, we are no less fully human and fully sexual. Deeply satisfying human intimacy, whether in marriage or outside, is in the end not dependent on copulation but on a faithful sharing of our hearts and lives with those whom we love, and a longing for their well-being and peace. For it is then that 'God can be God and love be gift.'[25]

11

Intimacy and the Family

*A person who has developed no family bonds will have a very
hard time developing any larger loyalties in later life.*

As an area of study, the family has come into its own in recent
years. Sociologists have joined social psychologists in exploring
the place it occupies in the lives of contemporary people. Anthony
Giddens has remarked, 'The study of the family used to seem to
many one of the dullest of endeavours. Now it appears as one of the
most provocative.'[1] This reflects in part the great upheaval in the
nature of theorizing about family life. The impact of both feminist
theory and postmodernist critique has been to challenge and
fragment any earlier consensus. There are now few 'orthodoxies',
and sociologists draw quite contradictory conclusions about the
nature, the meaning and the future of the family.

But the new interest in the family is only partly as a result of the
shifts in sociology. It also reflects the changes within the organization of the family itself. No longer does the nuclear family comprise
simply two married partners and their offspring, or the wider family
comprise all the other blood relationships. Now there are multiple
parents, half-parents, step-grandparents, half- and step-sisters and
brothers and a whole new meaning to 'extended family'. There
are also fears and uncertainties connected with the risks of more
unstructured relations. The Chief Rabbi, Jonathan Sacks, outlines
some of these changes:

> We have moved within the space of two decades from the
> convention of the stable nuclear family – husband, wife and
> children – to an extraordinary diversity of sexual and social
> arrangements many of which are consciously temporary and
> provisional. One projection suggests that by the end of the

century one child in two will have parents who were married when it was born and who stay together until it has grown up.[2]

The changes in family structure and organization are so pronounced that there is now a debate as to whether it is meaningful any longer to talk of *the* family as though it were something with a given structure. Norman Denzin feels the unidimensional view of a stable, fixed family is not relevant today and offers a much bleaker story: 'It is a single-parent family, headed by a teenage mother, who may be drawn to drug abuse and alcoholism. She and her children live in a household that is prone to be violent.'[3] The postmodern alternative is, therefore, to leave behind the big picture of a single entity, *The Family* (the 'metanarrative'), and talk instead simply of 'families'.

I shall not be going down that route. For my aim is not to look simply at the way families live, but to focus on the *normative* structure of the family. For 'family' is more than a socio-cultural concept, more than a pawn of patriarchy or capitalism. From a Christian perspective it is a structure of creation. That means the concept of the family is a crucial one, even though there might be many different ways of experiencing family life and living together. For God has so arranged the world that we are born into it through the family, and we gain our early identity from our place in that set of relationships.

The *meaning* of the family, then, is neither socially constructed nor is it neutral. In the Judeo-Christian tradition we are given biblical norms for family living: norms of parental care and nurturing for children, unconditional love, respect and honouring of parents by their offspring, commitment to each other's welfare by members of the family. This is not to be an economic or power relationship, but one of nurture, trust and love. The family is linked to marriage as the base from which children are born, where sexual boundaries are respected and through which they are nourished and taught. As with marriage, faithfulness and troth are to be at the centre of family living, and families are called to hospitality, justice and neighbourly love. They are to show kindness to the poor and generosity to those in need.[4] Evidence for the existence of these norms is widespread; they are apparent also in cultures which do not have roots in the

Christian faith for they are to do with the very meaning of the family itself. In biblical terms they are *creational*. So these norms are much more than 'rules'. They are the good soil into which we can put down roots for growth into maturity and emotional health.

Without wanting to hurt or stigmatize those who struggle with relationships or suffer at the hands of inadequate parents, it therefore needs to be acknowledged that there are good and bad ways of being family, and that some patterns of living bring greater blessing than others. There is a big difference between the extremes of nurturing, support and healing through which some families guide their members to adulthood, and the coldness, destructiveness and anger which can leave others emotionally crippled for life. There is a difference between the experiences of mutuality and communal care, and those of power enforcement and oppression. What is sobering is such 'casualties' are not always from 'broken' families, or those where power is exercised in a violent way. They can be found also within those which are outwardly very stable, and orderly. Sin can affect our relationships in profoundly contrasting ways.

Complexity of Family Intimacy

The key concern of this chapter is the complex issue of intimacy within the family. For family intimacy is different from the intimacy of marriage or even friendship in that there are many relationships involved, and these are thrown together by birth, not by choice or congeniality. The complex web of related people, with their temperaments, personal histories and attitudes to one another all play into the intimacy of the family. What is more the level of intimacy is never predictable, nor is it static. Those who enjoy a close bonding with siblings or parents in younger life can find that new experiences, changes of outlook or different friendships can create their own distance later. Conversely, those who have not enjoyed warm relationships within the family during adolescence or young adulthood may well find that the gap closes with age, or the birth of grandchildren, and a new sense of belonging ferments the interchange in later years. Like any other form of human intimacy, family closeness depends on reciprocal love and commitment, as well as good communication and a constant readiness to make allowances.

The family is a dynamic institution to which people relate through vital stages of growth in their lives. For many people it can provide them with a deep sense of continuity and personal identity, because family members are usually those who have known each other for a long time. Unconditional acceptance by the ones who know us best and love us constantly in spite of all our faults, gives us messages about ourselves which communicate our deep value as human beings. They also, even inadvertently, communicate messages about God, for God too does not demand that we 'prove' ourselves but accepts us in Christ, 'just as we are'. Yet, sadly, this is not the experience of everybody in families. What is increasingly evident is that people get stuck in their relationships, and do not grow together through the various stages and changes of life. Control by power, economic threats, fear of change, inability to handle situations, or hearing things of which they disapprove can lead family members to 'close off' against each other. But when disclosure is not allowed to take place, for whatever reason, the relationships do not mature.

Because several people make up the one family nexus, inevitably there are different temperaments, and personality characteristics relating in complex twos, threes, fours or more. Each extra person means a new set of relationships within the same group, which accentuates the complexity of the family. There will therefore be different emotional needs and emotional boundaries within one family, which might not always be fully appreciated. For example, most members of a given family might jog along contentedly with functional relationships, and even take the same contentment into later bondings in life. But there might also be one member for whom the emotional component of this family is very inadequate. For that person, close intimacy is lacking. It stops at a superficial level when what is longed for is a depth of encounter which the family seems unable or unwilling to provide. The consequence of this might be that this person is less identified with home than the others. There may well be a deeper longing within that person for understanding, warmth and closeness, not because it has been present in the family but because it has been absent.

The Family as a System

The myths of individualism need to be addressed. A family is not just a collection of individuals, but from a Christian viewpoint is meant for community. That means it is always bigger than the individual members it contains. People are inevitably shaped and influenced by the groups they belong to, and in most societies the family is one of the most powerful groups in anyone's life. Every aspect of the group structure is important. So the size of family we come from is significant. So is the age distribution and where a person comes in the 'line-up', whether (s)he is an only child, the eldest, middle, youngest, and so on. The gender composition is also substantial: whether a child is the only girl in a family of boys, whether the children are all the same sex, or whether each child has a brother and a sister. All of these considerations – size, age groups, gender – will influence each person in the family. And if the family breaks up, or re-forms with additional members this inevitably increases the complexity, and the emotional implications. It is not only what parents do or say which is significant in family life. Children also come to see themselves and take their place in relation to the rest. Some interesting patterns have been identified. Studies on 'high achievers' often find them to be the eldest of their siblings, or only children; studies on gregarious or easygoing people often point to the influence of their being the youngest and having more relaxed parenting than those above them.

In addition to the 'history and geography' of the family group there are other factors. People occupy a place in a family which is more than where they come in the line-up. One might be the 'fixer' – the one we turn to for practical help in a situation. Another (very often the mother) might be the 'manager' – the one who holds the family together, both physically and emotionally. This emotional manager 'interprets' members of the family to each other – father to children, and siblings to each other. Another might be the 'socializer', who fills the house full of guests; or the 'crutch' who supports the weaker members; or the 'idler', who never takes on their share of the work. There is seemingly no end to the different parts people might play, and family members reinforce the labels whenever another piece of behaviour fits in. So the 'phone occupier' will be the one we are sure is the culprit when we try to connect with home and find the line engaged; the 'moralist' will be the one we know will take the high moral ground usually in disapproval of something we find unimportant; the 'thief' will be the one who borrows things uninvited; the 'baby' will be the one we periodically indulge or dismiss, and who may find it hard to dislodge himself or herself and grow up, and the 'problem' member will give the whole family headaches and nightmares for years to come. The labels which a family often doles out to its members, are often the ones with which those people themselves identify, even if they dislike them.

In much psychology or counselling the family is now accepted as a whole unit which needs to be considered. For example, in trying to resolve any problem with an individual person, Family Therapy addresses the family as a *system*, and it will look at the way different members of the family uphold that system through the specific and complex contributions they make. Other therapists look at the patterns of control and power in a family and at how this is maintained. For family members often collude in more than overt labelling. They can work together much more subconsciously. There are often 'underfunctioners' in families: those people who seem inept and always in need of some help; and 'overfunctioners': those who take on the responsibility for others, sometimes not leaving them enough space to develop their own capabilities. There are 'reactive' members: those whose responses are driven by anxiety or concerns; or 'passive dependants': those who wait for the initiative from others. Within any family the set of bondings, associations, and role relationships can be very complex, and kept in place by the tacit agreement of the different members. Overfunctioners, for example, may more readily show anxiety, suffer sleeplessness, or blame themselves when something goes wrong in the life of another. Others are quite likely to collude, and agree that this is where the blame lies, when in reality the problem may have a very different source. It is not surprising that many problems which occur in the lives of individual members become developed and often stuck because of the complex relational dynamics within the family as a whole. In some of the more difficult scenarios a family 'selects' one person to be the problem focus. This maintains a rigid, inadequate family structure by consensus.[5]

Peter was referred to consultation because he had problems with truancy and long bouts of sulkiness at school, whilst at home he wet the bed and refused to cooperate with homework. After one session in individual therapy, Peter's whole family was seen by a family therapist. Systematic work with the family over a period of months revealed a complex patterns of painful relationships, many of which were held in place by the father who was frustrated at work and bitterly disappointed with life. His inability to communicate this verbally to anyone at home upset and irritated his wife who was unable to understand what was wrong yet was required to provide all the right responses. Unrelated and random rows between the parents affected the three children in different ways. Whereas his brother kept distance, and his sister tried appeasement, to little avail, Peter developed his already established position of 'problem child'. By providing them with behaviour that needed addressing, and a set of quite different issues to resolve, he gave them space from relentless rowing with each other, and kept the parents together. Without being able to articulate what he was doing, Peter had, with the collusion of the whole family, taken upon himself the brunt of the family's disorder. In biblical terms he had become the scapegoat for his own and everyone else's sins. Things could only begin to change for him once he was released from this role, and the parents were able to communicate with each other and sort through their own frustrations.

In talking about families I have been referring mostly to those where children are young. But this could reinforce a misunderstanding: that the family only plays a big influence in the emotional life of its members during childhood. This is far from the case. As people grow older relationships within the family can become more influential, not less, and patterns of control, dependency, passivity and reaction may continue throughout life. Middle-aged men and women can be just as affected by relationships with their parents or siblings as people in their adolescence. Adult siblings or cousins can still tiptoe around difficult issues, or find themselves with feelings which both bind and distance themselves from each other. Mothers who are octogenarians can still be reduced to tears by a son or daughter who hurts, rejects or disappoints them. The family remains a powerful force through our whole lives, even for those people whose experience of it is limited. That is why so many big family 'celebrations' are accompanied by grief. A lifetime of misunderstandings, still unresolved, or a gnawing desire for warmth when all advances seem to be rebuffed, can settle uneasily in any room when those members are together face to face. The bonding of a family is elaborate and complicated.

The emotional power of the family extends even beyond the grave. When a close relative dies so do the possibilities that might have been. The complex mixture of regret, remorse, sorrow, joy or relief can itself leave confusion and heaviness in its wake. Even when there has been much joy in the relationship, and there is little for which to reproach ourselves, we often find ourselves remembering something which could have been better. Where there has been little joy, it can be harder. A man who had suffered humiliation, indifference and rejection from his father throughout most of his life said with feeling, 'When the old man dies I shall order a crate of champagne and drink through the night.' But he did not. Instead he plunged into a deep depression where he ached for the love which his father had once clumsily and inadequately offered him, and fisted the table in anguish that he would never be able to make that offer again.

Problems with Intimacy

Some problems with intimacy scarcely need to be spelled out. Most people who have had any experience of families will be familiar with issues like jealousy, competition for attention, refusal to cooperate, or plain bad temper which arises in most households, in particular where there are young children. And how these are handled may well feed into and shape a person's emotional life later. When the family has broken up because of the separation of the parents such problems can feel much bigger.

Step families are now less likely to result from the death of a spouse than from the re-forming of marriage ties after divorce. And a family which includes step-parents and stepchildren may have to negotiate tricky areas of access to the other parent. In *Second Chances* Wallerstein and Blakesee show how a child may need to relate to two mothers or fathers, two sets of brothers and sisters, in addition to all the extended family relations.[6] Sorting out even the most basic issues – what to call step-parents – can be a problem at first and bring a confusion of feelings which can get out of hand. There can be jealousy of being replaced in the absent parent's life by a new family, or mixed emotions which come from sharing the other parent with children to whom they are now related by remarriage. The important fact is that the changes are not simply external ones which accidentally impinge on the lives of those people in families who want to get involved. Instead, 'these new forms of extended family ties have to be established by the very persons who find themselves most directly caught up in them'.[7] Forming stable step family relations calls for great commitment and generosity. When the children are split up themselves, however, to be taken into care or separated out for adoption the feelings of loss and helplessness can be very intense.

But first families who stay intact can also have problems! In many families there are 'hot issues' which are rarely confronted, but which leave a great emotional hole in the centre of relationships. Because nothing can be said, people often tiptoe round one another in an effort to avoid what might upset or antagonize other members, with the result that it never is dealt with. In their book, *Families and How to Survive Them*, John Cleese and Robyn Skinner discuss this 'screening off' process which can arise because of taboos in the family: 'The emotions we haven't learned to handle will feel very awkward to us. So we're likely to start by trying to hide them from others and end up by concealing them even from ourselves. We "screen them off" and then we don't even realize they're there.'[8]

In a family which fears conflict or discourages the expression of anger, each member will be encouraged to 'screen off' those feelings which might result in discord. Where this attitude has been passed down from the previous generation, conflict avoidance might have become quite skilled, and reinforced by dozens of subtle behavioural characteristics from parents or others. Of course, sometimes this might produce family relationships of high amicability, where there is no hostility. But it is more likely to produce a situation where there is an ever-growing pool of submerged emotions which cannot be handled. In individual family members it can also lead to depression, to what Myra Chave-Jones calls 'frozen rage'.[9] 'Screening off', however, does not only apply to anger. Any set of attitudes, feelings or opinions which are regarded as taboo or inappropriate might well have to be avoided and replaced by good behaviour. The problem is that this need for conformity to some unspoken family *status quo* can continue for years. As Cleese observed: 'If the family disapproved of the emotion, which is why it got shoved behind the screen in the first place, when you try to bring it out – even years later – you'll find the same disapproving feelings.'[10]

The way to deal with 'hot issues' is not straightforward, especially in a family which has kept them successfully under wraps for generations. Often it is only in a crisis that they emerge, and then dealing with them can be like amputating a leg without anaesthetic. It is more likely to be the case that one or two family members feel the need to face up to the real issue; to dismantle the screen and pull the mouldering problem out into the open where it can have the care and attention it deserves. Sometimes the issue is dragged out years later, not in the family context at all, because one of its members can deny that 'screened off' emotion no longer. Yet it is never easy. There is often much shame and fear connected with disclosure. When people finally allow others to see what has always been forbidden in them, it can cause a deep crisis of identity. For what is being uprooted are those things which, as far as the family is concerned, simply are not there. Yet it is important to remember that 'it's not "difficult" emotions that cause the problems, it's denying that you have these and find them uncomfortable . . .'[11]

From a Christian position this move is vital. For if there are issues which need healing, that healing is only possible if we have first discovered what they are. It is no use treating an ulcer as though it were mild dyspepsia ('we never have ulcers in our family . . .'). Similarly, if there are things which need forgiveness, and sorting out with God, we need first to have the courage to identify those things, and to have the willingness to go through some difficult heart-searching. We cannot be forgiven for spiteful jealousy if it always masquerades as harmless rivalry ('there's never been any jealousy in our family . . .'). Until then, what lies hidden and screened off lies out of reach, yet ready to reappear in a dozen different disguises.

Anger and Intimacy

'Screening off' is only one of the ways in which family problems are not properly faced. There is an opposite scenario where families give full vent to their feelings, constantly rehearsing old rows. They become trapped into destructive patterns of attack and counter-attack with no apparent way through. Many of these patterns involve blame and recrimination which goes back years. Yet the re-raking of old injustices or betrayals never lets go of the hurt. Rows can also set the stage for expressions of deeply rooted anger.

Anger is a crucial human emotion. It can be that which eradicates oppression, fuels social change, or rails against hypocrisy. Anger at the ill-treatment of others has led to the repeal of slavery, and the outlawing of exploitative child labour. There is much anger in the Psalms when the writers cry against injustice and shout about the way evil-doers seem to prosper. There is anger in the Gospels when Jesus sees that the place where God is to be worshipped has been turned into a 'den of thieves'. In its right place anger is essential. It produces great art, clever humour, and momentous songs of protest. But when it is annexed to irritation or small-mindedness it can also fuel the most humourless, trivial bickering, or petty behaviour. Most of us know only too well the difference between the two.

Most families have their share of anger, as one or other member displays annoyance about the way (s)he is treated, or displeasure about something else. But in some families anger is a much more regular and devastating visitor. For families who live under the constant threat of domestic violence, even an apparently mild disagreement can result in severe damage to people or things and the repercussions can be formidable. A woman who has a deep submerged anger can leave her children or husband emotionally paralysed, showing anxiety in any discussion where the wrath is likely to surface again. Where it is the mother who is the explosive one, however, it is less likely that she will vent her anger by sustained and systematic physical violence. Violent fathers are both more numerous and likely to generate a more dangerous outcome, not least because their physical strength is the greater. The terrifying process of releasing pent up anger and out-of-control rage can bring fury and brutality which is frightening in its unrestraint. It is also likely that these men in turn will have been inducted into violent behaviour during their childhood or adolescence and will follow patterns of denial, refusing to face the reality of the situation. Sometimes, of course, it might have been repressed in a man, 'screened off' only to surface with devastating consequences when he becomes a husband and a father.

Very often the violence is directed only against his wife, and the first abusive onslaught might have happened early in the marriage. In some families the wife might be utterly unprepared for its savagery, having nothing in her past family relationships which could have given her any hint of what it could be like. For other women, however, it is part of a long, complex pattern, where they are no stranger to violence. Not that the reasons for this are always well understood. One writer reports:

> A woman I know married a man who used to beat her up. Then she married a man whom she abused emotionally. Now she's entangled with a man who is rude, aggressive, sometimes violent. 'Why don't you find yourself a man you actually like?' I've asked her, but I know the answer. She's living out some unconscious drama dating from her childhood. She can't live without conflict, pain, rejection. It's an expensive game.[12]

There is some truth in this comment, for childhood experiences are often taken into adulthood and can continue until they are resolved. As we noted in an earlier chapter, some women do move from one abusive relationship to another. Evidence given to women's refuges shows that many wives stay in violent marriages for years until fear for children, or one beating too many eventually drives them to separate and save what they can of sanity and self-esteem. The role of 'victim' can be one which is 'accepted' implicitly as an insidious part as the family system. Nevertheless, there is a very dangerous misunderstanding here too. This writer implies, even subconsciously, that women are the ones to blame when they are persistently the victims of intemperate and violent partners. It is their 'need' for conflict and punishment that locks them into abusive situations. This distorts the understanding of the dynamics of family violence. For so long as the focus remains on women – whether on their victimization, supposed inadequacy, 'unconscious dramas', or passivity – the onus of the problem will never rest where it belongs. And when similar claims are made for the violence enacted on children, we are perilously close to justifying aggression by blaming the victim. Yet the real issue in cases of family violence is the culture of destructive power which is all too often passed down through the generations. The result is anger-driven brutality which is the very opposite of intimacy and the ultimate expression of defeat.

Although it is not impossible for a family caught up in such tragic patterns of pain to survive, it is extremely unlikely that it can ultimately break the bondage to violence without help. To start with, the silence which is usually at the heart of the family must be broken. This means that other people will inevitably have to be drawn in: those who are competent to work through the problems with the family, the couple, and with the abuser alone. The wider context of relationships which surrounds the couple is also important. The problem may need to be disclosed to a few close friends. It will need support and understanding from others. It will need a place of safety for those who are in danger, and a persistence and hope for the relationship despite the pain. Above all it needs from the abuser a full acknowledgement of his problem, and the sustained *will* to change. From my own observations it is often only when power and strength of a very different kind replaces the violence and destruction that healing begins. For the family is not simply a *creational* structure, made by God and now deeply affected by the sin and brokenness of human life. It is also a *redemptive* structure. It can be brought back into new relationships whatever depths of guilt and suffering have gone before. But it is usually only when people are prepared to harness the Holy Spirit of God to break the bondage of years that hope becomes a slow reality and new life can be found.

Relationships within the Family

Within the complex system of family relationships, pairs of bondings stand out as especially significant. Parent-child relationships often take on sets of characteristics which seem to 'belong' to the specific pair and not to others. Mother/daughter, father/son, father/daughter, mother/son all have different dynamics and nuances which have been the subject of much study. Many novels have explored these relationships: novels such as D. H. Lawrence's *Sons and Lovers*, which focuses on a man and his powerful tie to his mother; or Steinbeck's *East of Eden*, which tells the story of a strict father and the son who longs to please him. Contemporary biographies and anthologies draw out father/daughter relationships and how they affect an understanding of womanhood and self. Yet of all of these pairs it is probably the mother/daughter relationship which has received most attention in recent years, not least because of the considerable feminist involvement in the subject.

Mothers and Daughters

Nancy Friday's best-selling book, *My Mother My Self*, first published in the 1970s and reissued ten years later, spoke to two generations of women about themselves and their mothers. She analysed the extent to which mothers remain influential in the lives of their daughters and how so much of a woman's life involves coming to terms with that relationship with her mother. Unearthed were processes by which women learn to deny their feelings, and the driving power of ideologies of mother-love, along with the difficulties for daughters in accepting the independent existence of their mothers. A decade later Harriet Goldhor Lerner entitled one of her own chapters 'Our Mother/Her Mother/Our self' and wrote of the 'deep, inexplicable and ambivalent bond' which connects daughter and mother. The ambivalence is evident in the way we respond to predicaments. 'We may still be blaming our mother, trying to change or fix her, or we may still be keeping our emotional distance. We may be absolutely convinced that our mother is "impossible", that we have tried to improve things and nothing works.'[13]

For these American writers, the mother/daughter issues in the 1970s and 1980s highlighted some key enigmas. The first was how to cope with generational differences between women who lived within an almost entirely domestic context and those who have grown up to expect independence and a personal career. A second was the crucial issue of negotiating 'separateness',[14] where daughters found it far more difficult than sons to differentiate their own identity from that of their mothers. A third issue was that of understanding and dealing with maternal guilt, which was experienced in different ways by both daughter and mother. The issue of guilt provided a strong link with much other feminist writing because it explored the whole social context of mothering. 'Our mothers have let us all down because they have lived with impossible and crippling expectations about their role . . . Guilt is woven into the very fabric of womanhood.' That is why mother-guilt was never seen as the personal problem of individual women. Rather, 'It stems naturally from a society which assigns mothers the primary responsibility for all family problems, excuses men from real fathering and provides remarkably little support for the actual needs of children and families.'[15]

In the 1990s, many of these preoccupations have shifted, especially those stemming from the generational changes. Now, those women who are beginning work, or getting married, or starting out in a long-term relationship are far less likely to have been raised right through to adulthood by full-time homemakers. Probably, daughters will have watched their mothers go back to work, negotiate complex timetables, manage a home and family, and have expectations of a greater domestic participation from their husbands. Many daughters may have shared study space in the home with their mothers, or swapped worries over job interviews and career possibilities. Mothers may have their own stories of sexual harassment at work, or experiences of difficult choices. The great gap in lifestyles is now much smaller and more easily bridged. More contemporary worries are about the lack of time to continue a meaningful relationship through other pressures. As daughters may live at a distance from mothers the problems of separating geographically are far less acute than the problems of being able to find the time and energy to get together.

Yet in other areas far less seems to have changed. Although they may be more muted, issues of emotionally separating, issues of guilt and the complex nature of mothering are still evident, and the work of Nancy Chodorow, Dorothy Dinnerstein and Lillian Rubin offers perennial insight.[16] The suggestion is that mothers relate differently to their sons and daughters, recognizing, often unconsciously, that sons will need space to develop a male identity. But daughters are the same sex, and therefore this distancing does not take place. That is why letting go of a deep inner dependency on a mother can be a continuing struggle for a woman, for women are more likely than their brothers to have problems with separating. Consequently, the internal pressure to see, evaluate and experience ourselves through the eyes of our mothers can remain long after other pressures have disappeared.

Margo's mother was excessively anxious about food. She had a long list of forbidden everyday items which she would never serve up to anyone, because she had read in one of her articles that they could produce allergies. Her kitchen regime involved regular sterilization and scrupulous food preparation, and Margo's robust health was attributed to an absence of all banned substances. The few occasions when she had been sick had resulted in some other food being taken off the list, irrespective of the ailment.

Margo took her mother's detailed regime into her own marriage to Thomas. At first he found the various obsessions amusing. But as time went on, and children came, he became irritated with the way his mother-in-law's odd ideas had such influence over what his family ate. As a pharmacist he had little time for pseudo-science and failed to see why Margo invariably accepted her mother's version of reality, rather than his own. He finally negotiated a settlement where he and Margo should share the shopping and cooking, and each be free to cook what they wanted. Although Margo was unhappy and anxious about the agreement, she had little choice because of her teaching job. The arrangement seemed to work until Larry, their youngest son, became ill. Receiving a troubled phone call from her daughter, Margo's mother diagnosed that it was the food.

The heart of the problem in the family was, of course, nothing to do with eating. It was about Margo's relationship with her mother. For all of her childhood she had imbibed strong maternal attitudes, which her passive father had never challenged but simply ignored. Not that Margo's mother was a dominant person in other ways. She had given Margo every encouragement to develop her own talents and career. Her anxieties over health went back to her own family, where her parents' incessant bronchial and stomach diseases had eclipsed the sunny warmth of childhood. Helpless to do anything about the illnesses then had left her determined to do everything she could in the future. All of this was now wrapped up in the relationship with Margo who, without understanding their source, felt the fierce power of her mother's attitudes.

It was not at the level of rational acceptance, therefore, that Margo was functioning, but at the level of needing to affirm and somehow compensate for something to her mother. She needed also to be sure of her mother's approval and not to be the source of further concern and worry. She probably knew somewhere subconsciously that 'a daughter's "declaration of independence" can be especially hard for a mother who may feel she has nothing – not even a self – to return to after her children have grown.'[17] Meanwhile, she was passing on the same anxieties over food and health to her own children, and incurring the continued irritation of her husband. Until she could properly differentiate herself from her mother, and have space to form her own attitudes she was stuck. Unless she could work through to her own self-identity, she would be unable to properly handle relationships with any of them.

It is not only those women who are overly influenced by their mothers who find it hard to 'separate'. Women who are fighting their mothers, blaming them, keeping their distances or manoeuvring cautiously around them are all likely to be facing the same fundamental problem. For as long as our mothers are to blame or impossible to relate to we still have not grown into our own identity. But when we are confident about who we are, we can bring that self into a new relationship and take the first step towards a mature intimacy.

Sometimes the problems are less with a daughter separating than with the need to come to terms with a mother's differentiation from her. Many women find it hard to see their mothers as developing persons themselves, with need for open affirmation and encouragement. Nancy Friday shows how women's reluctance to accept their mothers' sexuality may lead to being both embarrassed and confused by it. The mother role is not one which can be allowed to be overshadowed by anything else. Sometimes women know little of the emotional experiences or the influences which have directed their mothers in their early lives. But it is only when mothers too are allowed a separate identity that daughters can 'reconnect' with them and share their lives together as two distinct people with personal histories of their own.

The writings of therapists provide us with strong insights into the problems of detachment and separateness which daughters and mothers often experience in relation to each other. So does the modern novel. In her Booker-prizewinning *Moon Tiger* Penelope Lively's main character, Claudia, is a strong, talented and dominant woman, with one daughter, Lisa. Even though Claudia is now elderly, sick, and at the end of her life the relationship is not able to move forward. The dynamics between the two have never fully matured, never opened up into intimacy.

For Claudia has never seen Lisa detached from Claudia. Lisa is extinguished by Claudia, always has been; even now, in the alien, dispassionate hospital room she sits warily, awaiting Claudia's next move. Claudia snuffs Lisa out – drains the colour from her cheeks, deprives her of speech, or at least all speech to which anyone might pay attention, makes her shrink an inch or two, puts her in her place. The other Lisa is not like that. The other Lisa, the Lisa unknown to Claudia, is positive while not assertive, is prettier, sharper, a good cook, a competent mother, an adequate if not exemplary wife.

Lisa talking to Claudia tells her mother what she wants her to know in a perfunctory way, and reflects on what she does not tell her:

> 'Well', says Lisa. 'It was the boys' half-term last weekend so Harry took them to a rugger match. And on Saturday night we all went to the theatre – the RSC *King Lear*. Very good. And dinner after at Rules – a treat for Tim's birthday. And . . . um . . . let's see . . .'

> And on Monday morning I visited the man who has been my lover for four years now and of whom you know nothing nor ever will. Not because you would disapprove, but because you would not. And since I was a small child I have hidden things from you: a silver button found on a path, a lipstick pilfered from your handbag, thoughts, feelings, opinions, intentions, my lover. You are not, as you think, omniscient. You do not know everything; you certainly do not know me.[18]

Lisa hates both her mother's pride and her lack of interest in her. She also despises her liberal attitudes which make no distinction between what is moral and what is not. But Lisa is still living with the older woman's attitudes and ideas. She is the trapped daughter of her mother. She has not been able to let go of her mother's forceful power and it still dominates the way she thinks and reacts. Even in rejecting her mother's assessment she cannot help but relate to it. Lisa can largely go her own way, but the relationship is a defeat.

Coming to full maturity is to accept one's own personal identity as a human being, and to accept that of other people. In Christian terms it is to recognize that our identity lies not in our identification with our mother, or any other family member, but in our relationship with God. It is to recognize and own our twin needs of separateness and bonding, and not to be engulfed by either one of them. In that context we are then able to assess who we are, and come to terms with where we need to change. We are then able to acknowledge for ourselves where our responsibilities lie. And for those women who have managed to rework strong, adult mother-daughter relationships, anything else seems easy!

Fathering

The place of the father in a family has often been grossly under-estimated. In the past it has so often received scant attention, and where there has been any focus it has usually been to identify fathers with discipline and decision-making. This was extolled at length by some Christian writers in the 1970s, often from the utterly mistaken assumption that this marked the Christian family out from the more worldly version. In reality it merely reinforced the secular stereotypes. Central tasks of nurturing and care were offloaded on to mothers, and fathers were warned against bathing the toddlers for this could seriously impair their gender identity: little boys would grow up not knowing what it was to be a man.[19] The result was that generations of children found mother as their only nurturer and became emotionally isolated from their fathers.

Decades on, we are wiser. We now know that the father's relationship with both sons and daughters is crucial in the development of a strong sense of self-worth. Attentiveness, a preparedness to listen, readiness to be involved with the details of a child's day convey messages which cannot be expressed in any other way. Problems within adolescence are far less intense when a father has already put quality nurturing into his child's life, and become a friend. For the message that one is important enough for a father to be around is in itself a massive confidence booster. And a family intimacy in which the father takes full part is the strongest foundation for good relationships in the rest of life.

Yet though we might know this, it is less easy to put it into practice. Many men still feel at a loss in the key areas of close family relationships. For they were often raised themselves by absentee fathers, whether the absence was physical or emotional. And today, men who are too career-involved to be at home much with their children communicate negative signals. The conclusion that one is less important than work, conferences or colleagues can be easily drawn by children whose fathers are regularly away.

It might be inaccurate, but it can be hard to dispel. A friend whose wife was driving him to work was horrified to hear his four-year-old son say to their visitor, 'And this is where daddy lives.' Harriet Lerner shares the popular joke in her profession about the psychoanalyst's son who says he wants to be 'a patient' when he grows up. ' "That way," the small boy explains, "I'll get to see my father five times a week!" '[20] But as the years continue and a child's father is still absent, the gap between them can become a chasm. For the times when he is available are likely to be times of silence, stilted conversation, or criticism. Because now the parent is in the company of those he hardly knows, and who do not know him. Before there can be mutual trust and real communication some painful re-evaluating might be necessary.

One key role in a father's nurturing is the affirmation of his children's sexuality. Especially as they move into puberty both daughter and son need to know that their sexual development is acceptable, and they are not becoming repulsive. Sadly, puberty is often the very time when many fathers retreat from physical intimacy, particularly with their sons because of an unspoken fear of encouraging homosexuality. So the boy who enjoyed a father's lap, and being hugged and kissed finds that at thirteen this pattern is not continued. It is not surprising if the message he unconsciously picks up is that there is something wrong with growing up. In fact this is a vital time in a boy's development for him to receive uncomplicated bodily affection from his father. Far from confusing his sexual identity it will contribute significantly to his development of secure masculinity.

A daughter too needs physical affection and endorsement during puberty, and to know also that the sexual boundaries will be fully respected. The way her father treats her mother will be very important in establishing this. If for his wife there is physical disrespect, or coldness, the attention the girl receives from her father will be problematic and unwelcome. When she knows that her mother is secure in her father's love and commitment, this is more likely to reflect on her own sense of value. Generous admiration, trust and approval, along with sensitivity from her father to her often inexplicable mood swings are of crucial importance to an adolescent. So is the recognition that there are no 'no-go' areas in conversation, that things can be talked through and feelings expressed. As with her brother, the regard and respect with which she is treated now will be crucial in her growth into maturity, self-esteem and acceptance.

Sibling Love

Love between sisters can be amongst the most intimate love which is on offer. Those who have shared so much of their early lives together, and confided their secrets and their stories are quite likely to keep in touch throughout a lifetime. Relationships between brothers usually take a different shape, and yet these also can remain close and committed whatever the geographical distance. Relationships between a brother and sister though frequently deep are inevitably more complex, for they carry within them many of the nuances of male-female relationships, as well as those of mother-son and age issues.

Any of these sets of relationship can run into problems, however. Issues or attitudes which are not resolved when the siblings were sharing a family home can be carried into adulthood and dominate the relationship for years to come.

In Shere Hite's *Report on the Family* she recounts

> 83 per cent of girls with brothers say their mother was often 'nicer', granted more freedom and privileges to their brothers than to them. Three quarters of young women now in their teens and twenties say their mother gave their brothers the right not to do dishes, more rights to go out of the house, more privacy and freedom ('You can't force him, he's a man, after all!')[21]

Often these attitudes mature over time and can be remembered with humour. Sometimes they do not and old, forgotten disputes can re-emerge later when some new crisis or change hits the family. There is a big difference, however, between the way people handle deep problems with siblings and the way they handle them with parents. By and large most people keep up some contact with parents and leave any problems on permanent hold, whereas they are far more likely simply to retreat from siblings and stay out of their lives altogether.

This raises some important issues. I have heard many people over the years say, 'I have no contact with my brother (sister). We have never got along, and I'm not really interested in finding out how (s)he is.' The lack of contact can continue for years, punctuated only by the next family wedding or funeral when some inexplicable family bond draws them together. Some even insist that their sibling means nothing to them. They are better without them.

In fact this is a common confusion. It is quite likely that such people do 'manage' better by keeping their distance from a brother or sister. But this is rarely because they mean nothing to them. It is more because the brother or sister means *too* much to them, that the feelings are too intense to be able to cope with the rows, misunderstandings and anxiety. And so the safest thing to do is to go for 'cut-off' and keep distance in the hope that these emotions will go away. It is preferable to the high level of anxiety which accompanies seeing one another and being confronted by what we think we know about each other.

So keeping distance is often nothing to do with an absence of feeling. For many people it is simply a way of managing potential emotional stress. Sibling love is very complex, because it is being forged often during difficult periods in people's lives. Dislike, envy, jealousy, blame, anger can become overlaid; attitudes of parents may well have rubbed off, as may struggles over power. It takes courage to take the first step towards a new, more open relationship, precisely because much of the past can be bound up together. Deciding for sibling intimacy can be a demanding choice, but life is impoverished without it.

Conclusion

Family intimacy is one of the deepest gifts from God, breathed into creation, for human sustenance and well-being. But, like all of life, it has become contaminated by sin. Family brokenness, anger, distance, hurt, violence and cut-off feelings all distort the meaning of family love and deprive us of its strength and power. That is why we need so much to hear the Christian message of redemption for the family. For the death and resurrection of Christ were not just historic events which began a church. They are good news for the family today. They announce that the way is open for reconciliation and new life, and this new life can touch all our relationships, even those which have been the most defeated by brokenness.

The relationship between parents and children has lifelong consequences. It begins in the quality of the marriage relationship itself. For the greatest gift a parent can give a child is to love the other parent. It is that love which puts down the foundation for most other areas of intimacy. Love, warmth, closeness, security and acceptance all communicate values which are essential for our growth as whole persons. They tell us about who we are and how much we matter. They tell us about the reality of God and the love of Christ. They enable us to help the generations yet to come to live in ways which are loving and not destructive. In a Christian sense intimacy within the family ultimately always reaches out beyond itself. For it knows something of God's love for the whole world, and has to be expressed in care and concern for other human beings who also need to be loved.

12

Finding Intimacy

I have come to the conclusion that human intimacy is only fulfilled when it transcends itself by means of a personal relationship with God.

Pat Collins

It is not that we have banned intimacy from the West. We have simply tried to take it over, putting up a sign saying 'Under New Management'. We have wanted to make it serve us, oil our wheels of commerce, keep the systems going. Or we have taken it into a cult of self and, bowing down before our own image, have made it into a religion. We have doled it out in small rations for good children or copied it for Mills and Boon to put on market stalls in cheap paperbacks. We have claimed it, sold it, reshaped it and abused it. And then we wonder why it cannot satisfy us.

The problem is that our culture has failed to recognize that ultimately intimacy comes from God. It is not something which we can command at whim, or buy and sell on the open market. It is given to us along with our humanness and is an intrinsic reminder of who we are. Made in the image of God, we need closeness with others in order to express and experience our personhood. And the God who calls us into being, the God who is relationship and love, also calls us into community. In community we are simultaneously taken out of ourselves and fully become ourselves. For we are and always will be persons-in-relationship; not on our own, not of our own making and not accountable to our individual wills.

This message must come again and again into the consumer-bound postmodern society which would deny the integrity of our humanness, and offer us cheap and worthless solutions to the deep longings of the human heart. It must speak to all those who grow up in a culture of loneliness, who do not reach out to others in love, but fill their lives with things which give them substitute meaning. The message is an urgent one, for with each passing year of these substitutes, real intimacy becomes ever more difficult to achieve.

The relationships of family, friendship, marriage, neighbourliness and fellowship are all God's gift to human life, and will continue to provide a context for intimacy as long as human society survives. Yet each of these relationships themselves must respond to the meaning of community. The biblical covenantal norms of troth, commitment, faithfulness and love are not options which we can discard for self-interest and still make our relationships work. They are what structure and define them, and breathe life into them. It is important to remember, though, that life-breathing is a dynamic process, not a static acceptance of rules. Marriages which become stuck in resentment, boredom, or a weary lack of affection may be faithful sexually, but they are still a long way from fulfilling the biblical norm. Friendships may observe the rules of congeniality but lack the openness and trust which gives them depth. Whatever the relationship there has to be the movement and growth which signifies that it is truly alive. There has to be the sense too of the *uniqueness* of this relationship: that it is not reduced to another, or treated in a cavalier fashion which robs it of its own identity and being.

Intimacy and the Church

The channel through which we learn about God, the Bible and therefore about intimacy is, in principle, the church. Yet ironically, churches have themselves been slow to grasp the relevance of biblical truth for our intimate lives. Their vision has too often been a narrow one, preferring the predictability of worship and sermonizing to trying to grapple with the meaning of God's love in a postmodern world. That is usually because our Christian priorities are elsewhere. A bigger worry is when our Christian faith is also elsewhere, drawn away into 'churchiness', or internal wrangling, rather than centred on the God whom we profess to worship. Reflecting on North America, Ronald Rolheiser discloses his own concern about this.

God and religion are given the same type of status and importance as is given to the royal family in England, namely they are the symbolic anchor for a certain way of life but they are hardly important in its day-to-day functioning. It is not that this is bad, it is just that one does not see much evidence that anyone is actually all that interested in God . . . Too much evidence suggests that moral philosophies, human instinct and a not so disguised self interest are more important in motivating [our] activities than are a love and a gratitude that stem from a personal relationship to a living God. Hence God is not only often absent in our marketplaces, he is also frequently absent from our religious activities (and religious fervour) as well.

This suggests . . . that there is more than a little unbelief among us believers. God is a hangover, a neurosis, a calling card, a religion, a cause . . . and only rarely a living, informing, comforting, challenging person whose reality dwarfs that of our everyday world.[1]

Without the living and challenging God at the very centre of our faith we cannot begin to understand the meaning of love or how that love relates to the rest of our lives today. We cannot experience the compassion of Christ or comprehend how the message of the cross can liberate people from the deepest forms of imprisonment. We cannot grasp the power of the Spirit and allow that power to bring encouragement and solace to those who are experiencing pain and loneliness in their lives. Without the intimacy of God in the very centre of our church life, we cannot take Christ's hope and redemption to a hurting world. Instead we are merely caught up in judgementalism or platitudes.

Judgementalism and platitudes are in fact the springs of two different traps into which many churches have fallen, both in Britain and the United States. For example, churches have often become locked inside moralism, ritualism, and otherworldiness, with the bulk of their energy consumed in maintaining a subculture. So the crucial vision of listening and speaking to people in the wider secular culture, and carrying to them the life-giving strength of the Christian gospel has not been grasped. Or churches have become self-indulgent and narcissistic, paying little heed to authentic biblical living and ready to embrace whatever feels important to our identity needs. Such a church is 'a supermarket for individuals in search of therapies, rather than the covenant community of God's people described in the Bible'.[2]

Neither of these options comes close to the biblical picture of the redemptive community of the church. For the church in the New Testament letters and Acts is that community which is to practice *koinonia*, to break down barriers between people, to call the scornful to repentance, and to draw believers into lives of integrity and grace. The church as a worshipping community is to bear testimony to God's love for the world in the reconciling life and death of Jesus Christ, and to live that out in its concern for truth and justice. Those who bear that testimony are called to worship and to live as sisters and brothers, who have deep claims on each other. For the way we relate to each other will not only enrich our own lives but will bear a much greater testimony to the reality of the Christian faith than will any preaching on its own. 'They will know that we are his disciples by the way we love one another,' writes the apostle John. So if the words we use in communication are undermined by the lack of respect and honour for others within the church our message will be compromised. If Christ's love is not demonstrated in power by the community that bears his name, then the secular unbeliever has the right to ignore our lofty words and eloquent cadences.

In the New Testament model, love within the church is therefore to be real, visible and accountable. It is to operate at a practical level of care and compassion – binding up the broken, supporting the poor, feeding the hungry, comforting the bereaved – for our quality of care for those in the church mirrors the reality of our love for God. 'If a brother or sister lacks daily food and one of you says to them "Go in peace, keep warm and eat your fill," and yet do not supply their bodily needs what is the good of that?' demands the apostle James. And in his own letter John adds, 'let us love, not in word or speech but in truth and action.'[3] But we are also to love at the level of identification, trying to understand the pain, suffering, temptations or joy in the life of another. Being available for those who need us is often the hardest and most neglected aspect of Christian living today, and yet without such availability the church will never be able to demonstrate the reality of Christ's life to the world.[4]

Therefore there is a crucial place for the church in the intimacy lives of believers. Whilst it is not required to be a place of close friendship it is to be a *place of listening*. We have to be ready to hear those who have hardly known where to turn with the grief, pain and emptiness of a broken relationship, rather than greeting their hesitant disclosures with superficial embarrassed responses or moralistic clichés. A Christian fellowship is challenged to be ready to open its heart to women who have 'fallen in love' with other women, or whose husbands are abusers or whose children are on drugs. For so often these people find it easier to leave the church, rather than share their pain and struggle with those who sit in the pews beside them. We can no longer insist that disturbing issues of a personal and private nature must be left at the church door when people come to worship. For the effects of this have often been disastrous. Not only have the unchurched been further distanced, but many Christians also have been left bereft, lonely and unable to seek help.

Sometimes we need help with listening. At a big church houseparty we led, we broke the old lecture-questions mould and asked people simply to reflect on their life at the age of sixteen: their family, school, work, what they looked like, their clothes, their friends, how they spent their time and so on. Then in groups of six they were each to tell their stories. It was an amazing eye-opener. In this church of widely mixed age groups and an enormous variety of backgrounds there came stories of anxiety, fear, breakdown, courage and hilarity, and the real histories of its members unfolded themselves in an atmosphere of growing curiosity, sharing and trust. The young and the old listened in rapt interest to one another's personal disclosures, and many of those who had never dared to share feelings of any depth found themselves slowly liberated. In the Bible reading and prayer time afterwards there was real thanksgiving and celebration for each other, and for the amazing power of God's love.

The church is also to be a *place of acceptance and encouragement*. There needs to be recognition in fact that struggles and brokenness are part of the normal Christian life. The Christian faith does not inoculate anyone from pain, emotional confusion and conflict, although it does give us grounds for hope and persistence. For the body of Christ is not divided into the 'problem people' and the 'successful' rest. To be human is to suffer, if not at this very moment, then at some stage in our lives. And this suffering comes despite or even because of our faith. Christians struggling with the temptation of adultery, with a promiscuous homosexual lifestyle or with the pain of betrayal might suffer even more, because they know what is required of them if they are to stay faithful to the gospel. The difference for the Christian is that we can have confidence that we never struggle on our own, but that the Holy Spirit of God is with us in every contest against the pain and brokenness of our world.

Then the church is to be a *place of compassion*. It needs to break rank with everything in our society that speaks of self-interest and look beyond its own doors at the hurting world. In the light of our contemporary fragmenting culture it is not enough simply to defy the critics and carve out for ourselves relationships where we feel comfortable. Greg Smith points to a more biblical alternative:

> Post-modern society, which tends to network only with people who share a common interest, does not match up well to Christ's ideal of neighbourly love. While we have more opportunity than ever before to engage in personal face-to-face community across the ethnic and social boundaries that divide our world, we retreat instead into our ghettos of family, race, ethnicity, social class, gender, religion, shared leisure pursuits and password-protected cyberspace. In doing so we fail to recognize and respond to human need or to hear the cry of the oppressed for justice, and we cut ourselves off from our own humanity and from God.[5]

There are some churches and Christian organizations who have responded to this call. They will be found working in community care, or on behalf of the homeless, organizing food aid, developing family and young people's projects, or running day centres. One church I know supports an incest survivors' group, another staffs a Christian hostel for young ex-offenders. For far more churches still, addressing the relational needs of others made in God's image should not be an optional extra in the Christian life, but an integral part of our service of God.

The church is also to be a *place of redemption and healing*. So many people are stuck in their search for intimacy because they have not known forgiveness in their lives, and because they have not forgiven themselves for things they hate. But the very heart of the Christian faith is the truth of *grace*, that God in Christ forgives utterly those who call to God in repentance. There is no question of whether we are morally upright, faithful friends, loving partners or exemplary parents. The past can be left behind and we can begin to experience the reality of Christ's words, that he makes 'all things new'. Redemption is available, whatever the condition.

Yet although receiving forgiveness and being brought into renewed relationship with God is effective the very moment we ask for it, healing and redemption in our relationships may take much longer. When we go to hospital for life-saving surgery we may have the diseased part of us cut out and know that all is now well, we will live. But healing by its very nature cannot be rushed. It needs time, and we need care. Our wounds will have to be cleaned and dressed. Our bodies will need rest. Other anxieties will have to be taken off our shoulders. In time we will realize that what happened in the operating room was indeed effective, and now we are whole. But in between, the pain might be as great as ever.

Churches are often very good at clarifying where we need surgery, but are much more impatient in coping with the long-term nursing. They also often confuse the two. A person who comes to God may need to be forgiven for hatred or resentment. But they may also need healing for what they have suffered, whether it is abuse, loss, neglect or just lack of love. The two must be diagnosed aright. Treating abuse, for example, as though it were a barrier between that person and God, rather than an area of their life which is calling out for God's love and deep soothing, can bring harm not blessing. A Christian support network needs to be a place of safety where wounds can be examined without fear, and where anxieties can be voiced and defeat shared. This is nothing profoundly radical. It is almost two thousand years since St Paul pointed out that for Christians to show patience, kindness, gentleness, and peace is simply to live with the fruit of God's Spirit.

Finally, if the church is to help people in the search for intimacy it needs to operate as the *body of Christ*. The image of body is used many times in the New Testament letters,[6] and sums up the deep interconnectedness which members of the church are to have with each other. 'Body' is very different from 'hierarchy'. It means that all are important and needed, all must work in cooperation with the rest, all must be given the space to develop their own gifts and all must stay related to the 'head of the body', Christ himself. And membership of the body cuts across every background, culture, ethnicity, and relationship – not negating nor replacing them, but drawing them together. So, for example, Christian believers who are married are both brother and sister as well as husband and wife. Children in a believing family are also brother or sister to their father and mother in addition to being sons and daughters. And whatever authority structures exist within the work or educational context, within the body of Christ these are not to take prior place. That is why St Paul was ready to entreat the wealthy Philemon to treat his fugitive slave Onesimus as a brother. It would not bring social equality, but it would recognize their parity of status before God.[7]

The church then is neither a circle of intimate friends, nor a welfare agency, but the church, and as the church it has a vital part to play in people's lives. Both in what it believes and how it lives, it needs to demonstrate that God is the source of intimacy and to help people break down those barriers which cut them off from others. And the way it is called to do this is through love. It has to be a living denial of what Jonathan Swift said nearly three hundred years ago: 'We have just enough religion to make us hate, but not enough to make us love one another.'

Conclusion

The need for intimacy is not a new discovery at the end of the second millennium. It is intrinsic to being human. Human beings are created for intimacy, to know and to be known, to love and be loved. The relationships studied in this book give us a glimpse of the breadth of that love, and of the varieties of ways in which it can be expressed. Whether in friendship or sisterly affection, in marriage or neighbourly care, in collegiality or sexual closeness, in fellowship or fatherhood, human society offers us great opportunities to fulfil our created need for closeness with each other. What is important is that we recognize that these relationships are not random and chaotic. They are structured, normatively, so that there is a shape to the intimacy within each, and that our freedom to love entails the need to respect the boundaries.

I have not only wrestled with intimacy as a created structure in this book. The presence of sin and brokenness has been an inescapable theme. Breaking down barriers, and letting go the pain of the past is essential if we are to know liberty in our walk with others. At its most basic level this might involve working through layers of misunderstanding and problems with communication. At its deepest it might mean allowing ourselves to be transformed, almost remade, into those who are able to love and respond to the promptings of love.

I believe this is now a pressing task. For although the need for intimacy is not new, the depth of the search for intimacy is new to our present age. For we live in a world which makes it hard to live fully as a human being, to be rooted in relationship, to experience interdependence as a normal way of life. Competitiveness and suspicion cut us off from each other. Commercialism reduces our value. And even though an increasing impersonality may be inevitable in the development of global technology and international communication, if it defines the way we live our intimacy lives it will increase our loneliness.

Yet our longing for love will not go away, because it is given to us by God. And a wonderful interlocking circle becomes unavoidable when we think about love. It begins with and constantly returns to God. For God is love. But love cannot exist on its own. It presupposes a relationship.[8] And the intimacy of relationship is at the very heart of God. There is a community between the Father, Son and the Spirit. That community is love. But this same God has designed *us*, made us, shaped us, and loved us into being. We are to be called 'God's image'. So love too is part of our own identity. And it is love which calls us back into relationship with God.

To know God is, therefore, to know the source and the meaning of intimacy. It is to begin to know ourselves, to find a home for our identity. And we can know God in a hundred different ways, for God does not hide from us. God is beyond creation yet can be experienced within it, for God's presence is everywhere. In the life and the words of Jesus, in the power and warmth of the Spirit, in the Scriptures, in prayer, in worship, in truth, in community, in the created world, in other people, in healing, in loving, in forgiving, in my parents, my child, my friend, my sister, my husband, myself – God is here. And when we draw close to God, we tap into that great source of intimacy which will sustain us and take us into deeper relationships with others.

Love is not an option for human beings, it is a requirement. It is the most profound statement of who we are. But in this world our love will always be incomplete. Our intimacy will always be partial.

For we are contending with brokenness and sin, which can hurt and destroy. In the words of St Paul, we are looking through a glass darkly, but one day we shall be face to face. Yet though the glass is dark it still reflects; it still tells us whose image we bear; it shows us that we are made in love. It is only when we give ourselves up to that love that we can come to know who we are, and all we can be. In the closeness of intimacy we begin to have faces.

Notes

1 Longings for Closeness

1. Dale Spender, *Man-Made Language* (London: Routledge & Kegan Paul, 1985), p. 6.
2. Edgar N. Jackson, *Understanding Loneliness* (London: SCM Press, 1980), p. ix.
3. Jacquelyn B. Carr, *Crisis in Intimacy* (California: Brooks/Cole, 1988), p. 3.
4. Richard Winter, *The Roots of Sorrow* (London: Marshall Morgan & Scott, 1985).
5. See Sue Atkinson's excellent book, *Climbing Out of Depression* (Berkhamsted: Lion Publishing, 1983) for understanding and help in this area.
6. Kathleen R. Fischer and Thomas N. Hart, *Promises to Keep* (London: Triangle, 1992), p. 13.
7. Mike Mason, *The Mystery of Marriage* (Portland, Oregon: Marc Europe, 1985), p. 117.

2 Intimacy and the Public World

1. Henri Nouwen, *Reaching Out* (New York: Doubleday, 1975), p. 19.
2. James Olthius, *Keeping Our Troth* (London: Harper & Row, 1986), p. 5.
3. Anthony Storr, *Solitude* (Portland, Oregon: Flamingo, 1989), p. 14.
4. Ronald Rolheiser, *The Restless Heart* (London: Hodder & Stoughton, 1988). p. 18.
5. E. F. Schumacher, *Small is Beautiful* (London: Sphere, 1974), p. 34.
6. Kenneth Baker, *The Times* (London, September 1991).
7. Olthius, *Keeping Our Troth*, p. 3.
8. *Key Data, 1993/94 Edition* (Central Statistical Office, H.M.S.O).
9. *Social Trends* (Central Statistical Office, H.M.S.O., 1993).
10. Jill Radford, *The Wandworth Study*.

11. Hammer and Saunders, 'Blowing the Cover of the Protective Male: A Community Study of Violence to Women', in E. Gamarnikov et al., *The Public and the Private* (London: Heinemann, 1983).
12. Olthius, *Keeping Our Troth*.

3 Intimacy and the Private World

1. A lengthier analysis of public and private is in Elaine Storkey, *What's Right With Feminism* (London: SPCK, 1985), chapter 8.
2. Mason, *The Mystery of Marriage*, p. 117.
3. Anthony Giddens, *Modernity and Self Identity* (Cambridge: Polity Press, 1992), p. 7.
4. Michael Schofield, *The Sexual Behaviour of Young People* (London: Longman, 1965).
5. Christine Farrell, *My Mother Said . . .* (London: Routledge & Kegan Paul, 1978).
6. Kaye Wellings, Julia Field, Anne M. Johnson and Jane Wadsworth, *Sexual Behaviour in Britain: The National Survey of Sexual Lifestyles and Attitudes* (Harmondsworth: Penguin, 1994). See chapters 2 and 3.
7. *Social Trends* (Central Statistical Office, H.M.S.O., 1994), vol. 24.
8. Carol Smart, *The Ties that Bind* (London: Routledge & Kegan Paul, 1984).
9. Gillian Hanscombe and Jack Forster, *Lesbian Mothers* (London: Sheba Feminist Publishers 1982), p. 153.
10. Ibid., p. 16.
11. Mary Stewart Van Leeuwen in her analysis of homosexuality in *Gender and Grace* (Leicester: IVP, 1990), pp. 224–7.
12. Jack Babuscio, *We Speak for Ourselves* (London: SPCK, 1988), p. 25.
13. Ibid., p. 124.
14. Clarence Tripp, 'Can Homosexuals Change with Psychotherapy?', 1977, quoted in Babuscio, *We Speak for Ourselves*, p. 126. Seventeen years later Julian Haffner repeats the point in what he mistakenly claims to be a radical, new book: *The End of Marriage: Why Monogamy Isn't Working* (London: Century, 1993).
15. Wellings et al., *Sexual Behaviour in Britain*, p. 183.
16. Jack Dominian, *Sexual Integrity* (London: Darton, Longman & Todd, 1987), p. 86.
17. See also Ken Plummer, *Modern Homosexualities* (London: Routledge, 1992).
18. Babuscio, *We Speak for Ourselves*, p. 125.
19. The True Freedom Trust is a counselling organization which works amongst gays and lesbians. Martin Hallett's book *I am Learning to Love* (London: Marshall, 1987) documents his own struggles and journey out of a homosexual lifestyle.

20. Norman Denzin, 'Postmodern Children', *Society*, 24, 1987.
21. Peter Wilmott and Michael Young, *Family and Kinship in East London* (1955); Norman Dennis, Fernando Henriques and Clifford Slaughter, *Coal is our Life* (1956); Viola Klein, *The People of Ship Street* (1957); Hannah Gavron *The Captive Wife* (1965).
22. Heidi Hartmann, 'The Family as the Locus of Gender, Class and Political Struggle', *Signs*, 6, 1981.
23. Elaine Storkey, *What's Right with Feminism* (London: SPCK, 2nd edition, 1995) has an explanation of these distinctions.
24. For contributions from different feminist writers see Veronica Beechey, *Unequal Work* (London: Verso, 1987); Sylvia Walby, *Patriarchy at Work* (Open University Press, 1986); M. Barratt and M. McIntosh *The Anti-Social Family* (London: Verso, 1982).
25. C. Smart, *The Ties that Bind*, p. 145.
26. See Roy McCloughry, *Men and Masculinity: From Power to Love* (London: Hodder & Stoughton, 1991) for an extended account of a men's group.
27. This is taken from my book *Mary's Story, Mary's Song* (London, HarperCollins, 1993).

4 The Origins of Intimacy

1. Stuart Miller, *Men and Friendship* (London: Gateway, 1983), pp. 17–18.
2. Quoted in Miller, *Men and Friendship*.
3. See Edward O. Wilson, *Sociobiology: The New Synthesis* (Cambridge, MA: Harvard University Press, 1975).
4. Richard Dawkins, *The Selfish Gene* (Oxford, 1976).
5. See discussion in Stewart Van Leeuwen, *Gender and Grace* and S. L. W. Meller, *The Evolution of Love* Freeman, 1981)
6. Garrison Keillor, *The Book for Guys* (Faber, 1994).
7. Miller, *Men and Friendship*, p. 18.
8. Ibid., p. 19.
9. Mario Puzo, *The Godfather* (London: Mandarin, 1969).
10. Foucault, *History of Sexuality* (London: Penguin, 1981), p. 225.
11. See R. Pearsall, *The Worm in the Bud* (Harmondsworth: Penguin, 1971).
12. Carr, *Crisis in Intimacy*, p. 49.
13. Ibid., p. 49.
14. Babuscio, *We Speak for Ourselves*, p. 10.
15. Carr, *Crisis in Intimacy*, p. 49.
16. Ronald Rolheiser, *The Shattered Lantern* (London: Hodder & Stoughton, 1994), p. 30.
17. Ibid., p. 140.
18. William Johnston, *The Mystical Way* (London: HarperCollins, 1994), p. 151.
19. Miller, *Men and Friendship*, p. 22.

20. Pat Collins CM, *Intimacy and the Hungers of the Heart* (Dublin: The Columba Press, 1991), p. 91.
21. Quoted in Vishal Mangalwadi, *Search of Self* (London: Hodder & Stoughton, 1991), p. 131.
22. Ibid., p. 131.
23. Johnston, *The Mystical Way*, p. 158.
24. Quoted in Mangalwadi, *Search of Self*, p. 130.
25. Gerald Priestland, *My Pilgrim Way* (Mowbray, 1993).

5 Barriers to Intimacy

1. A. Phizaclea 'Gender, racism and occupational segregation' in Walby, *Gender Separation at Work* (Buckingham: Open University Press, 1988), p. 52.
2. Harriett Goldhor Lerner, *The Dance of Intimacy* (London: Harper & Row, 1990), p. 8.
3. Rolheiser, *The Restless Heart*.
4. Nouwen, *Reaching Out*, p. 101.
5. Lewis Smedes, *Forgive and Forget*, (London: Triangle, 1988).
6. Rolheiser, *The Restless Heart*, p. 169.

6 The Power of the Past

1. Carr, *Crisis in Intimacy*, p. 79.
2. Jean Grigor, *Loss: An Invitation to Grow* (London: Arthur James, 1986), p. 9.
3. Judith Wallerstein and Sandra Blakeslee, *Second Chances* (London: Bantam, 1989), p. 308. See also Judith Wallerstein and Joan Kelly, *Surviving the Breakup: How Children and Parents Cope with Divorce* (New York: Basic Books, 1980).
4. Pat Collins, *Intimacy and the Hungers of the Heart*, p. 35.

7 Gender Differences in Intimacy

1. George A Rekers, 'Psychological Foundations for Rearing Masculine Boys and Feminine Girls', in *Recovering Biblical Manhood and Womanhood*, eds. John Piper and Wayne Grudem (Wheaton, Illinois: Crossway, 1991), p. 296. See also Michael Harper, *Equal and Different* (London: Hodder & Stoughton, 1994) and the review of it by Deborah Halling in *Third Way* (June 1994).
2. Gregg Johnson, 'Biological Basis for Gender-Specific Behaviour', in *Recovering Biblical Manhood and Womanhood*, eds. Piper and Grudem, p. 293.
3. Stewart Van Leeuwan, *Gender and Grace*, p. 88.
4. Keillor, *The Book for Guys*.

5. McCloughry, *Men and Masculinity*, p. 188.
6. McCloughry, *Men and Masculinity*, pp. 188–9.
7. Lillian Rubin, *Intimate Strangers* (Glasgow: Fontana, 1985), quoted in Michael S Kimmel, and Michael A Messner *Men's Lives* (New York: Macmillan Publishing Co, 1989), p. 364.
8. Kimmel and Messner, *Men's Lives*, p. 409.
9. Quoted in Collins, *Intimacy and the Hungers of the Heart*, pp. 115 and 122.
10. See also Daniel Lewinson, *The Seasons of a Man's Life* (N. York: Ballantine, 1978).
11. Rubin, *Intimate Strangers*, p. 129.
12. Miller, *Men and Friendship*, p. xi.
13. Joel Sherzer, 'A Diversity of Voices: Men's and Women's Speech in Ethnographic Perspective' in *Language, Gender and Sex in Comparative Perspective*, eds. Susan U. Philips, Susan Steele and Christine Tanz (Cambridge: Cambridge University Press, 1987), pp. 95–120.
14. Stuart Miller has some interesting stories in *Men and Friendship*, pp. 136–8.
15. Kimmel and Messner *Men's Lives*, p. 23.
16. Keillor, *The Book for Guys*.
17. Deborah Tannen, *You Just Don't Understand: Women and Men in Conversation* (London: Virago, 1992), p. 43. See also her *That's Not What I Meant* (London: Virago, 1992).
18. See also Jennifer Coates, *Women, Men and Language* (London: Longman, 1986); Carol Gilligan, *In a Different Voice* (Cambridge, Mass.: Harvard University Press, 1982); Spender, *Man-Made Language*.
19. Tannen, *That's Not What I Meant*, p. 110.

8 Friendship and Intimacy

1. Ecclesiasticus 6: 14–17.
2. James Olthius, *I Pledge You My Troth: A Christian View of Marriage, Family and Friendship* (London: Harper & Row, 1975), p. 109.
3. Kaye V. Cook and Lance Lee, *Man and Woman, Alone and Together* (Wheaton, Ill.: Victor Books, 1992), p. 194.
4. See two excellent articles: Howard E. Frost and Kaye V. Cook, 'Being Single in a Couples' World: Gender Roles, Identity and Contentment', and Kristin L. Ellins, 'The Never Married Woman: Coping in a Couple-Dominant Society', *Priscilla Papers*, vol. 7, no. 4, 1993, pp. 1–13.
5. C. S. Lewis, *Transposition and Other Addresses* (London: Geoffrey Bles, 1949), p. 58.
6. Ibid., p. 63.
7. Proverbs 27:6 (AV).
8. See Miller, *Men and Friendship*, p. 137.

9 Marriage and Intimacy

1. See, for example, Haffner, *The End of Marriage*.
2. Wellings et al., *Sexual Behaviour in Britain*, p. 252.
3. Wellings et al., *Sexual Behaviour in Britain*, ch. 6, pp. 245–8.
4. See Ephesians 5:32.
5. See Alan Storkey, *Meanings of Love* (Leicester: IVP 1994).
6. As described by the Chief Rabbi, Jonathan Sacks, in *Everyman*, BBC, September 1994.
7. See Matthew 19:3–9 and 1 Corinthians 7:10–17.
8. 1 Corinthians 7:4–5.
9. See also Hebrews 13:4.
10. It is interesting how much is made of the requirement of wives to 'submit' in Ephesians 5. Because Paul does not specifically ask it also of husbands it is often interpreted that husbands should not submit to their wives. Yet to apply the same exegesis to the whole passage would give the absurd conclusion that wives are never to love their husbands, for Paul does not require them to and only asks this of husbands.
11. Jack Dominian, *Make or Break* (London: SPCK, 1984), p. 48.
12. Jessie Bernard, *The Future of Marriage* (New York: World Pubg Co, 1972).
13. Wellings et al., *Sexual Behaviour in Britain*, p. 104.
14. See Alfred Demaris and Gerald Leslie, 'Cohabitation with the Future Spouse; Its Influence upon Marital Satisfaction and Communication', *Journal of Marriage and the Family*, February 1984.
15. *UK Household Survey 1989*, Office of Population Census and Surveys (1992), and *Social Trends* (1994).
16. Fischer and Hart, *Promises to Keep*, p. 55.
17. Quoted in Carr, *Crisis in Intimacy*, p. 137.
18. Dan Kiley, *Living Together*, *Feeling Alone* (London: Mandarin, 1991), p. 7.
19. Mason, *The Mystery of Marriage*, p. 80.

10 Sexual Intimacy

1. Henri Nouwen, *Intimacy* (New York: Harper & Row, 1969), p. 34.
2. Dominian, *Sexual Integrity*, p. 95.
3. Olthius, *Keeping Our Troth*, p. 7.
4. Cook and Lee, *Man and Woman*, *Alone and Together*, p. 228.
5. Mason, *The Mystery of Marriage*, p. 117.
6. Olthius, *Keeping Our Troth*, p. 12.
7. Phyllis Trible, *God and the Rhetoric of Sexuality* (Philadelphia: Fortress Press, 1978).
8. Sheila Kitzinger, *Woman's Experience of Sex* (London: Dorling Kindersley, 1983), p. 85. See also Nancy Friday, *My Secret Garden* (New York: New York Pocket Books, 1974).

9. McCloughry, *Men and Masculinity*, p. 168.
10. Wellings et al., *Sexual Behaviour in Britain*. See also the discussion of homosexual lifestyles, pp. 178–230.
11. Babuscio, *We Speak for Ourselves*, p. 118.
12. Ann Landers' study, quoted in Olthius, *Keeping Our Troth*, p. 115.
13. Shere Hite, *Women and Love. A Cultural Revolution in Progress*. (London: Viking, 1987), p. 5.
14. Trevor Stammers, *The Family Guide to Sex and Intimacy* (London: Hodder & Stoughton, 1994), p. 145.
15. Dominian, *Sexual Integrity*, p. 95.
16. Lewis Smedes, *Sex in the Real World* (Berkhamsted: Lion Publishing, 1979), p. 184.
17. Mason, *The Mystery of Marriage*, p. 80.
18. Donald Orr et al., 'Premature Activity as an Indicator of Psychological Risk', *Paediatrics*, 1991, pp. 141–7.
19. The sex education programme put out by Christians in Education is a much more rounded contribution to the learning experience.
20. Dominian, *Sexual Integrity*, p. 64.
21. Stammers, *The Family Guide to Sex and Intimacy*.
22. See correspondence in the *Church of England Newspaper*, September–October 1994.
23. Nouwen, *Intimacy*, p. 32.
24. Dominian, *Sexual Integrity*, p. 64.
25. Ronald Rolheiser, *The Shattered Lantern* (London: Hodder & Stoughton, 1994). p. 41.

11 Intimacy and the Family

1. Anthony Giddens, *Social Theory and Modern Society* (Cambridge: Polity Press: Stratford University Press, 1987), p. 23.
2. Jonathan Sacks, *The Persistence of Faith* (London: Weidenfeld & Nicolson 1991).
3. Norman Denzin, 'Postmodern Children', *Society*, 24, 1987.
4. Aspects of this normative framework are found in a number of passages in the Bible, for example: Deuteronomy 4:9–14; Deuteronomy 5; Leviticus 18:6–14, 19, 29; Psalm 22; Proverbs 31; Joel 1; Matthew 18–19; Mark 10; Luke 14:12; Ephesians 6; 1 Corinthians 5:1–2; Colossians 3; 1 Timothy 5; Hebrews 13:1–4; 3 John 5.
5. See Salvador Minuchin, *Families and Family Therapy* (London: Routledge, 1993).
6. Wallerstein and Blakeslee, *Second Chances*, p. 308.
7. Giddens, *Modernity and Self Identity*, p. 13.
8. Robyn Skinner and John Cleese, *Families and How to Survive Them* (London: Mandarin, 1989), p. 33.
9. Myra Chave-Jones, *Coping with Depression* (Berkhamsted: Lion Publishing, 1981).
10. Skinner and Cleese, *Families and How to Survive Them*, p. 121.

11. Ibid., p. 121.
12. Tom Crabtree, *The Search for Love*: *A Guide to Your Relationships* (London: Cosmopolitan Press, 1982), p. 16.
13. Goldhor Lerner, *The Dance of Intimacy*, p. 183.
14. See here the work by Lillian Rubin, *Intimate Strangers*.
15. Goldhor Lerner, *The Dance of Intimacy*, p. 186.
16. See Rubin, *Intimate Strangers*.
17. Ibid., p. 191.
18. Penelope Lively, *Moon Tiger* (Harmondsworth: Penguin, 1987), pp. 60, 56.
19. Larry Christenson, *The Christian Family* (Eastbourne: Kingsway, 1981).
20. Goldhor Lerner, *The Dance of Intimacy*, p. 186.
21. Shere Hite, *The Hite Report on the Family*. (London: Hodder & Stoughton, 1994) p. 171.

12 Finding Intimacy

1. Rolheiser, *The Shattered Lantern*, p. 17.
2. James Houston, 'I Am what I Am Has Made Me', *Third Way*, September 1993.
3. See James 2:14 and 1 John 3:18.
4. See 'Another Family – The Body of Christ', in Richard Winter, *The Roots of Sorrow*.
5. Greg Smith, 'You and Who Else?' *Third Way*, February 1995, p. 24.
6. See Romans 12; 1 Corinthians 12; Ephesians 4.
7. For a discussion of 'parity', see Ray Anderson and Dennis Guernsey, *On Being a Family*: *A Social Theology of the Family* (Grand Rapids, Mich.: Eerdmans, 1985).
8. See Sue Walrund Skinner, *Family Matters* (London: SPCK, 1988), p. 163.

Further Selected Reading

Allender, Dan B, *The Wounded Heart: Hope for Adult Victims of Childhood Sexual Abuse* (Colorado Springs: NavPress, 1990).

Baughen, Michael and Myrtle, *Your Marriage* (London: Hodder & Stoughton, 1994).

Bellah, Robert N., et al, *Habits of the Heart* (Berkeley: University of California Press, 1985).

Clouse, Bonnidell and Clouse, Robert G. eds, *Women in Ministry: Four Views* (Downers Grove, III: InterVarsity Press, 1989).

Dixon, Patrick, *The Genetic Revolution* (Eastbourne: Kingsway Publications, 1993).

Dominian, Jack, *Make or Break* (London: SPCK, 1984).

Dominian, Jack, *Sexual Integrity* (London: Darton, Longman & Todd, 1987).

Eden, Martyn and Wells, David F., ed., *The Gospel in the Modern World: A tribute to John Stott* (Leicester: Inter-Varsity Press, 1991).

Foyle, Marjorie F., *Honourably Wounded: Stress Among Christian Workers* (London: MARC/Interserve/EMA, 1987).

Gilder, George, *Men and Marriage* (Gretna, La: Pelican Publishing, 1987).

Griffioen, Sander and Balk, Bert, eds, *Christian Philosophy at the Close of the Twentieth Century* (Kampen: Kok, 1995).

Guiness, Os, *Fit Bodies, Fat Minds* (London: Hodder & Stoughton, 1995).

Heddendorf, Russell, *Hidden Threads: Social Thought for Christians* (Dallas: Probe Books, 1990).

Hite, Shere, *Women and Love A Cultural Revolution in Progress* (London: Viking, 1987).

Houghton, John, *The Search for God: Can Science Help?* (Oxford: Lion, 1995).

Hurding, Roger, *The Bible and Counselling* (London: Hodder & Stoughton, 1992).

Hurding, Roger, *Roots & Shoots: A Guide to Couselling and Psychotherapy* (London: Hodder & Stoughton, 1985).

Keillor, Garrison, *The Book for Guys* (London: Faber, 1994).

Kiley, Dan, *Living Together, Feeling Alone* (London: Mandarin, 1991).

Lyon, David, *Postmodernity* (Buckingham: Open University Press, 1994).

McCloughry, Roy, *Men and Masculinity: From Power to Love* (London: Hodder & Stoughton, 1991).

Miller, Stuart, *Men and Friendship* (London: Gateway, 1983).

Mitchell, Ella Pearson, ed., *Those Preachin' Women: Sermons by Black Women Preachers* (Valley Forge, Pa: Judson Press, 1985).

Nouwen, Henri, *Intimacy* (New York: Harper & Row, 1969).

Okin, Susan Moller, *Justice, Gender, and the Family* (New York: Basic Books, 1989).

Rolheiser, Ronald, *The Shattered Lantern* (London: Hodder & Stoughton, 1994).

Rolheiser, Ronald, *The Restless Heart* (London: Hodder & Stoughton, 1988).

Sampson, Samuel and Sugden, *Faith and Modernity* (Oxford: Regnum, 1994).

Seerveld, Calvin, *On Being Human: Imaging God in the Modern World* (Burlington, Ontario: Welch Publishing, 1988).

Smedes, Lewis, *Sex for Christians* (London: SPCK, 1988).

Storkey, Alan, *The Meanings of Love* (Leicester: Inter-Varsity Press, 1994).

Storkey, Alan, *Foundational Epistemologies in Consumption Theory* (Amsterdam: University of Amsterdam Press, 1994).

Storkey, Elaine, *What's Right with Feminism*, 2nd edn (London: SPCK, 1996).

Storkey, Elaine, *Contributions to Christian Feminism* (London: CI Press, 1995).

Stott, John, *The Contemporary Christian* (Leicester: IVP, 1992).

Tournier, Paul, *Guilt and Grace* (Sussex: Highland Books, 1986).

Trible, Phyllis, *God and the Rhetoric of Sexuality* (Philadelphia: Fortress Press, 1978).

Van Leeuwen, Mary Stewart, ed., *After Eden: Facing the Challenge of Gender Reconciliation* (Grand Rapids: William B Eerdmans; Carlisle: Paternoster Press, 1993).

Van Leeuwen, Mary Stewart, *Gender and Grace: Love, Work and Parenting in a Changing World* (Downers Grove, Ill: InterVarsity Press, 1990).

Wallis, Jim, *Agenda for Biblical People* (USA: Harper & Row, 1976, 1984; London: Triangle/SPCK, 1986).

Wellings, Kaye, Field, Julia, Johnson, Anne and Wadworth, Jane, *Sexual Behaviour in Britain* (London: Penguin, 1995).

Wolters, Albert M., *Creation Regained* (Leicester: IVP, 1985).

Wren, Brian, *What Language Shall I Borrow? God-Talk in Worship: A Male Response to Feminist Theology* (New York: Crossroad, 1990).

Wright, Christopher, J. H., *Living as the People of God* (Leicester: IVP, 1983).

Index